ROUTLEDGE LIBRARY EDITIONS:
SOCIOLOGY OF EDUCATION

Volume 1

I0129420

RISK, EDUCATION AND CULTURE

RISK, EDUCATION AND CULTURE

Edited by
ANDREW HOPE AND PAUL OLIVER

Routledge
Taylor & Francis Group
LONDON AND NEW YORK

First published in 2005 by Ashgate Publishing Limited

This edition first published in 2017
by Routledge
2 Park Square, Milton Park, Abingdon, Oxon OX14 4RN

and by Routledge
711 Third Avenue, New York, NY 10017

Routledge is an imprint of the Taylor & Francis Group, an informa business

© 2005 Andrew Hope and Paul Oliver

British Library Cataloguing in Publication Data
A catalogue record for this book is available from the British Library

ISBN: 978-0-415-78834-2 (Set)
ISBN: 978-1-315-20949-4 (Set) (ebk)
ISBN: 978-1-138-21993-9 (Volume 1) (hbk)
ISBN: 978-1-138-21995-3 (Volume 1) (pbk)
ISBN: 978-1-315-41413-3 (Volume 1) (ebk)

Publisher's Note
The publisher has gone to great lengths to ensure the quality of this reprint but points out that some imperfections in the original copies may be apparent.

Disclaimer
The publisher has made every effort to trace copyright holders and would welcome correspondence from those they have been unable to trace.

Risk, Education and Culture

Edited by
ANDREW HOPE

and
PAUL OLIVER

ASHGATE

Published by
Ashgate Publishing Limited
Gower House
Croft Road
Aldershot
Hampshire GU11 3HR
England

Ashgate Publishing Company
Suite 420
101 Cherry Street
Burlington, VT 05401-4405
USA

Ashgate website: http://www.ashgate.com

British Library Cataloguing in Publication Data
Risk, education and culture. - (Monitoring change in
   education)
   1.Schools - Risk management 2.School environment - Risk
   assessment 3.Students - Psychology 4.Teachers - Psychology
   5.Risk perception 6.Risk - Sociological aspects
   I.Hope, Andrew II.Oliver, Paul
   363.1'19371

Library of Congress Cataloging-in-Publication Data
Risk, education, and culture / edited by Andrew Hope and Paul Oliver.
      p. cm. -- (Monitoring change in education)
   Includes bibliographical references.
   ISBN 0-7546-4172-4
   1. Schools--Safety measures--Case studies. 2. Risk--Sociological aspects--Case studies.
   3. Schools--Risk management--Case studies. I. Hope, Andrew, 1969- II. Oliver, Paul. III.
Series.

LB2864.5.R55 2004
306.43--dc22

                                                                        2004057430

ISBN 0 7546 4172 4

Printed in Great Britain by Antony Rowe Ltd, Chippenham, Wiltshire

Contents

Preface

In recent years, education has become perceived as an area of risk. Highly publicised incidents such as armed massacres in schools, child abductions, students assaulting teachers, increasing vandalism and the introduction of Internet access have resulted in a greater awareness of the potential dangers lurking in teaching institutions. Indeed such incidents have resulted in a growing 'risk consciousness', which in turn has led to a re-evaluation of the potential hazards present in teaching processes and a questioning of how individuals construct strategies to avoid these perceived dangers. It is notable that contemporary concern about safety in education does not just focus on student welfare but also recognises that staff and the institutions themselves face serious threats to their well being.

Concern about risk in education has also been fuelled by the development of a multi-billion dollar risk alleviation industry and a growing awareness among educational organisations that there is a need to construct risk reduction strategies. Yet, anxiety about risk in education is not merely recognition of actual dangers but also reflects the increasing use of the concept of risk as political rhetoric. Within this context, discussion about risks within education may be used as a political device, securing funding or justifying policy positions. This is not to suggest that actual dangers do not exist in educational process but rather to recognise that risk discourses themselves do not necessarily relate to actual dangers. Furthermore, whilst in contemporary Western society discussion of risk is often linked with threats to the body, property or social groups, it should be recognised that risks can have positive outcomes. Thus with regard to education, certain risks can be utilised to enrich the learning process and achieve pedagogic goals.

In addressing the theoretical and practical implications of education and risk the importance of culture in the risk process needs to be recognised. Perceptions of risk are always culturally situated and are therefore specific to time and place. Any understanding of risks thus needs to be both culturally and historically situated. Additionally it is vital to recognise that differences may exist between expert and layperson, teacher and student, practitioner and academic risk narratives. It is essential to understand these differences on a pluralistic hermeneutic level. Neither reproducing existing power relations nor inverting power hierarchies will provide a sufficient understanding of risk as it applies to education.

Reinforcing the view that discussion about risk needs to be culturally situated, the following chapters offer varied interpretations of risk processes within education. The first four chapters, which constitute the first part of this book, focus upon theoretical considerations of risk. Issues such as the nature of risk in education, the impact of existential choice, the social construction of risk discourses and the plurality of worldviews in postmodernity are discussed. Comprising the second part of this book the remaining twelve chapters explore particular case studies relating to risk and education. The contributions cover a variety of subjects including the dangers that exist in schools, the hazards of providing practical vocational education, the role of risk in higher education, the models of risk management developed in work based educational environments and educational health discourses. Throughout each of these chapters the importance of understanding risk perceptions and processes in education from a cultural perspective is highlighted.

The first chapter offers an overview of cultural risk perspectives, whilst maintaining that risk is a dynamic process that can have positive outcomes in educational contexts. Suggesting that accessibility to specialised knowledge has expanded to such an extent that the notion of the 'expert' is systematically challenged, chapter two considers the freedom and accompanying risks of existential choice within education. The question of choice also underlies the discussion of the social construction of risk discourses within educational policy and practice in chapter three. In this contribution the authors reaffirm that risks can have positive outcomes and bemoan managerialist discourses that inhibit educational policy makers and practitioners. Part I of this book concludes with a consideration of risk and the plurality of worldviews inherent in postmodernity. It is argued that while educational systems are characterised by innovations and initiatives, the relativism inherent in risk processes in postmodernity makes the selection of criteria through which to evaluate such developments problematic.

Part II of this book, focusing on case studies, opens with three chapters exploring risks that are situated within schools. Chapters five and six both deal with issues arising from the introduction of modern technologies into schools. The impact upon staff of the media reporting of risks arising from chat-line use is considered in chapter five. It is concluded that staff do not simply adopt the views espoused in the 'moral panic' over chat-lines but rather in some cases adapt or reject these views by drawing upon their own experience. Thus, students using the Internet to chat are perceived in some instances as dangerous rather than, as represented in the media, simply being at risk. The issue of dangerous students also arises in chapter six in which the author considers risk and actuarialism before exploring how the introduction of Closed Circuit Television systems into schools has addressed certain dangers whilst reinforcing dominant ideologies of control. Reporting on a large scale empirical study chapter seven discusses young people's attitudes to drugs, alcohol and tobacco education within their schools. It is concluded that many young people are conceptually sophisticated in the ways in which they assess and manage risk on a personal level, and this sophistication is not always mirrored in the type of drug education received in school.

Considering the risks surrounding technical education in schools and colleges chapters eight and nine both explore problems of practice and curriculum development. In chapter eight it is maintained that while the role of Vocational and Technical Education in socio-economic development in Africa is vital the system that provides such education engenders uncertainty and risky. Offering an historical overview whilst considering specific managerial elements that expose the system to risks, suggestions are provided as to how African planners can alleviate risks by being more progressive in their thinking. Focusing upon safety issues and the pressures upon Design and Technology teachers arising from the demands of curriculum delivery, the author of chapter nine discusses the risks arising from funding problems. The conclusion is reached that the value of what remains in the Design and Technology curriculum needs to be questioned.

Chapters ten and fifteen address issues of risk in the Higher Education sector. The risk factors that need to be taken into account in the delivery of Higher Education courses in Further Education establishments are addressed in chapter ten. The hazards arising from the pursuit of policies of diversity and excellence in the Higher Education sector is considered in chapter fifteen. It is argued that the foundational idea that greater excellence will result from greater diversity is unproven, whilst the pursuit of excellence is implicitly a paradigm that seeks, ineffectively, to eliminate risk.

Focusing upon risk in work-based educational situations, chapters eleven through to fourteen seek to highlight the links that exist between risk education and work environments. Chapter eleven explores the processes for managing the delivery of health care programmes of education and clinical training, whilst considering the protection of students and the safeguards provided for those in their care. The author highlights the importance of safe work-based learning environments and risk management plans. Drawing upon personal teaching experience the author of chapter twelve examines how social work students are prepared through training to deal with risk in their working lives. It is concluded that risk is an integral part of social work and that through the provision of appropriate risk frameworks for students and staff challenging tasks may become ultimately satisfying. Chapter thirteen explores the relationships between risk, knowledge and training in the context of a metropolitan fire service. It outlines the attempt to reduce both financial and human risk by developing organisational views of tasks, which centre on the capture, rendering and subsequent use of operational procedures that list aspects of good practice. The notion of risk in the context of vocational and career psychology is considered in chapter fourteen. In understanding the risk from academic and lay standpoints, the author reflects upon how it is possible to capitalise on the strengths of the risk management perspective in one's life career development. It is concluded that in career development individuals need to learn to locate or embed the risk construct within a more holistic, resilient and constructive thinking frame.

Finally, chapter sixteen examines the health discourse constructed in official educational material about donor insemination. The authors analyse the way in which risks are presented to both recipients of donor insemination and sperm donors. They also draw attention to strategies for containing the risks, such as, matching recipients with donors to reduce the visibility of the genetic 'difference', reinforcing a shared physical family identity; containment through donor anonymity and screening to exclude unsuitable donors. Ultimately the authors conclude that embedded within these strategies are versions of risky and less risky identities.

Viewed as a whole these sixteen chapters underline the importance of examining risk perceptions, processes and practices within the field of education. Whilst a variety of perspectives are adopted in exploring risk, education and culture, with the contributors drawing variously upon aspects of the psychometric paradigm, 'risk society' theories, cultural hermeneutic approaches and discourse analysis, all the authors reinforce the importance of understanding risk as an historic, culturally situated dynamic process. In conclusion, an attempt to examine risks and education would be impoverished if it did not consider the central role played by culture processes.

PART I
THEORETICAL
CONSIDERATIONS OF RISK

Chapter 1

Risk, Education and Culture: Interpreting Danger as a Dynamic, Culturally Situated Process

Andrew Hope

Introduction

As Caplan (2000, p. 1) notes at the start of the new millennium risk is a topic that is difficult to ignore. Indeed, it can be argued that in recent years Western society has become obsessed with the probability of damage, illness or death. Concern about such things as the spread of disease, food production and global terrorism have encouraged individuals to increasingly think of everyday activities in terms of danger and risk alleviation. Following recent disasters, even mundane experiences such as rail travel have been perceptually trans-formed into hazardous undertakings. One might be forgiven for thinking that the contemporary world is much more dangerous than the one that existed a few decades ago. However, it is not necessarily that society is more dangerous, rather people have become 'risk obsessed' (Giddens, 1991). Within the current political climate, it is hardly surprising if individuals start to perceive common place practices and institutions as 'risky'. Yet, there are specific reasons why educational institutions in particular have become perceived as 'risk environ-ments' in recent years. Highly publicised incidents such as armed massacres in schools, child abductions, child abuse, students assaulting teachers, increasing vandalism and theft, road safety outside schools and the spread of illnesses, such as meningitis, have resulted in a greater awareness of the dangers that potentially lurk in teaching institutions.

In considering the area of risk, education and culture there are many issues that compete for attention. Indeed the variety of subjects tackled in the subse-quent chapters of this book attest to the richness and diversity of this field. This chapter focuses upon the definition of key terms and the consideration of different cultural risk perspectives. In the first section the terms culture, education and risk are defined, whilst the links between these three concepts are discussed. The next section considers risk and culture, focusing on four different risk theories, namely the psychometric risk paradigm, the 'risk society' perspective, cultural hermeneutic approaches to risk and risk discourse analysis. Whilst considering these four theoretical frameworks, references are made as to how they might be applied in educational research, however there is no attempt to suggest that one framework is better than another. Rather such judgements depend on an individual's own theoretical disposition, the research question to be addressed and the exact area being researched. After discussing four cultural risks perspectives the focus shifts to consider two key features of risk as a cultural phenomenon. The first is that risks, despite a tendency to be constructed in negative terms, can have positive consequences. The second point is that risk is best understood as a dynamic process. Finally, in the conclusion some areas are suggested that might prove fruitful for future research into risk, education and culture.

Risk, Education and Culture

Risk exists at many different levels in education. While a variety of dangers may threaten the physical and psychological wellbeing of students as well as staff, decisions at a policy level can create new hazards that may compromise the effective functioning of teaching institutions. Before considering the ways in which risk, education and culture are inherently intertwined with one another, it is necessary to define these key terms.

Culture is a collective noun, signifying the symbolic and learned aspect of human society (Abercombie et al., 1994, p. 98). It is a sweeping concept that 'may be taken as the 'way of life' of an entire society and... include codes of manners, dress, language, rituals, norms of behaviour and systems of belief' (Jary and Jary, 1995, p. 139). Despite the existence of social consensus about many key issues in contemporary society, the recognition that there is a plurality of life-worlds has led some sociologists to question the idea of a unified cultural system, preferring to focus instead on fragmented and diversified cultures. Drawing upon ideas of cultural diversity Anglo-American sociologists commonly employ differentiated concepts to highlight particular aspects of these multiple cultures, such as 'belief system', 'values' or 'ideology' (Abercombie et al., 1994, p. 99). Nevertheless, the concept of culture is still widely used, with academics stressing its historical nature, relativity and diversity.

Knowledge of culture is gained through a complex social process (Jary and Jary, 1995, p. 139) that can be broadly labelled education. In its widest sense, education refers to the process of rearing or developing an individual. While traditionally the term education is most commonly associated with the formal compulsory system that seeks to instruct children and youths, it is increasingly recognised that education is a life-long process, which can occur outside of formal teaching institutions. Indeed it is recognised that 'all parts of the social structure can have an educational influence' (Musgrave, 1983, p. 105). Education is central to the process of socialisation and therefore plays an essential role in the acquisition of cultural knowledge. While much educational research focuses on the formal provision of cultural and technical knowledge in schools, colleges and Higher Education institutes, it is important not to disregard the learning that takes place in the workplace, home or in public spaces such as libraries and art galleries. Culture impacts on all such activities and is something that can be acquired through education. Importantly not all education processes should be seen as primarily providing cultural knowledge.

Like the form, content and focus of education, risk perceptions are culturally constructed, being built up through social processes. In this sense risks are not given, but rather the product of cultural processes. Individuals learn to label certain things as dangerous. Hence, not all cultures consider the same things to be risks. Whether they are perceived to exist at the level of structure or agency, risks in contemporary society can be associated with danger and threats to individuals and / or their property. According to Furedi:

> Risk refers to the probability of damage, injury, illness, death or other misfortune associated with a hazard. Hazards are generally defined to mean a threat to people and what they value (Furedi, 1997, p. 17).

Nevertheless, while most commentators such as Furedi associate risk with negative outcomes, it should be noted that positive consequences could also ensue from risk. As the focus shifts to considering how risk, education and culture are intertwined this will be considered in more detail.

Literature that deals with risk and education often focuses upon certain threats to the wellbeing of students. In particular the emphasis is often upon a range of possible threats such as educational underachievement, youth unemployment, bullying, child abuse, substance misuse, youth crime, teenage pregnancy and sexually transmitted diseases (e.g. Furlong and Cartmel, 1997; Dwyer and Wyn, 2001). Yet, educational staff may also be at risk from stress, intimidation or violence. Such possibilities are all too frequently ignored in writings on risk and education. Beyond considering possible threats to the wellbeing of students and staff there is also the issue that institutions themselves might be at risk. Thus vandalism, theft, cuts in funding or incompetent management might result in educational institutions closing. Another group that might be exposed to risk as a result of the education system is local communities and neighbourhoods that border educational establishments. Although such concerns have been largely ignored by the literature, it is conceivable that the spread of vandalism, road traffic congestion and the potential existence of a large unsecured space after school hours may create certain hazards for local residents. Ultimately risk and education are connected by the question of who or what is at risk. Answers to such questions, as well as those about the exact nature of risks, are culturally constructed. Beyond considering who is at risk there is also the issue that individuals are often educated about certain risks and how to avoid them. Such culturally constructed risk education might take the form of primary school children learning how to cross busy roads or patients been given health advice when they visit a doctor's surgery.

Furthermore, risk can be used in the educational process to gain positive learning outcomes. In this context, educators might use 'role-plays' about hazardous situations as part of the learning process. It is also not uncommon to hear of teachers taking 'risks' in adopting unusual pedagogic approaches in an attempt to engender creativity and achieve more rewarding learning outcomes. Finally, risk, education and culture share certain common features. They are all relative, dynamic social concepts that are best understood in terms of historically situated processes.

In considering risk, education and culture, certain issues that have already been touched upon will be further developed. In particular a variety of cultural risk perspectives will be explored. Then the notion that risk can have positive consequences will be discussed before finally exploring the idea that risk, like education, is best understood as a process.

Risk and Culture

In social science literature the phenomenon of risk tends to be situated somewhere in or between the realist / social constructionist perspectives. Realism can be defined as the belief that the external, material world can be measured in an objective manner to arrive at 'absolute truths'. Thus the realist approach, which emerged from such disciplines as engineering, statistics, epidemiology and economics, treats risk calculations as 'objective facts' (Bradbury, 1989, p. 382). Consequently from this perspective risks can be 'identified through scientific measurement and calculation and controlled using this knowledge' (Lupton, 1999, p. 18). Social constructionism is the process whereby a phenomenon is constructed through social processes rather than being a natural occurrence. From this perspective risks are always social, built up through cultural and political processes. Drawing upon the fields of social anthropology and interpretative sociology the social constructionist risk perspective emphasises the aspects that realist approaches are accused of neglecting, namely, the social and cultural contexts within which risks are understood and negotiated. From this perspective, risk knowledge is connected to the sociocultural contexts in which it is generated. According to this approach as knowledge is never value free, debates about risks always involve questions of cultural representation, meaning and political position. Lying somewhere between these two 'ideal types' of scientific realism and social constructionism is a position that has been labelled 'critical realist'. From this perspective there is an assertion of the objective nature of risks, whilst recognising the role played by the state, scientific community and media in rendering such dangers perceptible. In the context, the social world does not simply 'exist' independently of risk discourses. However, while risk knowledge that individuals have of their social world affects their behaviour, such knowledge may be partial or even distorted. Cottle (1998) argues that such a perspective contains elements of ontological / epistemological slippage.

This section focus on four different cultural risk theories, namely the psychometric risk paradigm, the 'risk society' perspective, cultural hermeneutic approaches to risk and risk discourse analysis. Whilst these risk perspectives have some features in common they should nevertheless be seen as distinct approaches. Although some commentators might label the psychometric risk paradigm as strongly 'realist' rather than cultural, recent developments have meant that this approach has adopted a more cultural position, drawing on social concepts such as stigma, globalisation and media amplification. Both the psychometric risk paradigm and the risk society approach adopt a realist position. However, it should be noted that writings on 'risk society' have increasingly moved towards what has been labelled as a critical realist standpoint. While cultural hermeneutic approaches to risk occupy a moderate social constructionist position, risk discourse analysis can be perceived as adopting a strong social constructionist approach.

The Psychometric Paradigm of Risk

Emerging from empirical studies of probability assessment and decision-making processes, psychometric approaches to understanding risk are situated firmly within the field of psychology. Pioneered by Starr (1969) this approach focuses on risk perceptions and stresses the existence of a set of mental strategies, or heuristics (Kahneman et al., 1982), which are used to make sense of an uncertain world. As Slovic (1998) notes this strategy for studying perceived risk seeks to develop taxonomy for dangers that engender understanding while allowing some degree of prediction regarding likely public responses. Most commonly, this is done using psychophysical scaling and multivariate analysis to produce quantitative data that provides a 'cognitive map' of risk perceptions. Thus people make quantitative judgements about the desirability of certain risks and these judgements are then related to certain pre-selected properties such as voluntariness, possible benefits and the number of fatalities. Such an approach allows for the consideration that certain risks may mean different things to different people. Research in this area seems to indicate that perceived risk is both quantifiable and predictable. Nevertheless, conceptual frameworks have been designed to describe how psychological, cultural and political factors interact to amplify risk perceptions (Kasperson et al., 1982). Within this perspective it has been noted that the perceived seriousness of a risk occurrence, the media coverage received and the long-term costs are determined partly by what the event portends (Slovic, 2000; p. xxiv).

In more recent years concepts drawn from other disciplines such as stigma (Goffman, 1963), globalization (Giddens, 1990) and media amplification (Katperson et al., 1982), have been utilised within this paradigm. Nevertheless, psychometric analysis of risk tends to underplay the importance of culture and politics in the social construction of risks. Indeed, there is a tendency within this approach to accept the labelling of certain dangers as 'risky' as unproblematic, failing to effectively explore the processes through which these

issues are selected. To some extent, this reflects that this perspective is primarily concerned with accessing existing risk perspectives. Whilst the psychometric paradigm seeks to quantify and predict risk perceptions it would be harsh
to dismiss it as purely realist in nature. Rather its attempts to draw upon wider
social theory and differentiate between risk cultures indicate acceptance of
the manner in which risk is socially constructed. With regards to the field
of education the importance of this risk perspective lies in it's exploration of
adolescent risk-taking behaviour (Benthin et al., 1993) and research into risk
education (Slovic, 2000). Insofar as quantitative, predictive research into risk is
popular with administrators, mangers and politicians, this approach is likely to
be utilised when addressing educational issues at a policy level.

'Risk Society' and Macro-Political Processes

Since the mid-1980s, a body of work has emerged from sociology exploring the
politics and macro-level meanings of contemporary strategies of risk (Lupton,
1999, p. 58). Drawing primarily upon the writings of Beck (1992) and Giddens
(1991), the 'risk society' perspective can be seen as combining an environmental consciousness with a belief that modernity is undergoing a transformation.

Beck maintains that western society has experienced three distinct stages of
social change, namely pre-industrial, industrial and 'risk society' (Beck, 1995,
p. 78). Within the 'risk society' perspective dangers are perceived as relating
either to physical hazards that destroy life or social and cultural insecurities.
Thus the production of pollutants, toxins and radioactivity threatens the
physical well-being of individuals, while the dissolution of traditional forms of
class culture, gender and family roles creates new forms of insecurity. While
Beck's earlier writings on risk tended to adopt a realist approach, focusing
upon 'given' hazards situated in the natural world, his position has shifted
towards critical realism, where he acknowledges the social and cultural processes through which risk perceptions are mediated. He implies that greater
anxiety about risks is related to the production of a greater number of risks in
late modernity. Not only is there an increase in hazards but also a growth in
mechanisms for the construction and labelling of such 'bads'. However,
Giddens (1991) maintains that the obsession with risk in contemporary society
is related to the growth in risk perceptions rather than an actual increase in
hazardous situations.

While Beck acknowledges that risks are not an invention of modernity, he
argues that contemporary risks are of a different nature. In 'risk society' 'natural' hazards, such as drought, earthquakes and hurricanes, are augmented by
'manufactured risks' arising from nuclear power, environmental pollution and
technological systems. Such risks exist at a global level, thus the life of a blade
of grass in the Bavarian forests comes to depend on international pollution
agreements (Beck, 1992, p. 23). Furthermore, consequences of hazards can
spread across future generations. For example, many of those affected by
dangers such as the fire at the Chernobyl nuclear plant are not yet born (Beck,

1996, p. 15). This suggests that the outcomes of risk in late modernity can be open-ended, making them more difficult to accurately describe and alleviate. Problematically many hazards such as toxins in foodstuff or nuclear threat also escape everyday perceptions (Beck, 1992, p. 21). Overall, Beck concludes that risks in contemporary society can only be minimised, never entirely removed (1995, p. 76).

Beck argues that in 'risk society' a process of reflexive modernisation dissolves the traditional boundaries of industrial society (1992, p. 87). This occurs as individuals react to the emergence of global risks, a process that is reinforced as industrial society itself becomes perceived as a 'risk society' (Beck, 1996). Yet for Beck reflexivity in this context does not denote mere reflection but rather self-confrontation (1994, 1996) encouraging labour mobility, a tendency towards 'classlessness' and the relative freeing of gender / sex status (1992, pp. 88–9). This dissolution and self-confrontation is connected with 'individuation', 'an historically contradictory process to societalization' (Beck, 1992, p. 90) in which individuals become the reproduction unit of the social in the lifeworld and are forced to construct their own biography. Individuation is fraught with risk (Beck and Beck-Gernsheim, 1995) Social movements come into existence as a reaction not only to new risks but also as a way for individuals to experiment with social relations. Individuals' also experiment with their bodies in alternative subcultures in an attempt to create new 'certainties' and combat the insecurity created by risk in contemporary society.

According to Giddens (1991) this reflexivity is not merely an individual process but is also institutionalised in organisations which have increasingly become disembodied in time / space contexts. While for Giddens (1994) reflexivity in the risk society occurs through expert institutionalised systems dependent upon lay peoples trust, Beck (1992) asserts that reflexivity is a critique of expert systems based on an inherent distrust. As a consequence of greater critical reflexivity, individualisation and questioning of expert systems the ability of individuals to construct their own biographies is privileged. Thus, inequalities and failures are increasingly perceived as a reflection of personal inadequacies (Beck, 1992, p. 100). The inability to protect oneself from risks such as unemployment, ill-health or marital breakdown may be considered the result of an individuals poor decision-making rather than wider social processes (Lupton, 1999, p. 72). Despite the existence of such uncertainties Giddens (1991) draws upon the concept of *umwelt* to argue that there are systems of competencies on which the basis of trust is constructed as a normal condition, allowing for remote risks to be bracketed out. Thus with smoking, it could be argued that the time between the current behaviour and the future possibility is sufficiently distant to allow the risk to be bracketed out. Furthermore, Giddens (1991) argues that individuals actually cultivate risk taking, experimenting with perceived trust through undertaking such activities as dangerous sports.

Beck and Gidden's writings on 'risk society' have been the focus of some criticism. Thus, it has been argued that their early work largely ignored cultural aspects of risk (Lash, 1994; Day, 2000), that the association between material processes and public risk perceptions is somewhat simplistic (Goldblatt, 1995), that their arguments are heavily rhetorical, whilst being empirical sparse (McMylor, 1996) and that they have understated the power of capital (Rustin, 1994). Nevertheless, despite an extensive critique arguments about 'risk society' have been hugely influential within the field of sociology. Due to the focus on macro-political processes present in the 'risk society' perspective educational research within this tradition tends to focus on structural factors and the impact of government policy on such issues as educational careers, employment opportunities and lifestyle issues (e.g. Furlong and Cartmel, 1997). Thus, the 'risk society' approach attempts to understand hazards that operate at a macro-political level. Within this risk perspective there is a focus upon globalisation, which would lend itself to a consideration of how local educational communities are affected by broader international issues, such as those relating to environmental education, global terrorism or the impact of new forms of information communication technology.

Cultural, Hermeneutic Approaches to Risk

Drawing upon social anthropology and interpretative sociology, cultural, hermeneutic approaches maintain that risk is always social (Douglas and Wildavsky, 1982). Therefore, any understanding of risk needs to be situated within the cultural and political settings that gave rise to it.

Over a period of many years, the anthropologist Mary Douglas has written extensively on risk, co-authoring a volume with Aaron Wildavsky in 1982, before writing two solo works on risk acceptability (1985) and blame (1992). Douglas (1992) argues that each society, subculture or organisation elevates some risks to a high point while depressing others. In this context risks are not 'given' but rather are selected through social processes. Thus, the decision as to what becomes labelled as a 'risk' gives an indication of the sort of community or society in which people wish to live. Being able to control what gets labelled as risk is a position of power, especially as numerous competing claims often exist. Within this perspective risk is best understood as a cultural artefact, something at least partially fashioned by social agents. Literature in this field draws upon a variety of other concepts including 'otherness', pollution and boundaries.

Douglas argues that the 'other' is a key concept in risk formation, being frequently associated with pollution and exclusion. The 'other' is conceptualised as different from the self, leading to the creation of boundaries between inside and outside the body / society (Douglas and Widalvsky, 1982). Certain marginal and stigmatised groups that are labelled as 'others' tend to have anxieties and fears projected onto them becoming perceived as 'dangerous' or 'at-risk' (Lupton, 1999, p. 124). Excluding and reinforcing boundaries that bar these 'others' enables individuals, communities or societies to deal with their fear of real or imagined dangers. Yet, 'otherness' is reinforced not just by exclusion but also through inclusion. Reaffirming belonging to a body / group whilst identifying what it would involve to be expelled reaffirms boundaries. In short, 'otherness' can be seen as a strategy for dealing with risk.

While pollution can be used in a purely physical sense it also has symbolic dimensions (Douglas and Widalvsky, 1982, p. 36). Thus Khare (1996, p. 437) notes that societies relate pollution to their moral values, with rites and practices aimed at reducing risk and danger to their people. However, Douglas contends that pollution rules do not strictly correlate with moral rules. She argues that some kinds of behaviour may be judged wrong and yet not provoke pollution beliefs, whilst others not thought very reprehensible are seen as polluting and dangerous (Douglas, 1966, p. 160). Nevertheless, pollution beliefs are closely associated with ideas of risk. Many environmental hazards are discussed in a manner that seems to suggest that risk and pollution are almost synonymous. For example, in schools staff and students, describe undesirable on-line material as 'dirty', 'filthy' and 'garbage'.

Pollution implies adulteration or transgression, providing a way in which individuals can express concerns about the integrity of boundaries (Douglas, 1966). Boundaries provide a demarcation, allowing a classification, distinguishing between social groups, the self and other, the 'civilised' and 'barbaric'. They instil an identity of belonging to that which is included whilst highlighting the 'difference' and 'otherness' of that which is excluded. Cohen notes that boundaries may be structural or symbolic, maintaining that '[i]t is in the symbolic that we now look for people's sense of difference, and in symbolism, rather than structure, that we seek the boundaries of their worlds of identity and diversity' (1986, p. 2). Concern about boundaries reflects the preoccupation of human societies with the question of how to deal with risks to the body, environment, community or wider society. Douglas (1966) maintains that pollution ideas can be used to describe four forms of risky situations where boundaries are compromised. Namely, external threats to boundaries, transgression of boundaries from the inside, internal contradictions within a boundary and uncertainty at the margin of boundaries.

Importantly, it should be noted that being excluded is not always a negative experience. Neither is the transgression of boundaries always undesirable or frowned upon in mainstream society. Thus, the rituals and celebrations of carnival seek to confuse boundaries at least for a time, allowing freedom from traditional restraints, encouraging inversion, excess and hybridity (Lupton, 1999, p. 166).

While Douglas's work provides a persuasive critique of the realist approaches, emphasising that risk judgements are political, moral and aesthetic, it has been criticised for reducing real dangers to little more than metaphor, trivialising real hazards and 'eliminating danger altogether' (Kaprow, 1985; 347). Furthermore, her writings are frequently re-interpreted as implying that lay perceptions of risk involve inaccuracies and errors of judgement because of the contaminating influence of cultural and social processes.

Central to the idea of understanding risk as a cultural artefact is the notion that danger needs to be understood hermeneutically. Hermeneutic in this sense relates to a social realist tradition, in which an understanding of actions is sought within the larger framework of the life world that produced it (Pawson and Tilley, 1997, p. 21). For example, whilst studying claims that the herbicide 2, 4, 5-T was harmful to farm workers in Cumbria, Wynne (1989) noted that scientists who claimed that the product was not hazardous if properly used, ignored the fact that because of work contingencies, it was rarely prepared and used according to the safety instructions. Within this tradition it is argued that it is important to understand the risk perceptions of both scientific experts and lay-people on a hermeneutic level (Wynne, 1989, 1996). However, this does not mean privileging the experiential truth of lay actors over the propositional truth of experts. This would merely invert the existing scientific knowledge hierarchies (Szerszynski et al., 1996, p. 7).

While the cultural hermeneutic perspective has not been extensively used in considering education and risk, there nevertheless exist certain aspects of this approach that recommend its adoption in exploring key educational issues. The use of anthropological concepts such as 'otherness', pollution and boundaries would offer new ways of interpreting problems such as bullying, exclusion from schools and the negative impact of technology. They would draw attention to the processes of cultural construction and labelling, whilst underlining that risk situations and environments need to be understood on a hermeneutic level.

Disciplinary Discourse and Risk

The analysis of risk that focuses solely upon social discourse is often ignored in the broader risk literature (e.g. Caplan, 2000). A reason for this neglect is that in concentrating purely upon discourse the threat posed by actual dangers, such as pollution, disease or natural disasters, is ignored. Rather researchers in this tradition are interested in how risk discourses are used as instruments of social control. Adopting a strong social constructionist position, writings focusing upon risk discourse draw heavily upon the work of Foucault. While Foucault did not dwell specifically upon the topic of risk in his writings, much of what he wrote about government and modernity has been applied by scholars, such as Castel (1991), to the analysis of risk as a socio-cultural phenomenon. Drawing on Foucault's (1991) writings on mass surveillance, monitoring, and observation, risk can be constructed as a disciplinary, moral technology.

From this perspective, it is argued that only through disciplinary discourses, strategies, practices and institutions is risk known. Thus, it is maintained that the nature of risk itself should not be the focus of study. Risk is seen as a 'calculative rationality', not as a thing in itself (Dean, 1999). As expert knowledge about risk has proliferated in late modernity, the various strategies that individuals are required to practise upon themselves to avoid risk have equally proliferated. Bauman (1993) argues that strategies dumping risk-avoidance behaviour on the individual help to create an enormous market in risk avoiding devices, from vitamins to video-surveillance systems. In this sense risk-avoidance is not so much a chance for the future as a way of maintaining a billion-dollar industry. He points out that there are massive vested interests in maintaining the structure of 'risk society' in its current form. This line of argument is difficult to avoid when the environmental risks attached to the motor car, plastics, cheap food and so on are considered. For Bauman (1993) these factors all cast doubt on Beck's notion that once we know about the risk we can begin to try to reduce it. He is also doubtful of the role of technology in dealing with these risks, after all technology created these problems and feasibly any technological solutions will create more difficulties.

An important characteristic of risk discourse in contemporary society is the 'apparent' ability to calculate risk through statistical processes. This 'knowledge' about risk can allow for a sense that technology is in control. The reflexivity of modernity and the surveillance of individuals and institutions strengthen this feeling of security. Yet, Bauman makes the point that attention to the major causes of risk is deflected by 'the type of reflexivity in which the public is trained by risk-assessments offered for popular knowledge and use' (1993, p. 203). Thus with regard to health, if the message is communicated that a healthy lifestyle is within an individual's control, then a person who succumbs to a health risk can be assumed to be responsible for their own condition. This is often reinforced when inquiries into disasters produce individualised accounts of simple causal chains. In late modern societies to not engage in risk avoiding behaviour is considered 'a failure of the self to take care of itself – a form of irrationality, or simply a lack of skilfulness' (Greco, 1993, p. 361).

The risk discourse approach is useful insofar it draws attention to rhetoric as an instrument of control and introduces the idea that risk perceptions might encourage self-policing. Yet, this approach ignores the existence of actual danger. Drawing upon this perspective research in education tends to focus upon how notions of risk are constructed through institutional processes, government policies and media coverage. Indeed Swadener and Lubeck (1995) have criticised much of the literature focusing on young people 'at-risk'. They argue that risk labels have been used unscientifically to stigmatise and mistreat certain groups as if their problems were unique and entirely their own fault. In this sense risk discourse research in education parallels much of the existing work on the process of labelling and self-fulfilling prophecies.

One feature common to all the risk perspectives that have been considered is their tendency to utilise the concept as a negative term, something that harbours the potential for harm or damage. This inclination to perceive risk solely in fatalistic terms ignores its potential beneficial aspects. It is to this consideration, of risk as positive process, that the focus now shifts.

Risk as Positive Consequence

The emergence of risk as a concept is associated with maritime ventures and the growth of the insurance market (Lupton, 1999, p. 5). In this context, it was used to describe the possible perils, such as storm, flood or epidemic, which might beset maritime ventures (Ewald, 1991). During the eighteenth and nineteenth century the concept of risk was increasingly used in terms of calculable probability, allowing for the possibility that risks could be both 'good' and 'bad' (Douglas, 1992). However, such usage has been eclipsed and in contemporary western societies, the concept of risk inherently invokes thoughts of negative impacts on the lives of individuals, communities or societies. As much of the current academic literature dealing with risk focuses upon ecological and health issues this is hardly a surprising consequence. Thus the word risk is now associated with danger. As Short notes '[w]hile risk and cost benefit analysis focus on both positive and negative potential outcomes, benefits tend to receive short shrift in these analyses as do positive aspects of risk' (Short, 1984, p. 711). Not only is there such a thing in strictly realist terms as a 'good risk' (one with high probability of gain and low probability of losses) but importantly engaging in risk behaviour can in itself be beneficial.

As the growth of 'extreme sports' in recent years indicates, risk taking can be a pleasurable activity. The display of daring, skill and resourcefulness that may be involved in taking risks can create an excitement which everyday mundane existence lacks (Giddens, 1991). In such circumstances the hazard itself becomes secondary to the potential pleasure from avoiding the negative consequences. Risk taking can act as boredom alleviation. Lyng (1990) uses the term 'edgework' to describe why some individuals voluntarily engage in dangerous activities which take place around cultural boundaries, such as those between sanity / insanity and life / death. Here boundary confusion and transgression is actively pursued for pleasure and in some cases to construct an identity as a risk taker. Indeed Lying (1990) stresses the importance of risk taking as skilled performance, ostentatiously displaying the ability to maintain control in a chaotic situation and overcome fear. Thus taking part in dangerous activities can be entertaining, physically and mentally stimulating, a display of skill or daring, and a process of identity construction. Furthermore, wilfully engaging in certain risks might be seen as an attempt to challenge authority, reject societal discourses relating to the safety of self and others. Deviant activities such as students hacking into school computer networks, truancy and even joy riding may all be seen as displaying aspects of 'edgework'. Arguably, such activities may provide entertainment, display daring, construct an identity as a risk-taker and challenge authority. Labelling such risk taking activities as having possible positive outcomes underlines the argument that risk consequences are interpreted through social, cultural and political processes.

The displays of skill sometimes involved in undertaking dangerous activities hints at the educational potential of risk taking. Indeed risk can be an important part of the learning process. Early socialisation in schools often seeks to teach students about a variety of risks that need to be avoided, such as crossing busy roads or talking to strangers. Yet as students develop, engaging in certain risk activities can be educationally beneficial, stimulating creativity. Teachers might actively pursue educationally 'risky' activities in the hope of greater pedagogic gains. In this context, risk can be associated with the concept of play. Play is type of 'free activity', it is a way to learn, to manage energies and to inspire improvisation within (and outside) rule governed behaviour (Schecher 1994, p. 621). There is an aesthetic in play, which relates to the pleasure gained from such an activity. Like intentional risk taking there is a delight in play in acting, engaging, focusing and even resisting. Play is everywhere and nowhere, liminal, essentially elusive (Turner, 1983, p. 234). Liminality in this sense represents a transitional stage between two distinctly different entities, identities or sites (Lupton, 1999, p. 133). While as Douglas and Wildavsky (1982) note it is in liminal areas that risks are often situated, it is also in such areas that the greatest potential for creativity and educational gains lie.

In conclusion, it should be noted that as risk perspectives are culturally constructed opinions may often differ as to likely positive or negative outcomes. Indeed, it is possible that the same activity will have differing interpretations as to the positive or negative nature of its outcomes. Over time, the various interpretations of the benefits or dangers of a particular risk will possibly change, reflecting that risk itself is a dynamic process. It is to this issue of risk as a dynamic process that the focus now turns.

Risk as Dynamic Process

One element that the various approaches to risk have in common is an appreciation that risk itself is a dynamic concept. The dangers that people fear in contemporary society are not necessarily those that will cause fear in the future. While some risks such as child abuse seem to occupy positions as on-going hazards in the public perception others such as the salmonella virus fade from the public sphere once outbreaks have been dealt with and the threat is deemed to have passed. This suggests that some risks fade from popular perception largely because they are no longer seen as a significant danger. However, drawing on Douglas and Wildavsky (1982) it should be recognised that deciding whether something is labelled as a risk is always a cultural and political process. Certain risks may capture public perception because they offer a real and present danger to the well being of individuals and society, yet the newsworthiness of risks is a significant factor in influencing what gets reported. For example, the cases of mothers being imprisoned in the United States of America for 'foetal endangerment' through refusing to take medical advice or give up certain drugs (Handwerker, 1994) is rarely given media coverage. On the other hand, the media exaggerate and sensationalise certain risks, such as the threat posed to children from Internet use (Lawson and Comber, 2000). In such cases, while the actual threats may exist, public perceptions of these dangers might be exaggerated due to media influence. Nevertheless, concern about certain risks can be transient.

Even where risks come to dominate the public perception for substantial periods of time the exact form that such hazards are perceived to take may change. As Szerszynski et al. (1996) note while nuclear technology has been a cause for concern for over four decades the focus has shifted from fear of a nuclear strike during the Cold War, to anxiety about unsafe nuclear power plants, back to fear of weapons of mass destruction and 'dirty bombs'. There is a long history of concern about the activities of paedophiles, yet the precise manner in which this risk has been socially constructed and discussed in the mass media has changed over time. For example, the murders of Holly Wells and Jessica Chapman resituated the fear of child abuse within educational institutions. Furthermore, the growth of Internet use by children and youths has meant a shift in concern to the on-line activities of paedophiles in recent years. Indeed as Bauman (1993) notes technology in contemporary society is the focus of much risk discourse and indeed many of the 'technological fixes' for such hazards seem to generate their own problems. The degree of attention that individuals and society give to particular risks can fluctuate over time. Concern about particular risks such as road traffic safety outside of schools may increase after a fatal accident, whilst other dangers such as underage smoking stay constant despite thousands of tobacco related deaths each year. Nor is the amount of attention paid to a risk a necessary function of the actual extent of that danger. In particular exaggerated and sensationalistic media coverage can lead to 'moral panics' where fears become grossly distorted.

Risks themselves are dynamic and are best understood as processes. While new risks might emerge, such as Internet addiction, others, like the spread of tuberculosis in industrially developed countries, are largely ameliorated. Understanding the process involved in the development of a risk is not just important in mapping the historical career of a particular danger. Rather to understand risks from a culturally situated perspective it is essential to understand them as processes.

Drawing upon top down models of policy processes it can be suggested that for a risk to occur it needs to go through several stages (Figure 1). Firstly the elements that can lead to a particular danger need to be present (existence of risk elements). Secondly these elements need to be active ensuring the danger-ous event happens (risk occurrence). Thirdly, there is an immediate effect of the risk occurring (risk output). Finally, there are the longer-term effects of the event (risk outcome). Admittedly, while detailed risk assessment exercises recognise the possibility of multiple risk outputs and outcomes, discussion about risk often takes place around the existence of risk elements with the latter stages of the process only tacitly acknowledged. For example, consider the issue of students accessing pornographic material using the school Internet. Research on staff risk perceptions (Hope, 2002) indicates that while many would label this as a risk there are several different interpretations of the actual

Existence of risk elements → Risk occurrence → Risk output → Risk outcome

Figure 1. The risk process

nature of possible dangers. Thus some staff were concerned about the corruption of innocent minds, whilst others feared the effect that students accessing such material in schools might have on the institutional reputation or staff authority. In this case, the actual risk of on-line pornography has several possible different risk outputs and outcomes. Drawing a stark distinction between the existence of risk elements and risk outputs and outcomes redirects attention to the important question of who is actually at risk. As Oswald (1998) notes with regard children and Internet regulation different answers to this question can lead to children effectively being differentially labelled as 'at-risk' or 'dangerous'. Differentiating between immediate and long-term effects acknowledges that some risk impacts will not be felt for many years. Finally, if risk is understood as a process then it should be recognised that feedback can occur at any stage, which could ultimately lead to new risk outputs and outcomes. In this context the risk process illustrated in Figure 1 is best seen as a basic analytical tool to encourage consideration of the processes inherent in risk. For as Bourdieu (1990, pp. 10–11) notes with regard to linear series and diagrammatic representations one should always be aware of the their ability to create a synoptic illusion of coherent, logically structured cultural forms.

Conclusion

Risk within education needs to be understood as a cultural phenomenon. Educational researchers need to adopt the cultural risk perspective that best suits their research question and theoretical disposition. Furthermore, it should be recognised that risk is a dynamic process, with inputs, occurrences, outputs and outcomes. Failure to adequately distinguish between the risk occurrence and risk output or outcomes endangers effective analysis and amelioration. Finally, particularly with regard to teaching strategies, it must be noted that risk may have positive consequences, not just negative ones.

Risk, education and culture is an area where more research needs to be carried out. Whether focusing on the potential dangers of introducing new forms of communication technology into the classroom, examining the impact of Closed Circuit Television on educational settings or exploring how to use this concept to engender creativity in the learning process, risk is a rich seam waiting to be tapped.

References

Abercrombie, N., Hill, S. and Turner, B.S. (1994) (2nd Edition), *The Penguin Dictionary of Sociology*, Penguin, Harmondsworth.

18   *Risk, Education and Culture*

Bauman, Z. (1993), *Postmodern Ethics*, Blackwell, Oxford.

Beck, U. (1992), *Risk Society: Towards a New Modernity*, Sage, London.

Beck, U. (1995), *Ecological Politics in the Age of Risk*, Polity Press, Cambridge.

Beck, U. (1996), 'Risk society and the provident state', in S. Lash, B. Szerszinski and B. Wynne (eds), *Risk, Environment and Modernity: Towards a New Ecology*, Sage, London, pp. 27–43.

Beck, U. and Beck-Gernsheim, E. (1995), *The Normal Chaos of Love*, Polity Press, Cambridge.

Benthin, A., Slovic, P. and Severson, H. (1993), 'A psychometric study of adolescent risk perception', *Journal of Adolescence*, vol. 16, pp. 153–168.

Bourdieu, P. (1990), *The Logic of Practice*, Polity Press, Cambridge.

Bradbury, J. (1989), 'The policy implications of differing concepts of risk', *Science Technology & Human Values*, vol. 14(4), pp. 380–399.

Caplan, P. (2000), 'Introduction: Risk revisited', in P. Caplan (ed), *Risk Revisited*, Pluto Press, London, pp. 1–28.

Castel, R. (1991), 'From dangerousness to risk', in G. Burchell, C. Gordon and P. Miller (eds), *The Foucault Effect: Studies in Governmentality*, Harvester/Wheatsheaf, London, pp. 281–298.

Cohen, A. (1986), 'Of symbols and boundaries, or, does Ertie's greatcoat hold the key?' in Cohen, A. (Ed), *Symbolising Boundaries: Identity and Diversity in British cultures*, Manchester University Press, Manchester, pp. 1–19.

Cottle, S. (1998), 'Ulrich Beck, "Risk Society" and the Media: A Catastrophic View?', *European Journal of Communication*, vol. 13(1), pp. 5–32.

Day, S. (2000), 'The Politics of Risk among London Prostitutes', in P. Caplan (ed), *Risk Revisited*, Pluto Press, London, pp. 29–58.

Dean, M. (1999), 'Risk, calculable and incalculable', in D. Lupton (ed), *Risk and Sociocultural Theory: New Directions and Perspectives*, Cambridge University Press, Cambridge, pp. 205–228.

Donnerstein, E. and Smith, S. (2001), 'Sex in the Media', in D.G. Singer & J.L. Singer (eds), *Handbook of Children and the Media*, Sage Publications, London, pp. 289–307.

Douglas, M. (1966), *Purity and Danger: An Analysis of the Concepts of Pollution and Taboo*, Routledge & Kegan Paul, London.

Douglas, M. (1985), *Risk Acceptability According to the Social Sciences*, Russell Sage Foundation, New York.

Douglas, M. (1992), *Risk and Blame: Essays in Cultural Theory*, Routledge, London.

Douglas, M. and Wildavsky, A. (1982), *Risk and Culture: An Essay on the Selection of Technological and Environmental Dangers*, University of California Press, Berkley, California.

Dwyer, P. and Wyn, J. (2001), *Youth, Education and Risk: Facing the Future*, Routledge / Palmer, London.

Ewald, F. (1991), 'Insurance and risks', in G. Burchell, C. Gordon and P. Miller (eds), *The Foucault Effect: Studies in Governmentality*, Harvester/Wheatsheaf, London, pp. 197–210.

Foucault, M. (1991), 'Govermentality', in G. Burchell, C. Gordon and P. Miller (eds), *The Foucault Effect: Studies in Governmentality*, Harvester/Wheatsheaf, London, pp. 87–104.

Furedi, F. (1997), *Culture of Fear: Risk Taking and the Morality of Low Expectation*, Cassell, London.

Furlong, A. and Cartmel, F. (1997), *Young People and Social Change*, Open University Press, Buckingham.

Giddens, A. (1990), *The Consequences of Modernity*, Polity Press, Cambridge.

Giddens, A. (1991), *Modernity and Self-Identity*, Polity Press, Cambridge.

Giddens, A. (1994), 'Living in a post-traditional society', in U. Beck, A. Giddens & S. Lash (eds), *Reflexive Modernization, Politics, Tradition and Aesthetics in the Modern Social Order*, Polity Press, Cambridge, pp. 56–109.

Goffman, E. (1963), *Stigma*, Ptrentice-Hall, Eaglewood Cliffs, NJ.

Goldblatt, D. (1995), *Social Theory and the Environment*, Polity Press, Cambridge.

Greco, M. (1993), 'Psychosomatic subjects and the "duty to be well": Personal agency within medical rationality', *Economy and Society*, vol. 22(3), pp. 357–372.

Handwerker, L. (1994), 'Medical risk: Implicating poor pregnant women', *Social Science and Medicine*, vol. 38(5), pp. 665–675.

Hope, A. (2002), *School Internet Use: Case Studies in the sociology of risk*, Unpublished Ph.D. Thesis.

Jary, D. and Jary, J. (1995) (2nd Edition), *Collins Dictionary of Sociology*, Harper Collins Publishers, Glasgow.

Kahneman, D., Slovic, P. and Tversky, A. (1982) (eds), *Judgement under uncertainty: Heuristics and Biases*, Cambridge University Press, New York.

Kaprow, M. (1985), 'Manufacturing danger: fear and pollution in industrial society', *American Anthropology*, vol. 87, pp. 342–356.

Lash, S. (1994), 'Reflexivity and its doubles: structure, aesthetics, community', in U. Beck, A. Giddens & S. Lash (eds), *Reflexive Modernization, Politics, Tradition and Aesthetics in the Modern Social Order*, Polity Press, Cambridge, pp. 110–173.

Lawson, T. and Comber, C. (2000), 'Censorship, the Internet and Schools: a new moral panic?' *The Curriculum Journal*, vol. 11(2), pp. 273–285.

Lupton, D. (1999), *Risk*, Routledge, London.

Lying, S. (1990), 'Edgework: a social psychological analysis of voluntary risk taking'. *American Journal of Sociology*, vol. 95(4), pp. 851–886.

McMylor, P. (1996), 'Goods and Bads', *Radical Philosophy*, vol. 77, pp. 52–53.

Musgave, P. (1983), 'Education', in M. Mann (ed) (1983), *MacMillan Student Companion of Sociology*, MacMillan Press, London, p. 105.

Oswell, D. (1998), 'The place of "childhood" in Internet content regulation: a case study of policy in the UK', *International Journal of Cultural Studies*, vol. 1, pp. 131–151.

Pawson, R. and Tilley, N. (1997), *Realistic Evaluation*, Sage, London.

Rustin, M. (1994), 'Incomplete modernity: Ulrich Beck's Risk Society', *Radical Philosophy*, vol. 67, pp. 2–12.

Schechner, R. (1994), 'Ritual and Performance', in T. Ingold (1994), *Companion Encyclopedia of Anthropology*, Routledge, London, pp. 613–647.

Short, J. (1984), 'The social fabric at risk: Toward the social transformation of risk analysis', *American Sociological Review*, vol. 49, pp. 711–725.

Slovic, P. (1998), 'The Psychometric Paradigm: Perception of risk', in R.E. Lofstedt and L. Frewer (1998), *The Earthscan Reader in Risk and Modern Society*, Earthscan Publications, London, pp. 31–43.

Slovic, P. (2000), *The Perception of Risk*, Earthscan, London.

Starr, C. (1969), 'Social benefit versus technological risk', *Science*, vol. 165, pp. 1232–1238.

Swadener, B.B., and Lubeck, S. (eds) (1995), *Children and Families 'At Promise'*, State University of New York Press, Albany.

Szerszynski, B., Lash, S. and Wynne, B. (1996), 'Introduction: Ecology Realism and the Social Sciences', in S. Lash, B. Szerszinski and B. Wynne (eds), *Risk, Environment and Modernity: Towards a New Ecology*, Sage, London, pp. 1–26.

Turner, V. (1983), 'Body, brain and culture', *Zygon*, vol. 18(3), pp. 221–446.

Wynne, B. (1989), 'Frameworks of rationality in risk management: towards the testing of naïve sociology', in J. Brown (ed.), *Environmental Threats: Perception, Analysis and Management*, Bellhaven Press, London, pp. 33–47.

Wynne, B. (1996), 'May the sheep safely graze? A reflexive view of the expert-lay-knowledge divide', in S. Lash, B. Szerszinski and B. Wynne (eds), *Risk, Environment and Modernity: Towards a New Ecology*, Sage, London, pp. 44–83.

Chapter 2

Knowledge, Risk and Existentialism

Paul Oliver

Introduction

In contemporary society there is an increasing variety of procedures by which we may gain access to specialized knowledge. In the pre-modern period and during modernity this was much less so, and indeed knowledge tended then to be distributed in relatively direct proportion to social, economic, and political status. There was also the important factor of the relationship between knowledge accessibility and religious authority. The electronic networks of the postmodern world have democratized the availability of knowledge to the extent that the role of the 'expert' is being radically altered. In areas of human activity often associated with the notion of the profession, specialist expertise, once almost unchallengeable, may now be called to account on the strength of understanding gleaned from computer-based sources. The undoubted advantages of increased understanding may be to some extent counterbalanced by risks associated with the uncertainty of a social world in which the individual may possess sufficient knowledge to challenge all, but insufficient understanding for certainty of action. In a world of uncertainty and freedom, the individual is faced with a series of existential choices. Educationalists may once have been regarded as possessing unique insights, partly be virtue of having received a specialist education. Now their decisions and policies are challenged by students, parents, and the electorate, ushering in an environment of complexity and some uncertainty.

Knowledge

The extent to which different forms of knowledge have found public acceptability and validity, has been very much associated with the manner in which power and authority have been distributed in the society of the time. The theocracies of the medieval period supported knowledge which was amenable to their doctrines and ideologies, but were unforgiving about ideas which did not mesh with the prevailing orthodoxies. Knowledge existed within a closed world, in the confines of which individuals understood broadly that which it was permissible to believe, and that which was beyond the boundaries of

acceptability. It was also relatively transparent with such a society, that theocratic power was synonymous with the capacity to define valid knowledge.
Those who held positions of power and authority within the theocratic hierarchy were able to make and sustain epistemological definitions. It might be
realistic to mount extremely minor challenges to traditional and orthodox
belief systems, but religious authority was not challenged lightly. The penalties
for dissidence could be severe.

In the modern period, the rise of scientific and technological understanding
resulted in a form of technocracy in which the new scientific entrepreneurs
were able to establish rather more rational grounds for epistemological judgements. Other forms of justification remained, including those related to traditional economic and political power, and also to the authority derived from
the inheritance of land and wealth. The capacity to define that which was
socially-acceptable as valid knowledge was also related to social class, and to
the differential educational opportunities which derived from those distinc-
tions. Nevertheless, despite the remaining traditional influence over the status
of knowledge, there were far more opportunities for individuals and groups to
redefine received wisdom. Within this atmosphere of transition however, there
still remained the notion of the expert and the authority, who were able to
define that which was perceived, and would be perceived, as legitimate.

As we move into the postmodern world, one of the most significant social
characteristics which has emerged, is the exponential growth in the number of
different world views, and perspectives upon the issues of the day. For every
viewpoint, belief, assertion, and claim to truth, there appears to be a profusion
of counter-claims. Almost as soon as evidence is assembled to support one
stance, then data emerges which seems to point in a different direction. As
Goldblatt (2000, p. 156) has argued, throughout history there will have been
conflicts and differences of opinion about that which is to be regarded as
accepted truth, but the key feature of such disputes in the contemporary age is
that they tend to be worked out much more in the public domain. As a very
broad generalization it could be argued that in the past many people were in
effect presented with the agreed stance of large organizations or institutions
without having any appreciation of the internal conflicts within such bodies. In
postmodernity however, as Woodward and Watt (2000, p. 29) have suggested,
the mass media are a central factor in the dissemination of both accepted versions of reality, and of definitions contrary to those most commonly accepted.
Programmes which present analyses of current affairs and political policies are
frequently structured in terms of a debate between opinion holders of opposite
polarity, with the chaired discussion being confrontational to a greater or
lesser degree. Although the ostensible purpose of such debate may be to enable
non-expert members of the public to clarify their own views on current issues,
the discussion may also, in effect, be seen as primarily entertainment, rather
than as two experts with opposing views attempting earnestly to shed light
upon, and to approach somewhat nearer the truth of a complex and difficult
issue. Viewers and listeners may sometimes take the view that participants

have not been motivated primarily by the desire to assist the public in forming a balanced and well-informed view. The prime difficulty with this very public debate about what may be regarded as valid knowledge, is that people may be left in what appears to be a position of great uncertainty. An example is that of economic debate, where several extremely well-educated, well-informed, and experienced economists who each take very different views on current economic imperatives, may produce detailed but apparently contradictory data to support their various claims. It is very difficult to know where this leaves the non-expert member of the public who is watching or listening. It is sometimes difficult to know how such debates can help them in making an informed choice at an election.

The enhanced availability of knowledge in the contemporary world, and in particular the extent to which knowledge is disseminated by electronic media, have had a considerable effect upon the capacity of people to analyse the comments of politicians, scientists, doctors and other specialists. As Goldblatt (2000, p. 156) further argues, people have access to sufficient understanding to reflect critically upon the pronouncements of experts, and to form judgements as to when it might be appropriate to suggest counter explanations and interpretations. Not only do people tend to possess both the education and the access to information to enable them to challenge authority more and more, but in a variety of ways, professional experts are increasingly held accountable for their actions and decisions. Such accountability has been increased at least partly through the intervention of legislation, but also by the intervention of the media in drawing attention to cases where the judgement of experts has either been patently wrong, or indeed culpable. The result has tended to be a shift in emphasis, from a near absolute belief in the authority of the expert, to a situation where people feel more and more confident in challenging the views of authority. Although this is in many ways a desirable trend, it does raise considerable concerns. If, for example, everyone is to feel that in principle they are their own expert, then it is difficult to see how society could function effectively, with everyone forming their own individual view and taking their own decisions. One might imagine that such a situation could lead to the fragmentation of society, and to a lack of consensus over important questions. While it may be extremely undesirable that society blindly follows those who are defined as experts, there does need to be some measure of consensus in society. Such a consensus probably depends upon the definition of certain norms, values, standards and criteria. While we may not wish power to reside in the hands of those defined as experts, without the restraints of effective social control, we may still consider that society will function the better for the exercise of some form of power within society.

In the medieval, and also to a large extent in the modern period, the definition of valid knowledge took place substantially within a hierarchical system of influence. Sarup (1993, p. 74) has pointed out in his discussion of Foucault, that power and authority now seem to permeate society in complex networks, rather than in linear relationships. One of the results of this is that the nodes of power are often difficult to identify, and the mechanisms whereby people are influenced are sometimes difficult to ascertain. In the postmodern age, the exercise of power may be more subtle, and be implemented for example, by the process of encouraging people to emulate certain fashions or modes of action. In mass media advertising for example, people are encouraged to adopt certain lifestyles, to copy certain ways of doing things, to have certain attitudes, and to respond to situations in specific ways. Not only does advertising seek to make preferential definitions of knowledge, but also seeks to exercise power in persuading people to adopt these definitions.

In the medieval period, the acquisition of knowledge was an incremental process, often lasting many years. It tended to involve a gradual initiation into a particular form of intellectual life, often associated with ecclesiastical doctrine and a related way of life. It was, in a sense, a form of apprenticeship, involving the transfer of knowledge and understanding from those who had undergone the process, to the novitiates. The circulation of such knowledge was very much restricted. In pre-printing days this was to a certain extent because of the slow process of reproducing manuscripts, but was also related to the prevailing concept of the purpose of knowledge. The inculcation of a body of knowledge was not simply about the transmission of information, but was part of the larger process of developing the whole person.

Through the modern age and into contemporary times, we can see the evolution of the concept of knowledge, from being concerned with the development of the person, through the pragmatic notion of using knowledge as the basis for industrial and commercial expansion, to the concept of knowledge as described by Lyotard (1984, p. 4) as a commercial product or saleable commodity. The existence of knowledge in the marketplace is a widespread phenomenon, encouraged by the multiplicity of forms of electronic transfer of information. Whether we consider subscriber television channels, the provision of books in a variety of electronic media, or the internet, it is evident that knowledge is a product to be sold, and a very valuable product at that. The expansion of education, and in particular of higher education, is further evidence of this trend. However, like all commodities, it is a debatable issue whether the consumer really needs the range of knowledge products which are available. Just as consumers may be persuaded that it would be desirable or beneficial to consume a new food product, so they may be persuaded of the hypothetical advantages of having access to further knowledge.

Lyotard (1984, p. 6) has further argued that knowledge could be conceptualized in the same way as money. The expansion of educational systems, particularly in the western contemporary world has resulted in the proliferation of qualifications and certificates which may be 'purchased' through the medium of tuition fees. One may then view such qualifications as a means of monetary exchange, in so far as the skills and knowledge which they represent are exchanged for well-paid employment. Companies and organizations may also invest in highly-qualified people to the extent that they will employ individuals who have studied at prestigious universities, not so much because they can realise that potential for the company immediately, but because it is believed in the long term, they will be able to generate saleable commodities for the organization.

The French philosopher Baudrillard has drawn our attention to a number of important phenomena in postmodern knowledge. In particular he has highlighted the way in which 'simulacra' in contemporary society, seek to represent at some considerable distance, a purported reality. So far distant are they however, from the knowledge they attempt to represent, that finally they are indicative only of themselves. Best (2003, p. 260) provides the example of news in the media, and the events which they purport to represent. If we consider the case of an event somewhere in the world, that event may or may not be selected for inclusion in a news programme. This is the first stage of the process of representation. Even if selected, only certain elements of the event may be selected for incorporation in the representation of that event. During this process, that particular event may be integrated with other events, and contextualized in readiness for the final presentation. Finally, the text is written which will seek to present the original event to the listeners or viewers. However, that text is arguably so far distant from the original event, that it may not in any real sense represent it. The news has become merely a collection of images and words, which are almost self-defining, rather than being defined in terms of the reality of the original knowledge.

In the context of Baudrillard's writing, Benton and Craib (2001, p. 169) have argued that society has in effect moved through several stages in terms of representing reality. As an example, we might consider representation in art and the reproduction of works of art. The Mona Lisa would originally have been da Vinci's attempt to create a likeness of a specific person. In common with artists of his period, he attempted to create 'a likeness' while at the same time revealing something of the character of the person being portrayed. So popular did the painting become, that in the modern period, with the advances in printing technology, it was no longer necessary to visit the Louvre in order to see the painting. One could view it in art books, on postcards and as a poster. In the postmodern world however, such art has passed beyond being merely the physical reproduction of a painting. It appears so widely in so many contexts, and as an accompaniment to so many different symbols, that it has virtually ceased to be connected with the original painting. It is now the Mona Lisa as multi-media image, and representing only itself. The ultimate separation occurs when people seeing the image, recognize it as a popular and common image, yet do not know its name, nor where it came from. If they are not aware that it is a copy of a famous painting, then the separation of image and reality is complete. We have then moved into the world of the hyperreal, a world in which the signs and images relate to nothing but each other.

Linked with this proliferation in the symbols which have but a tenuous link with that symbolized, has arisen a multiplicity of varieties of knowledge. Forms of mass electronic communication have been instrumental in the dissemination of many different forms of life and many different world views. These may have manifested themselves in alternative political ideologies and systems, in different religious and spiritual patterns, in different ways of marketing goods and of relating to the world of commerce, and in different forms and patterns of employment. The result is that individuals have a far greater choice than in modernity. Such choice can be stimulating in that it opens up different potentials for the individual, and in principle, provides far more opportunities for exploring the world. It can however, be also extremely confusing, in that the individual may not possess the understanding of the sophistication of this new world, to make informed decisions. As Spybey (1996, p. 9) has suggested, one result of this increased variation in society, is that individuals may have enhanced ideas concerning the potentiality of human life. One might argue that should this remain unfulfilled, then the individual may develop a negativity concerning social organization.

Travel and migration have always been a feature of human life, but as Spybey (1996, p. 12) has also pointed out, some features of postmodern society have led to certain types of migration for economic reasons. The expansion of electronic communication and in particular, the internet, has enabled people in all parts of the world, and perhaps most significantly in those countries which are economically and industrially underdeveloped, to see the affluence and consumerism which are features of the technologically-developed world. This has to some extent resulted in a completely-understandable momentum of migration in order to access the perceived advantages of such a social world. People are often willing to undergo the severest hardships in order to try to be part of the industrially-developed world. Such migration has raised ethical questions for developed countries, as the economic differentials across the world are brought into very sharp focus. It has also raised important conceptual issues about definitions of migration and the legitimacy or otherwise of peoples' claims to be able to move from one country to another. Additionally, the process of migration for economic reasons, has brought people of diverse cultures and ethnicities into contact with each other, and in the process different social definitions of knowledge have become contrasted with each other. This is yet another dimension of the phenomenon of globalization, and the tendency in the postmodern world for the widespread dissemination of cultural and epistemological systems.

Knowledge is central to the new globalized economic and commercial structures. At the heart of contemporary wealth-producing systems, are electronic and computer infrastructures which depend for their existence and maintenance upon a sophisticated, and well-educated workforce. As Castells (1998, p. 345) has argued, education, and the knowledge which accompanies it, is a fundamental supporting mechanism for world systems. In modernity, certain characteristics were required of the workforce. To different extents, these characteristics might have included physical strength, the capacity to work long hours in very difficult physical circumstances, and the capacity to adjust to not only often a single form of employment for life, but also to the monotony of many employment lifestyles. The physical nature and in some cases, the physical danger of employment in modernity, has been replaced with a workplace which is often bewildering in its complexity and the rapidity with which it can change. It may not be necessarily as physically dangerous, but it generates considerable psychological pressures, through its emphasis upon rapidly changing cognitive demands, and in the requirement for continuous professional updating. At its heart, is an almost insatiable demand for more and sophisticated understanding and knowledge in its employees. The knowledge required to obtain a specific job today, may be overtaken and become obsolescent in a matter of months. A knowledge of only the latest computer systems may be adequate to gain specific employment. Such trends seem unlikely to change in the near future.

As Castells (1998, p. 345) has further indicated, there is, in the contemporary world, a constant attempt by those in employment to ensure that they remain current with their knowledge and skills. If they do not manage to achieve this, then there remains the possibility that they will either have to eventually fill less technologically-sophisticated jobs. Not having the requisite skills is thus not only a phenomenon of the so-called 'underdeveloped' world or Third World, but is a characteristic of advanced industrial societies. As computerized technology becomes more and more sophisticated, then the capacity to interact with such technology will become a rarer and rarer commodity. It will become a commodity which can be traded. Those increasingly fewer individuals who possess such knowledge and skills will be more in demand, and those without the relevant knowledge, will either need to extend their education, or may face the prospect of less-skilled employment.

The essential nature of education in the postmodern employment infrastructures is that it enables people to interact flexibly with the rapidly changing needs of manufacturing and industry. So technologically-sophisticated are manufacturing systems, that someone who is able to function well within a system today, may find that a lengthy period of training becomes rapidly redundant as the system is changed for something more efficient or productive. Castells (1998, p. 341) has argued cogently that one of the most significant functions of education is to enable the individual worker to adapt rapidly under such circumstances, and to absorb the requirements of the new process. On the other hand, the person who is well-trained, but within fairly limited parameters, will not be able to adapt when the requirements of manufacturing change.

Risk

Some of the features of knowledge in the contemporary world, as outlined above, introduce a number of threats to the functioning of society, and contain inherent risks for the individual seeking to identify a meaningful and secure role in contemporary social life. One of the distinct features of training and education in both pre-modernity and in modernity, was that it functioned in a significant way to support the concept of the specialist. Individuals, usually at

an early stage in their lives, were invested, often after a lengthy period of training, with the skills and knowledge required to perform a particular function in
society. There was also, thenceforth, a tacit assumption that the individual
would perform that function usually for the remainder of their life, and would
in addition, introduce the next generation to these same skills. This subdivision
of knowledge into precisely-defined trade groups and professions, was on the
one hand reassuring in that it located knowledge within carefully-defined
parameters, and in addition, it provided to some significant extent, a stability
and predictability within society. It was a social system which changed but
slowly. There were of course, technological advances, but these tended to be
understood, to develop, and to be implemented in an evolutionary manner,
rather than in a way which would transform procedures rapidly. In the
postmodern world however, this has changed radically.

There have first of all been a considerable number of social forces which
have in effect conspired to undermine the notion of the individual who was
respected in society because of specialized knowledge and expertise. The
widening availability of education at an advanced level, has given a large
number of people a sufficient appreciation of specialist areas, to at least enable
them to seek precise clarification on issues, and even to mount a coherent
challenge to the expert analysis of a problem. Not only are people more able to
identify situations in which experts have made errors, but there is an increasing
intolerance of such errors. Experts are more easily and readily called to
account, and consumers, whether within the education system, or other sectors
of society, are eager to demand a very high quality of service.

The rapid changes in the nature of the work environment have also had a
considerable effect upon the social context of the 'expert'. As the demands of
the employment market become marked less by a sense of permanence and
predictability, but by a sense of rapid transformation and frequent changes in
workforce requirements, the role of the expert becomes to some extent undermined, and replaced by the role of the flexible technocrat who can adapt
readily to new situations. In contemporary society however, the traditional
expert is not always willing to relinquish the long-established role, and conflicts will inevitably occur. The expert will sometimes tend to view challenges
from other members of society as being based upon an inadequate understanding and a restricted access to relevant evidence. The expert may seek to reinforce traditional territories of knowledge by pointing to the range and depth of
knowledge which experts alone can access. Others, outside this specialist field,
may consider that this is merely an attempt to exercise societal and economic
power, based upon a less than perfectly established expertise. The potential
conflicts between expert and lay person have been documented by Lash,
Szerszynski and Wynne (2001).

Such a situation carries some potential advantages, but also a significant
risk. The localization of expertise in society has functional advantages, in
terms of knowing immediately how to access specialist knowledge. However, if
that specialization is undermined for any or all of the reasons discussed above,

then there may well be functional disadvantages. While the democratization of access to knowledge may be desirable from a philosophical or ideological viewpoint, there may well be residual uncertainties when people have the need to seek specialist advice.

One of the main difficulties in the hypothesis of the democratization of knowledge, is that even though we live in a society apparently permeated by computer-based technology, access to that technology is in reality, not uniform. Ready and convenient access is related to such factors as wealth and type of employment, and even to whether or not people are employed. Without a uniform access throughout society to the means of disseminating knowledge, there can be no true democratization of knowledge. Discussions of the relationship between information technology and society are contained in Lyon (2001).

The fundamental risk involved in these scenarios is that individuals in society are left to make many decisions for themselves, in contexts where they have either imperfect access to information, or simply inadequate knowledge. This could be viewed as a significant problem for society, leading to inconsistency of action, and a wide variety of ways in which societal issues are addressed. On the other hand, it could be seen as an opportunity whereby individuals may make personal choices and define the nature of their own individuality.

Existentialism, Existential Choice and the Implications for Education

In a contemporary world which sees to some extent the diminution of the strength of some social norms, and value systems existing in a state of evolution, existentialism views the dilemma of humanity as the making of the necessary moral choices. For the existentialist, and in particular Sartre, the nature of the human is to experience existence prior to any decisions about the essential nature of human beings. In other words, one of the defining characteristics of human beings is their freedom to analyse the nature of the world, and then to make autonomous decisions about the way in which life should be lived. The philosophical position that human beings exist in advance of the determination of their essential character is discussed in Masters (1974, p. 13) and Marill-Alberes (1964, p. 36).

Moreover, for the existentialist, human beings have the capacity to create the nature of their own existence. This is not decided for them by some inexorable process of predetermination. They are able to examine the world, and to decide the manner in which they will interpret it; the manner in which they will relate to other human beings; and the manner in which they will seek to make sense of the world. The world is not a series of given realities. Rather it consists of a range of interpretations, conducted by beings who at every twist and turn of their existences, can make choices about their own individual reality and the reality of the society in which they find themselves. The individual human being as the product of individual decision-making is discussed in Caws (1984, p. 112).

The need to make existential choices is at the heart of the human condition, and in a contemporary society in which the role of the expert is declining, the importance of those choices is enhanced. In a modern society it was more possible for individuals to leave decision-making to those people deemed by virtue of education or expertise to be qualified to take such decisions. In postmodern societies however, there is arguably more likelihood that people will need to take significant decisions. For the existentialist, and for perhaps Sartre in particular, this is an intrinsic part of the condition of humans. We need to accept the responsibility of taking decisions, and to face up to the consequences of those decisions.

Through this process we cannot avoid becoming involved with our fellow human beings and with society in general. In other words, we have to become engaged with the problems of society. Existentialists might argue that to avoid being engaged is impossible; that to be a social actor in the world entails of necessity, participating in individual and collective decision-making. In a world with an increasing dissemination of knowledge and data, it arguably becomes increasingly difficult or indeed impossible, to remain detached from being engaged. The concept of engagement is discussed in Masters (1974, p. 56).

In the modern age, education was a very systematic activity. There was a defined body of knowledge; defined by those who possessed the power to sustain those definitions. The curriculum appropriate to different situations was predetermined and was transmitted by those 'experts' defined by society as possessing appropriate knowledge and qualifications. This system remained largely unchallenged until the gradual opening-up of the educational system across social class and other divisions. The provision of open-access and distance-learning higher education provision was perhaps one of the most significant of these changes and challenges. The change to a comprehensive school system was another. These and other changes ushered in a process of enormous transition in education, characterised by a democratization of knowledge, and of institutions. Formerly there had been a relatively restricted definition of what should be considered valid knowledge, and this was replaced by multi-polar conceptions of different world views. In terms of what should be accepted as valid knowledge, the contemporary world is characterized by a range of relativities, and a corresponding degree of uncertainty about appropriate strategies for determining the most appropriate for a given situation.

Herein lies a considerable risk for education. Such an environment encourages the development of a multiplicity of different ideologies of teaching, of assessment, of learning styles, of curriculum development, and of educational management. It is a world which appears to encourage the exponential growth of initiatives, without providing a clear means for distinguishing between them, and evaluating their effectiveness in comparison with each other. The risk is that the educator is left adrift among a range of different developments, uncertain which to adopt, and in danger of being bewildered by the rapid transition from one initiative to another. Although any teacher must clearly operate within the constraints of a particular system or institution, it is surely important that at the same time, any educator exercises intellectual critical faculties in making existential choices between competing paradigms and developments, and is able to justify those choices on rational, intellectual lines.

References

Benton, T. and Craib, I. (2001), *Philosophy of Social Science*, Palgrave, Basingstoke.

Best, S. (2003), *A Beginner's Guide to Social Theory*, Sage, London.

Castells, M. (1998), *End of Millennium*, Blackwell, Oxford.

Caws, P. (1984), *Sartre*, Routledge and Kegan Paul, London.

Goldblatt, D. (2000), 'Afterword', in D. Goldblatt (ed), *Knowledge and the Social Sciences: theory, method, practice*, Routledge, London.

Lash, S., Szerszynski, B. and Wynne, B. (2001), 'Risk, Environment and Modernity: Towards a new ecology', in A. Giddens (ed), *Sociology: Introductory Readings*, Polity, Cambridge.

Lyon, D. (2001), 'Information Technology and the Information Society', in A. Giddens (ed), *Sociology: Introductory Readings*, Polity, Cambridge.

Lyotard, J-F. (1984), *The Postmodern Condition: A Report on Knowledge*, Manchester University Press, Manchester.

Marill-Alberes, R. (1964), *Jean-Paul Sartre: Philosopher without Faith*, Merlin, London.

Masters, B. (1974), *Sartre: a study*, Heinemann, London.

Sarup, M. (1993), *An Introductory Guide to Post-structuralism and Postmodernism*, 2nd edn. Harvester Wheatsheaf, London.

Spybey, T. (1996), *Globalization and World Society*, Blackwell, Oxford.

Woodward, K. and Watt, S. (2000), 'Science and Society: Knowledge in medicine', in D. Goldblatt (ed), *Knowledge and the Social Sciences: theory, method, practice*, Routledge, London.

Chapter 3

Risk and Education:
A Distortion of Reality

Linda Eastwood and Chris Ormondroyd

Introduction

Though their explanations vary in keeping with theoretical preferences, all major contributors to theories of change agree that either advanced modernity or post-modernity has changed the nature of the relationship between people and society. There is insufficient space here to fully expound this debate as our focus is on the way in which discourses arising from the risk / trust spectrum have colonised education along with other former public institutions in the United Kingdom (UK). We argue that this has created a climate of exaggerated anxiety; one that is at the polar extreme from the state's rhetoric about preparing for uncertainty. It is our intention to show how such a regime of truth constructs an environment in which those very attributes necessary for dealing with uncertainty are blocked, constrained and disciplined.

Our two key themes will address the agenda of control underpinning the 'managerialist' discourse and a more optimistic, positive alternative where risk taking is re-defined as a possible foundation for innovation and creativity. These themes will explore the way in which government policies and their contingent external assessment bodies have distorted education to the extent that success is only that which can be measured. The sovereignty of league tables, Quality Assurance reports, official inspections and Further Education National Training Organisation standards confine educational institutions to narrow definitions of performance. Failure to conform results in risk assessment and special measures being enforced to remedy the situation. A main thrust of our argument is that such techniques create a negative and controlling aspect of risk and 'risk society', whilst distorting other possible directions for education. Directions that we believe are necessary in a less than predictable world.

We argue that managerialism has exceeded its jurisdiction in transcending issues of accountability to govern what we teach, how we should teach; what students learn and how they should learn it. Does the rigidity of curriculum developments and assessment accountability lead to inspections that create a positive developmental framework for teachers or do they instil fear, threat and conflict? (Beck, 1994, p. 5)

The Emergence of Risk

Risk has become part of the agenda of researching contemporary society because of the impact of change arising from advanced unpredictability, as the world becomes increasingly complex. Giddens' explanation for its emergence sees social fragmentation as the key issue. Giddens uses the term disembedding to identify ways in which local networks are replaced by the uncertainties of the global economy. In such a disembedded environment, expert systems guarantee expectations across wider dimensions of time and space, but they are impersonal and abstract, stretching social systems and requiring a different kind of trust (Giddens, 1991, p. 2). Trust in Giddens' advanced modernity is about a process of developing confidence in the reliability of a person or a system. It exists in a calculative form. Trust is ambivalent because it involves confidence in abstract and faceless systems. Compared with the localised systems of the past such as kinship, community and religion, modernity offers personal relationships, abstract systems, future thinking and a perception of threat produced by modernity's increasing uncertainty.

The response to such perceptions of risk, danger and hazard influence both lay people and expert alike. The limits of predictability of such a complex world can produce a pragmatic acceptance, an interest in survival. It can also generate a sustained optimism based on faith in reason or god or a cynical pessimism where risk is dealt with by the use of black humour. Finally, there is the possibility for radical political engagement in various social movements. It has been suggested by Giddens, that:

> To live in the universe of high modernity is to live in an environment of chance and risk (Giddens, 1991, p. 109).

In summary we live in a culture highly sensitive to risk – threats are everywhere from the air that we breathe, to our own bodies, our partners, families and strangers.

Impact on Policy Formulation

Drawing on Giddens, we would suggest that the response of the British state over the past thirty years has been to utilise outmoded techniques of reason in order to implement a re-establishment of control as an adaptation to uncertainty and risk. Such techniques coalesce into a discourse of managerialism, which has rippled through the public and private domains, constituting subjects in keeping with its inherent anxiety about change. Such a development can be identified with Henderson's (1987) first zone of transition when 'Riding the Tiger of Change'. Confronted by the inability of experts to predict the future in the face of increased complexity, Henderson identifies three possible responses. Zone one – where institutions resist change until they become brittle and shatter or simply stagnate and decay. This is the Breakdown zone (Henderson, 1987, p. 148). The political arena of this zone is identified by Henderson as:

> The politics of the last hurrah a maladaptation to change where governments rigidify and defend their borders against waves of globalisation challenging their cherished national sovereignty. Politicians wrestle with domestic unemployment, trade, retraining and industrial policies (a hopelessly outdated concept) in a rational planning exercise, which is defied by the uncertainties and instabilities of the global market place (Henderson, 1987, p. 148).

In zone two, Henderson suggests that social institutions are involved in fibrillation, as when the human heart muscles temporarily vacillate under stress. The consequences are either death or a re-stabilisation. In this zone, crises reach their zenith and a severe re-examination of institutional practices and values is required. Henderson argues that this is in itself a high-risk strategy, as processes in zone one must be challenged. This zone is also littered with confusing contradictions as those who interpret change come to terms with added risk and uncertainty. Henderson identifies zone three as the breakthrough zone. This is a zone of optimistic development, where it is acknowledged that new international relationships are emerging; where there is a new compact between north, south, east and west. Henderson sees an emergence of a global values system that reconciles human beings with the processes of their planet. For Henderson this represents the era of new green technologies and reciprocal relationships – nothing less than a politics of reconceptualisation (Henderson, 1987, p. 159).

Despite rhetoric about modernisation and change, the evidence would suggest that zone one is exactly where the UK finds itself, the result of an inherently inward looking, conservative regime where risk is used to generate public fear and anxiety, which can then be placated by more technologies of control. In terms of its impact on educational strategies and practitioners, this general over-arching discourse comes to have serious and we would argue counter productive consequences. Foucault's (1972) work suggests that we are now far more disciplined by discourses that order our being:

> Disciplines are defined by groups of objects, methods, the interplay of rules and definitions, of techniques and tools: all of these constitute a sort of anonymous system, without there being any questions of their meaning or their validity being derived from whoever happened to invent them (Foucault, 1972, p. 222).

The case that we make is that in responding to an initial fear about financial insecurity, coupled with fears and anxieties about global competition and the threat of the 'other', the dominant discourse in the UK for the past thirty years has been managerialism. Such a discourse has transcended traditional political boundaries and manifested a regime of truth, which ensures that our major institutions, including education are firmly trapped in Henderson's breakdown zone. We should like to concentrate on how socially constructed mythologies, shaped by risk and the responses to it, influence and shape our educational practices.

Managerialism has been criticised since its emergence in the early 1980s as the embodiment of New Right thinking. Despite antagonisms against it, the strength of the newly constructed discourse has been such that its academic opponents have been reduced to the status of 'chattering classes' by Mr. Blair (Hall, 1998). In this, there can be seen to be no departure from Mrs. Thatcher's pro-managerialist position. Total Quality Management (TQM) is founded on claims to objectivity and factual analysis. The whole raft of TQM measures, which now govern institutional practice, are designed to enhance accountability, efficiency and transparency. The person in the street's trust is placed in the processes that produce league tables and make organisational performance visible. Risk is minimised by a menu of performance from which decisions can be made. Thus, the client is presented with reassuring data in an uncertain world. This is how the theory goes, and its support comes from government rhetoric, which roundly justifies it. However, it doesn't take too much investigation to recognise the serious flaws in both the institutional practice of TQM and in its founding principles. We argue that on three counts, managerialist techniques fail to achieve their claims. The first is that their pedigree is the result of a flawed cultural misunderstanding. The second is that they are inefficient and costly. The third is that as institutional practices supposedly gearing the UK up to meet an uncertain future, they are ineffective.

McWatt (2002) explains the 'distorted understanding' about 'quality' in its journey from American management gurus in Japan through UK business and UK Government. Despite their best attempts, the Japanese attempt to clear some of the cross cultural misunderstandings about the concept of 'quality' fell upon deaf ears. McWatt observes that the Americans ignored key fundamental principles of 'quality' as expressed by the Japanese in their annexation of the concept.

> To most Japanese, quality has an almost religious significance and the attitudes of craftsmanship are protected at all costs (Clark & Itoh, 1983, p. 111; cited in McWatt, 2002).

McWatt suggests that this principle, exemplified in the Zen arts, blends together elements in a holistic fashion. In eastern archery the arrow, bow and target harmonise as one with the archer, as in Japanese craftsmanship. This view of holistic quality never emerged in the American Business solution to organisational change. The emphasis was directed to consumer choice and the importance of customer requirements and best customer use and selling price (McWatt, 2002). This seems a far cry from educational provision and the public's trust in it, but the impact of the new business techniques on public service reorganisation from the 1980s to the present does have relevance. Before the consequences of such changes are addressed it might be worth stating that the new techniques failed to make much of an impact on American successes in the global market place. We hear politicians constantly endorsing such techniques to guarantee our requirements for a well-trained flexible work force fit for the challenges of global markets. They might pause to reflect that with the American interpretation of 'quality' General Motors operates with ten times the work force of Toyota and produces less cars (McWatt, 2002). Using Americanised concepts of quality, (McWatt identifies this as static quality in Robert Pirsig's metaphysics), General Motors is less flexible, less reliable and slower than its Japanese competitor.

The fate of institutional practice is nevertheless sealed. Tagg (2002) argues that auditors didn't prevent the collapse of the Allied Irish Bank or Enron. Neither is it the case that more auditors are the solution. Critics point to the static rule based approach to accountancy and audits as problematic. As long as companies can tick off boxes to verify compliance with certain rules, the job is considered as done (McWatt, 2002). This mind set leads to an over concern with rules and narrow tangible goals. Practitioners in education will be familiar with the techniques and the consequences will be re-visited later. In relation to education, Richard Gombrich suggests that British universities follow a 'fitness for purpose' range of techniques arising from Fordist and Taylorist practices:

> The factory mass produces qualified students, thus adding value to the raw material. The academics, the workers on the shop floor are there merely to operate the mechanical procedures which have been approved by management and checked by the inspectorate (Gombrich, 2000, p. 3; cited in McWatt, 2002).

Avis supports this view, arguing that application of competency models and measured objectives has a reductive effect on both students and tutors. The system reproduces managerialist control over all concerned (Avis, 2000). It would seem that we are paying a huge price for a conservative response to risk and uncertainty. The particular obsessive emphasis on learning outcomes gives rise to a specific regime of truth. It is a mechanism from which neither practitioners nor students find it easy to escape and it reinforces in the public mind that trust can be maintained in the processes that guarantee not quality, but the prevailing discourse. As Foucault (1980) observes:

> Each society has its regime of truth, its general politics of truth: that is, the types of discourses which it accepts and makes function as true; the mechanisms and instances which enable one to distinguish true and false statements, the means by which each is sanctioned; the techniques and procedures accorded value in the acquisition of truth; the status of those who are charged with saying what counts as true (Foucault, 1980, p. 131).

This argument contends that such managerialist regimes of 'truth' production and 'truth' maintenance are founded neither on empirically verifiable criteria of success, nor even on their claims to efficiency and effectiveness, but rather as a need to order security in an unpredictable and risk beset world. Managerialism's second claim to credibility is that its techniques guarantee fiscal discipline and cost effectiveness. An investigation of the costs hardly supports this view. The cost of a Total Quality Audit in Higher Education has been calculated at £250,000 (McWatt, 2002). The total cost since implementation in 1995 is reckoned by the Times Higher Education Supplement to be £100 million. This is in addition to the £3–£5 million per year spent on administration of Quality Assurance (McWatt 2002). On the basis of these figures, of the £2 billion overspend in Higher Education, a half is attributable to the audit arm of managerialism alone. Such investment in bureaucratic and control measures hardly squares with the claim that we are creating organisations that are more effective.

It is the intent of the chapter thus far to establish that the practices and procedures of educational institutions have been predicated over the past 30 years on a forever spiralling and costly regime of managerialism. However, its effects have been to transform functioning organisations into lumbering top heavy institutions like General Motors, where the emphasis is on responding to regimes of evaluation and audit rather than the encouragement of learning, the treatment of ill health or the apprehension of criminals. In terms of its capacity to engage with practices that allow a transition to a globalised world, such techniques are not only inadequate, but damaging. In her Reith lecture of 2002, Onora O'Neil exemplified the growing concern for the disparity between public trust and transparent data from audits. She was also mindful of the extension of this regime of truth into the hearts and souls of institutional life.

In the past two decades the quest for accountability has penetrated our lives like great draughts of Heineken's, reaching parts that supposedly less developed forms of accountability did not reach (O'Neil, 2002, p. 2).

It could be argued that many public sector professionals find that the new demands damage their real work. Teachers aim to teach their pupils; nurses to care for their patients; university lecturers to do their research and to teach; police officers to deter and apprehend those whose activities harm the community; social workers to help those whose lives are for various reasons unmanageable or very difficult. Each profession has its proper aim and this aim is not reducible to meeting set standards following prescribed procedures and requirements (O'Neil, 2002, p. 3). O'Neil continues to demonstrate the counter productive consequences of modern managerialist practices, which result in more paperwork for practitioners and less emphasis on the traditional role.

Performance indicators are chosen for ease of measurement and control rather than that they measure accurately what the quality of performance is (O'Neil, 2002, p. 5).

The lack of public trust then becomes one fashioned by the managerialist mind-set. Institutions are berated by the public for lack of conformity to the accountability measures they are urged to maintain. The public are not mistrusting of the intrinsic requirements for being good nurses and teachers, good doctors and police officers, but rather of the response rate to externally imposed targets and initiatives. The system produces a tautology, an inescapable false logic that pervades both institutional practice and public response. Thus as with many other institutions, expectations of education are part of a manipulative discourse that seeks to break the trust between patients and doctors; students and lecturers; pupils and teachers. This managerialist discourse never had at its heart any concern for the human condition – quite the reverse. Clarke and Newman identify managerialism as a theology

> Dogmatic and sectarian, requiring the existence of believers (bureaucrats) and heretics or dissenters (those who fail to see the vision) (Clarke and Newman, 1997, p. 36).

With its emphasis on regulation, disciplined budgets, audits, quality management and a vision of nouvelle cuisine – less is more, the new discourse created a value schism. The legacy of this has had repercussions for the past 30 years. Clarke and Newman (1997) suggest that it continues to create a challenge for practitioners in education and other former public service institutions. Indeed old notions of progress based on the solving of social problems have been displaced by a limited version privileging more effective service delivery and improved customer responsiveness (Clarke and Newman, 1997, p. 37). The new discourse, with its emphatic stress on 'change,' fuelled by 'folk devils' and 'moral panics' about survival in a new era of global competition created a discourse, which had a dramatic impact on practitioners. They were now to be embroiled in the confusion of its implementation. As Clarke and Newman observe:

> 'Subjected by' points to what might be called the ideal effects of discourses – the production of new subjects who identify with it and enact it in their practices. By contrast, 'subjected to' suggests the experience of being regulated by and disciplined through a discourse without it engaging beliefs, enthusiasms or identification (Clarke and Newman, 1997, p. 54).

There is no alternative (TINA), has been a consistent feature of both New Right and New Labour dogma. Clarke and Newman (1997) observe that practitioners under this regime are encouraged to focus on compliance rather than professional commitment (Clarke and Newman, 1997, p. 54).

When managerialism intervenes in the relationship between tutors and students, what consequences result? One impact on the educational practitioner is the swift conversion into management at entry into the profession. Whereas once they were managed, they now become responsible for managing some course, area of development or initiative (Avis, 2000). A second impact is that practice is also structured by the discourse. Avis argues that Government initiatives such as 'Learning to Succeed' set up the framework. The emphasis is on:

Self assessment and action planning; obtaining and responding to the views of students and other customers about opportunities and services offered; setting in place effective mechanisms to receive, investigate and respond to concerns raised; target setting using benchmarking based on relevant and consistent performance indicators (DfEE, 1999, pp. 44–45; cited in Avis, 2000).

This framework exemplifies the technicisation of practice. That is the taken for 'grantedness' of the need for modernisation, whether this be a response to fears of holding a place in the global marketplace or a more hidden agenda based on the re-assertion of masculinism, which Williamson (1995) sees a corporate governance model as reflecting. If managerialist techniques and assumptions are evaluated in terms of the rhetoric about 'uncertain futures' then questions might be asked of the apparent discrepancy between their means and ends. Is the whole discourse of disciplinary control commensurate with preparations for uncertainty? The fear of the unknown seems to have imbued both New Right and New Labour with a pressing desire to fashion more 'risk' eliminating strategies in institutional life at a time when 'being risky' might offer more appropriate solutions to uncertainty. Certainly, to arrive at zone two of Henderson's scheme there is a requirement to recognise the maximum number of opportunities to shift gears, reconceptualise, re-design and re-structure to 'ride the tiger of change' into the third zone (Henderson, 1987). Henderson offers the observation that

High-risk strategies are often most effective, while doing nothing can be the most dangerous action. Any change that is not reconceptualised and remapped might well lead to an action that is maladaptive and relegate the system/person back to zone 1 (Henderson, 1987, p. 153).

One might suggest that the entire edifice of Managerialism is concerned with pedantic mechanisms of controls – hardly a strategy likely to create effective change. At an economic level this also begs the question as to whether the fit does exist between the government's perceived needs of the economy and the needs of the people. Avis (2000) suggests that it's a false assumption to link the two.

Education per se cannot create jobs. Indeed some have suggested that the relationships between the economy and educational development is the reverse, with economic success enabling investment in education, which in turn leads to the raising of standards (Ashton and Green, 1996, p. 40; cited in Avis, 2000).

We might pose the principle of paradox to elucidate the response to risky uncertain futures. At a time when our practices could be justifiably targeted on skills for imaginative, creative innovations demanding vast multi-level thinking, we have opted for a discourse of narrow cognitive measurable outcomes. The pressure generated by operating within constraint results in practice, which is dumbed down to dovetail with the mundane grey practices of a consumerist market place existence for the bulk of the population. Policies seem to favour controlling and disciplining the rear of the train while the engine accelerates out of sight. We are nowhere near a mind-set advocated by Henderson, where in zone three – the breakthrough zone, politics reconceptualises all the basic assumptions and conditions underlying the problems and crises of zone two – all within global frameworks (Henderson, 1987). Education could be at the spearhead of this reorientation, with a much more positive and less narcissistic vision. But what managers, teachers and learners labour to establish, maintain and fuel is managerialism (Avis, 2000). Trapped in the tautology that the system has created, what options are there for practitioners? How is the Further Edication or Higher Education practitioner to deal with the system's fear of the unknown, anxiety about fiscal stringency and the new heresy of democracy? For Governments of the past 30 years have encouraged the construction of a monster that now seeks to direct its own perverse logic back at those who gave birth to it. More rational logic is demanded of the political centre, which sacrifices older democratic values for the new evangelising movement. Totalitarianism emerges with the implementation of yet more rational procedures. 'Risk' is the new witchcraft, the new communism, the new terrorism – it must be ruthlessly eliminated, whilst simultaneously maintaining a 'moral panic' in the minds of the population in order to justify more managerialist techniques and measures.

If this is a pessimistic view of our institutional practices, it is intended. We should like to counter this with a view of educational practice that eschews both the means and ends of the dominant discourse. We advocate that what the current discourse lacks is the positive and enervating dimensions of risk. A bungee jumper is well aware of the exhilaration that results from embracing the risk associated with stepping into thin air. The second theme of this chapter will now address this aspect of risk and consider its consequences for education and specifically for educational practitioners.

Risk-Taking and Creativity in Teacher Education

A serious cause for concern in the twenty-first century is a more tightly prescribed and fragmented curriculum that arises from the consequences of managerialism. In the Post Compulsory Education and Training (PCET) sector, regulatory bodies such as the Further Education National Training Organisation (FENTO) and the Office for Standards in Education (Ofsted) certainly do not encourage risk taking. Bleakley (1999) criticises the FENTO framework and identifies serious flaws with them, including anti-intellectualism, over-determinism, prescription and instrumentalisation. This leads to:

A narrow and inappropriate model of education and training...which has reduced individual opportunity for educational self-realisation within the FE sector (Reeves, 1995, p. 105; cited in Wallace, 2002).

It is with this in mind that attention should be refocused on the positive aspects of risk-taking and creativity that makes teaching exciting, innovative and challenging. Are teachers really encouraged to take risks in their teaching in an ever accountable and unpredictable educational world? Certainly one of the factors that inhibits risk-taking in the teaching process is having to work with inflexible structures with regard to New managerialism's ideologies and rhetoric. What images are provoked when creativity in teaching and learning are being considered? Is it people being creative? Is it being imaginative, artistic, taking risks, being challenging? Is creativity about the new and unexpected? Or is it about finding new routes to existing destinations, seeing things in new ways and breaking rules? It is probably all of these and more, but certainly one major theme surrounding creativity is the necessity to take risks on several different levels. As Craft suggests, teaching can:

> also mean taking some risks, risking hearing things which you didn't know you were seeking, and which you may not know how to accommodate. It is guaranteed to bring change and development (Craft, 2000, p. 127).

> In some social contexts, risk-taking is actively encouraged as a means of escaping from the bounds of everyday life, achieving self-actualization, demonstrating the ability to go beyond expectations ... (Craft, 2000, p. 171).

There are many situations other than encouraging creative teaching where risk-taking might be seen as positive, pleasurable and enjoyable from bungee jumping and parachuting to raise money for charity, to white knuckle rides at the theme park. In this counter discourse the agenda is a different one. To encourage the activity, to know exactly what the risks are but to still go ahead with the event. Taking risks and challenging accepted ways of teaching can also be a pleasurable experience.

Creativity itself is an elusive concept that it is set within social, cultural and academic boundaries. Traditional definitions surrounding creativity are set within dominant psychological discourses (Fritz, 1943; Jeffrey and Craft, 2001). Bleakley (2003) breaks the paradigmatic mould when he posits that the reason creativity is so elusive as a concept is that its meaning is contingent upon how different people in different settings breathe meaning into it. This social construct approach is useful when consideration is given to what is meant by risk taking and creativity and how culturally bound and socially constructed images provide definitions of what a good teacher is. Examples from popular culture tend to provide the image of the good teacher as someone who is very risk-taking such as in the films *Dead Poet's Society*; *Dangerous Minds*; *Good Will Hunting* and *Mr Holland's Opus*. However, would these be the examples that others would use to stress the qualities of good teaching outside of the popular culture arena? Cultural acceptance is important with regard to the identification of perceptions of good teachers particularly in a risk society where;

> No one is an expert, or everyone is an expert, because the experts presume what they are supposed to make possible and produce (Beck, 1999, p. 9).

In the world of education these experts might be the teachers themselves but it is more likely that they will be those external bodies responsible for inspecting and assessing. Such bodies will engender new managerial ideologies where risk consciousness reflects a culture of blame in which 'the system' is the scapegoat and society is prone to moral panics (Douglas, 1992). Lupton (1999) suggests that the emergence of the word 'risk' is often associated with notions of early maritime incidents where accidents at sea were blamed on the elements and not those of human responsibility. If you died at sea it was the fault of the weather. Society today might now seek to blame human behaviour. For example, if a child dies on a canoeing adventure whilst on a school trip it is not the elements that are at fault but the teacher who organised the visit and the risk assessment that was inadequate. Does this mean that teachers and trainee teachers should be discouraged from taking students on trips because they might end up responsible for incidents? Hence, the 'moral panics' which now surround these adventures. Take this idea of 'moral panics' one step further and place it in the classroom. It becomes evident how personally and publicly constructed myths can distort images of what is meant by a 'good' teacher and a 'good' lesson. Are the risk takers really perceived to be the 'good' teachers? In teaching, what passes for creativity among many practitioners is often governed by a restricted view and there is always the danger that teachers will be too busy just doing their jobs to think about risk-taking and creativity. As Woods states:

> The teaching profession, whilst demanding creativity, does not in fact foster it in its members (Woods, 1995, p. 84).

Yet risk-taking is proposed as a central platform to creative teaching and teaching for creativity (DfEE, 1999). It enables individuality and enables teachers to be in control of the situation rather than being restricted by formal regulatory bodies and new managerialism ideologies. Creativity has been debated and discussed in several areas of education for many years, such as Early Years, Primary Teaching and Arts and Design education (Lytton, 1971; Slater, 1971; Duffy, 1998). It has become a buzz word in UK policy debates and yet recently articles and letters in the education press have focused on how the current climate of testing, across the education system as a whole, may be constraining teachers' creativity and inhibiting them from taking risks. Wragg (2003) writing in the Guardian argued that creativity is:

the crucial element in each generation's renewal and enhancement of itself. Without it society would not even stand still, it would roll backwards ... No less a figure than Chris Woodhead (and there is no less a figure than Chris Woodhead) once wrote that it was dangerous for teachers to think up their own ideas. Dangerous? Setting fire to your pants, or swallowing a cup of razor blades is what I call dangerous. But thinking up fresh ideas is what teachers are paid for (Guardian, 10/06/03).

So, is risk-taking and being creative dangerous? Certainly when most people think about the dangers of education they might have in mind accidents on school trips, pupils stabbing each other in the playground, debates about whether it is safer to walk the children to school or take them in the car. Each of these examples might be considered risky. They might think of the terrible incidents in the summer of 2002 at Soham. Few would perhaps initially think that the practice of creative teaching might be dangerous. When looking at the 'risk society' and taking it to its extremes Beck (1994) suggests that:

> Reflexive modernization' means the possibility of a creative (self-) destruction for an entire epoch: that of industrial society. The 'subject' of this creative destruction is not the revolution, not the crisis, but the victory of Western modernization (Beck, 1994, p. 2).

The idea that creativity might lead to self destruction could be applied to the teaching situation and it is one of the areas of creativity that has been recently debated. Bleakley has introduced a post-modern view of creativity by producing a map of creative discourses. The ten discourses of creativity he identifies are creativity as an ordering process, creativity as rhythm and cycle, creativity as originality and spontaneity, creativity as the irrational, creativity as problem solving, creativity as problem stating, creativity as inspiration, creativity as serendipity, creativity as resistance to the uncreative and creativity as withdrawal and absence (2003, pp. 7–18). His 'creativity as the irrational' certainly follows this dangerous, self-destructive approach where creativity arises from a discourse that includes transgression and impulse:

> a breaking free from order, rules and regulations. From the 'day world' perspective the irrational is seen as dangerous, courting lunacy or destruction. From the 'night world' perspective of Romanticism, creativity is experimentation, the instinctive and animal side of life, ferment, the suspension of intellect, the primitive raw. Harnessed as a political force, this is breaking an old social order in revolution. Its social side is intoxication. Its extreme is annihilation: destructive as a creative act (Bleakley, 2003, p. 11).

Is this 'reflexive modernization' set in an educational context? In this discourse risk-taking becomes powerful and empowering. If we really believe that the future is uncertain and unpredictable then surely uncertainty demands a level of education, which embraces creativity, risk-taking and innovation, because only imaginative thinking can deal with uncertainty. Not narrow cognitive measurable outcomes, but vast, multi-level thinking and action to take advantage of innovative technological markets. If we really want to educate individuals to function in a technological globalised world then risk-taking and specialist creative and imaginative skills are surely the way forward. This has to be developed despite the strict controls of new managerialism.

Conclusion

To conclude, we return to Wragg's (Guardian, 10/06/03) views on creative teachers. If innovative and creative teachers are viewed by the state as dangerous, who is in danger from their practice? It would appear that we have not escaped the 1980s fear of destabilisation. The state continues to portray an anxiety about change and a rejection of anything that promotes challenging, open and empowering skills. Yet, we have argued that to meet the uncertainty that the globalised world presents, these are a necessary part of the toolkit that the population requires. Risky teaching contravenes most taken for granted assumptions in the managerialist discourse. It changes the focus from narrow cognitive and employment skills to the dynamic relationship that exists as a potential between tutors and students. Such a dynamic is less predictable, less programmed and less measurable in terms of its outcomes. In an unpredictable world, the value of the innovator is massive. Rigid, top-down systems and control mechanisms hardly stimulate potential.

Perceived risk arises from discourse. The creation of moral panics provides a justification for policy making. Such policies and techniques have led to a very limited, constrained and threatened discourse not only in education but in the ways that individuals live their lives.

In its institutional form we have argued that managerialism acts as a constraining discourse which limits possibility. Not only, are innovations and creativity restrained, but any consideration of options, alternatives or discourses of possibility are also blocked. Till now the key concern amongst many professional practitioners has been the erosion of social justice and autonomy arising from managerialist practices. We should like to suggest that whilst relevant as an argument, this nevertheless is of limited value. Ensuring social justice is a laudable agenda, but being aware of how the future might be anticipated is another relevant concern for educationalists.

We have argued that our practices confined us to Henderson's (1987) breakdown zone. We consider that a more creative and innovative form of educational practice might pave the way to explore some of Henderson's zone three – the Breakthrough zone. In this education might deliver new structures, forms goals and values (Henderson, 1987, p. 147). Perhaps the only way to achieve this is to re-visit our a priori assumptions about risk itself. Whilst operating with negative interpretations of risk, we further reinforce anxiety, fear, apprehension, low morale and stress. A positive interpretation of risk would encourage innovation, creativity, celebration and liberating forms of practice both in education and across the public domain.

References

Avis, J. (2000), 'Policing the Subject: Learning Outcomes, Managerialism & Research in PCET', *British Journal of Education Studies*, vol. 48(1), March.

Beck U., Giddens, A. and Lash, S. (1994), *Reflexive Modernization: Politics, Traditions and Aesthetics in the Modern Social Order*, Polity Press, Cambridge.

Bleakley, A. (1999), 'Are the FENTO Standard up to Standard?', Paper presented to the *Further Education Development Agency Research Conference*, Cambridge, 9th December.

Bleakley, A. (2003), 'Constructions of Creativity', Paper presented to the *SRHE Conference, Innovation and Creativity in Teaching*.

Clarke, J. and Newman J. (1997), *The Managerial State*, Sage.

Craft, A. (2000), *Creativity Across The Primary Curriculum*, Routledge, London.

Davies, T. (2003), 'Communication: the essence of a creative approach to teaching, learning and assessment', Paper presented to the *BERA Conference*, Edinburgh, 12th December.

DfEE (1999), *All Our Futures: creativity, culture and education*, DfEE Publications, Suffolk.

Douglas, M. (1992), *Risk and Blame: Essays in Cultural Theory*, Routledge, London.

Duffy, B. (1998), *Supporting Creativity and Imagination in the Early Years*, Open University Press, Buckingham.

FENTO (1999), *Standards for Teaching and Supporting Learning in Further Education in England and Wales*, FENTO, London.

Fritz, R. (1943), *The Path of Least Resistance*, Salem, Stillpoint.

Giddens, A. (1991), *Reading Guide to Consequences of Modernity*, Polity Press, Cambridge, www.arasite.org/giddmod2.htm.

Guardian (10/06/03), 'Creative teachers should be positively encouraged, not made to toe the line'.

Henderson, H. (1987), 'A Guide to Riding the Tiger of Change – Three Zones of Transition', in W.I. Thompson (ed.), *Gaia – A Way of Knowing*, Lindisfarne Press.

Jeffrey, B. and Craft, A. (2001), 'The Universalization of Creativity', in A. Craft, B. Jeffrey and M. Leibling, (eds), *Creativity and Education*, Continuum, London.

Lupton, D. (1999), *Risk*, Routledge, London.

Lytton, H. (1971), *Creativity and Education*, Routledge, London.

McWatt, A. (2002), *The Misleading Use of the Word Quality Within the Higher Education System*, www.moq.org/forum/mcwatt.

O'Neill, O. (2002), 'A Question of Trust', *BBC Radio 4 Reith Lectures*, www.bbc.co.uk/radio4reith2002/lectures.

Slater, G. (ed) (1971), *Education and Creative Work*, Hull Printers Ltd, Hull.

Woods, P. (1995), *Creative Teachers in Primary School*, Open University Press, Buckingham.

Wallace, S. (2002), 'No Good Surprises: lecturers' preconceptions and initial experiences of further education', *British Educational Research Journal*, vol. 28(1).

Chapter 4

Risk, Education and Postmodernity

Paul Oliver

Introduction

It is scarcely contestable that we live in an era of extremely rapid change, and that in addition the nature of contemporary society is dramatically different from that of even the seventies and the eighties. The pervasive impact of electronic technology has taken place in perhaps two decades, and initiated not only considerable lifestyle changes for individuals, but also extensive structural changes in society. Almost in parallel there have been fundamental changes in economic, political and employment patterns. The basis of western economies in extractive and manufacturing industry has been superseded by an emphasis upon knowledge-based industries. The modern has been displaced by the postmodern. The individual is no longer restricted to a role in either the obtaining of naturally-occurring materials, nor in their use for the manufacture of consumer artefacts. The society based upon knowledge provides a multiplicity of social and employment roles, within a bewildering display of images and identities. Plurality is initially very enticing, but it holds within itself the seeds of uncertainty and confusion. The risk of a society based upon a multiplicity of roles, is a risk of lack of identity for the individual, and a prevarication in decision-making. Within educational systems, such uncertainty can be associated with a lack of sense of direction. But postmodernity, by its very nature and by its other characteristics, does offer prospective solutions. The individual is no longer constrained by the great ideologies of the past, and the tensions which developed between them. The resulting sense of freedom and liberation, counterbalances the uncertainties of plurality, and holds the promise of a different but self-determining future.

Risk

The starting point for much of the debate about postmodernism has been the contention of Lyotard (1984) that one of the significant features of postmodern society is an increasing disregard for, and suspicion of metanarratives. The end of the modern period was to some extent characterized by the existence of a number of dominant ideologies, which although often in competition with each other, held sway within certain parameters. The doctrine of liberal economics was in conflict with the *dirigisme* characteristic of Marxist political systems. The ideology of an accepted corpus of knowledge which could be legitimated in more or less absolute terms, and justified for transmission within an education system, was contrasted with a relativism in epistemological terms, based upon the arguments that knowledge was created and recreated within specific social contexts. Lyotard's argument is that these have declined in importance and acceptance in postmodern society, although some might still want to argue that western capitalism, for example, still represents an important and influential form of metanarrative. Lyotard's general arguments in terms of metanarratives are discussed in Boyne and Rattansi (1990).

The risk implicit in a declining acceptance of metanarratives is that individuals in society may no longer possess the structuring framework within which they can make sense of their lives. While there may remain broad, general explanations for the nature of society, the trend within postmodern society appears to be towards a more and more fragmented understanding of the social. Ultimately, to carry the argument to the extreme, we are left with a plurality of understandings, and some difficulty in harmonising these differences. The risk for the individual is a form of philosophical isolationalism in which each human being looks out at the world with a specific world view, and the challenge is to forge ways of communicating with other world views. There is moreover, the difficulty of attempting to compare and evaluate differing perceptions of the world.

The challenge to the great narratives of the past has come from a variety of sources, but in particular from the enormously increased potential for communication in a global age. This has come largely, but not exclusively, from the increase in electronic communication. While it is difficult to establish clear causal connections, there would appear to be a number of significant, interrelated factors. The internet and mass media enable people in one part of the globe to have a vision of the lifestyle and economic standing of people in other areas. While not the sole cause, this may be one factor in the increased trend for both legitimate and illegal economic migration. Coupled with the dramatic increase in business and tourism travel, there are increasing opportunities for people to see alternative lifestyles, cultures, religions, economic and social systems at first hand. Such experiences almost inevitably encourage comparisons, and invite reflections on one's own world view. Interaction of this type, may tend to lead to a world which is on the one hand far more aware of other cultures and world views, but also to a world which generates some challenges to the former apparent certainties. Lyon (1999, p. 63) has discussed some of the possible consequences of this type of interaction.

A related trend in the postmodern has been the exponential growth in media images, and the apparent resulting confusion between an object or idea of itself, and its representation in the media. Ultimately, there appears to be the real possibility that truth and reality may be more associated with the media image than with the original object or idea. In such a world of hyperreality, to use Baudrillard's term, there is a significant increase in the range of subjective definitions of the world, derived from media images. Hence it becomes increasingly difficult to find an anchor in a large-scale intellectual, explanatory system. The large number of potential explanatory systems reflects the large number of media images. Ultimately there is a reduction to individual, subjective interpretation. The relationship between media and reality in the thinking of Baudrillard is discussed in Norris (1990, p. 128).

In postmodern society the concept of power is arguably less significant than in modernism. In the latter societal system, political and economic power were important factors in ensuring the maintenance of industrial production and manufacture. The industrial infrastructure was dependent upon a large workforce which in its turn reflected the social and class systems of the day. Ultimately society was hierarchical, and the maintenance of this system of stratified authority depended upon the mechanisms of social power. In the postmodern, the application of power within a relatively rigid hierarchical system, has become much changed, with an increasing emphasis upon a diffused and dispersed system. In the contemporary world, power is far more multipolar, and is exercised in different ways by many different organizations and systems. Political power, as exercised by the government of the day, is restrained and influenced by the media. Not only are journalists and commentators able to exert a restraining influence upon political and economic power, but by providing a means by which small groups or even individuals can give voice to their feelings and arguments, they are able to publicize counter-views which can have an effect upon government policies. Many other groups can exercise considerable influence in society. These may include the legal profession; the medical profession; academics; the financial institutions and many others. It is almost impossible to weigh the different degree of power exercised by different bodies, but it is evident that in our current society, although ultimate power may be vested in government, there are so many different influences on government that it is difficult to analyse all of the factors and influences which might contribute to a particular policy decision.

The risks in society from such a diversity of power loci is that people may never be totally certain as to when or when not, to accept instructions. Certainly, even within a postmodern society, most people exist within at least one form of hierarchy, and so are familiar with the exercise of bureaucratic power. Nevertheless, we are increasingly familiar with situations which have involved a successful challenge to bureaucratic authority, and although a good thing this may well be under given circumstances, it does leave a context in which there is to some extent a feeling of uncertainty. An individual, aware of the potential for a challenge to authority, may be unsure whether to accept instructions or to mount an argument against what is required. Depending upon one's perspective, such a scenario may be viewed as functional for society, or to contain implicit risks. The principal advantage would appear to be that within such a social framework there are fewer opportunities for unrestricted hegemony, and far more checks and balances within society. On the other hand, the risk is that there will exist a lack of decision in society, with each individual wanting to challenge every initiative and instruction. The result could conceivably be a society which develops a significant lack of sense of direction. Inherent in such an analysis of postmodernism however, is that there will be a focus upon the micro structures of society, at the level of small groups and organizations, and even of the individual. Such an analysis may well be at the expense of a legitimate consideration of the wider-ranging social forces which influence society.

Foucault has been one of the major critics of the exercise of power in the modern era, and the manner in which rational empiricism came, so it could be argued, to have a dominating effect upon the life of human beings. For Foucault it is difficult to accept that the great explanatory models of modernism, can totally reflect the social reality of the world. The world is a far too complex place to be understood from one perspective, and in the postmodern, it is necessary to select a wide range of perspectives in order to begin to comprehend society. Foucault's approach to the nature of power in society is discussed in Best and Kellner (1991).

It is perhaps interesting to consider the possible factors which have resulted in an apparently enhanced awareness of risk in contemporary society. Certainly when one looks at the social conditions of medieval and modern society, it would appear that the life of the individual was threatened in a greater variety of ways than at present. There were certainly more health-related risks for example. In addition, although one appreciated all too well the symptoms and results of certain illnesses, the causes were often not understood at all. Although many of these illnesses have now been explained and in some cases remedies found, there have arisen within postmodern society, other forms of risk. Since the Enlightenment, the often self-imposed challenge for humanity has been to gain greater and greater control over the environment, and the rationality of the scientific method has played a greater and greater part in this enterprise. Nevertheless, we have begun to see in the postmodern era, the limitations of this enterprise, ranging from accidents in the space programme to the unanticipated results of interference in the food chain. One of the social and human consequences has arguably been an increased suspicion of empirical science in general, and perhaps in its capacity to control the world. We perhaps now see science as not conquering the natural world, but rather being subject to its existing forces. This has perhaps created a feeling of uncertainty and lack of confidence in empirical science, and a heightened sense of risk. The feeling is perhaps that the human race has lost control of the scientific enterprise. Such issues are discussed in Miles (2001, p. 124).

One of the implicit dangers of the acceptance of the diversity of postmodern society is that in a rather subtle way one may come to tolerate the adverse features of such a society. Such arguments, for example from Harvey (1990) are discussed in Delanty (2000, p. 145). In a globalized, post-industrial economy there are certain to be many winners and many losers. As companies move knowledge, technology and production around the world, seeking for example a more and more cost-effective workforce and locality, some will gain and some may find their livelihoods taken away. The global movement of capital inevitably entails a wide range of social consequences. One might seek to at least partially justify such a society by pointing to the diversity of views and the multiplicity of different lifestyles. However, the postmodern, post-industrial world is not a society without the existence of significant power structures. Such power distributions may be different in nature and in scope from those of modernity, but they still have a very great influence over the lives of individuals. It is important that any explanation and analysis of such a society should not ignore the potential influence of such power systems. If the need for such an analysis is not acknowledged then there is a risk that the potential consequences of the exercise of such power will be overlooked. Individuals may not have an appreciation of the causal systems operating in society, and hence will not be able to plan effectively for their own lives and for the immediate social groups to which they belong.

On one level, the entire process of arguing within the framework of postmodernism is, in an epistemological sense, rather self-contradictory. The prevailing assumption about knowledge within postmodernism tends to be a rejection, to varying degrees, of the rationalism and scientific approaches of the enlightenment and of the industrial modern age. The logic and rationalism of that era is viewed to some extent as having been part of a system of bureau-cratic control which was characteristic of the time. Yet one might argue that in order to analyse and challenge such rationalism, then one has to adopt procedures of that very rationalism which one is seeking to argue against. There is the risk here of an untenable thought process, which may be seen as undermining the intellectual position of postmodernism. These issues are evaluated in Benton and Craib (2001, p. 171).

If modernist thought is characterized by the presentation and analysis of empirical evidence, then that of postmodernism may be viewed as rather less rational, rather less based upon empirical analysis. Perhaps one of the factors here is the sheer diversity of postmodern society. In a world of great disparity and diversity it becomes rather difficult to classify phenomena. Yet such classification is often at the heart of the rational process. Rationality and logic often seek to place phenomena in increasingly complex classificatory schemes, which in turn seek to examine and establish relationships between categories within those schemes. The problem and indeed the risk here, is that this is difficult within postmodernism, and the writers and thinkers of this era may need recourse to more intuitive thought processes. The result is a style of discourse about postmodernism which may appear both individualistic and idiosyncratic, and less capable of presenting in a clear way, the precise aspects of the era (see Delanty, 1997, pp. 108–9).

Nevertheless, there is still the danger in the contemporary world, of too great an emphasis upon the significance of knowledge. The facility with which knowledge and information may be transmitted around the world, can tend to give an enhanced pre-eminence to the status of knowledge, and to intellectual explanations of the social world. The rationalist and empiricist explanation of the world derived from the Enlightenment is but one means of interpreting the environment in which we find ourselves. Competing paradigms may not be given the consideration which they deserve, and there is hence the risk that we seek explanations for phenomena which are exclusively grounded in the analysis of empirical evidence. If we make the assumption that one prevailing paradigm will ultimately be replaced by another, or at the very least will have to amend its fundamental assumptions, then it may well be a limitation to progress if we surround ourselves with restrictive ways of looking out at the world. The risk is that we perhaps become relatively closed to other ways of seeing and understanding, and fail to see the potential in fresh visions. The potential dominance of knowledge is discussed in Gergen (1999, p. 17).

Education

Wagner (2001, p. 165) has argued that the relative uniformity of the modern period has given way to a society in which the individual is represented in a much more separated, fragmented manner. We can find a number of examples of this from within the world of education. In the modern period, the world of higher education was far more standardized, with a greater uniformity of curricular provision. Although relatively-speaking far fewer people were able to take advantage of higher education, there tended to be a greater consistency in terms of the overall provision within a particular subject area, with the result that when a person graduated within a specific subject, then the areas which they had studied were broadly understood and appreciated. However, this has changed dramatically with the expansion of higher education within the postmodern world.

One of the principal changes which has taken place is that education has become significantly commodified. Higher education institutions have become seen as corporate entities which place considerable emphasis upon marketing their courses and trying to ensure that they recruit the requisite number of students. Courses have become commodities to be promoted and sold as a commercial product. Of course, this is not to deny that they remain connected with the eternal values of education, such as the maintenance and transmission of the accumulated culture of humanity, but ultimately consumers need to wish to purchase them, otherwise the educational purposes of the product cannot be achieved. The commodification and commercialization of educational courses as product, has taken place within a clearly capitalist context in higher education. Universities are in competition with each other, not only in terms of the traditional issues of research quality and output, and that difficult-to-define concept of academic reputation, but also in terms of such measurable criteria as income and hence the ability to provide better and more prestigious facilities. The external market place between universities is not only within one country, but between universities in different countries. So universities compete internationally in the capitalist market for the best research minds, and for the best graduates and students. They also compete internationally for the most lucrative sponsorship from corporations willing to support higher education. Not only this, but universities within themselves are also creating an increasingly internal market place, where academic departments are competing with each other for resources, which include funding for additional staff appointments, research funds, and buildings and infrastructure.

In an attempt to meet the demands of this commodification of education, institutions have tried to develop more and more varied courses, in order to fill apparent niches in the market, and also to attract more and more students. In many cases, these are students who would not traditionally have attended university, but are now encouraged to do. New degree courses are constructed in a variety of ways in order to compete in the new educational market place. Subject areas may be combined together in order to try to meet new vocational trends. Scientific subjects or technical subjects may be combined with a humanities subject such as languages or media studies, in order to create an area of study which might lend itself to employment in an evolving area. In other cases, vocational areas which had not previously required systematic study at higher education, are being used as the basis of new degree programmes. This also reflects the increasingly sophisticated nature of many jobs, and the incorporation of information technology within its various systems.

. These societal changes have had a number of apparently beneficial effects. More and more people have had the opportunity to experience higher educa-tion, and to extend their horizons both in terms of potential employment, but also in terms of a personal exploration of knowledge. If we also wish to evaluate this trend in a perhaps more specifically functional, pragmatic sense, then industry and commerce has also had the advantage of gaining a better educated and more sophisticated workforce. There are however, some intrinsic risks with these developments. In broader societal terms, a widely expanded higher education system must be financially supported both at the level of government and institutions, but also at the level of the individual who must find a means of self-support during the period of study. Moreover, the increas-ingly diversified nature of degree courses can make it very difficult for employ-ers and others to compare the content of programmes, and hence to under-stand the exact nature of the academic background of potential employees. In a world where many people possess a university degree, employers may find that it is difficult, if not impossible, to base a selection procedure upon academic qualifications, and they may need to have recourse to their own structured selection process. To some extent, that does perhaps begin to challenge the nature and purpose of a widely-expanded system.

If it is difficult for employers to identify future employees from their higher education studies, then it also becomes difficult for younger students to select their preferred course in higher education. It becomes more and more difficult to select a programme of study which will become a good investment for the future in career terms. Moreover, in a capitalist society, it is arguably not irrelevant to think of higher education courses as an investment, since the considerable personal expense involved may easily necessitate one thinking about the course in terms of that which one may tangibly gain afterwards.

There is also an analogy between commercial and industrial products and education. The market economy drives commercial enterprises to be continually changing their products in order to meet subtle changes in market needs. In the same way, there is a drive for continual change in higher education courses, in order to try to gain a market advantage. Such continual change has been helped by the modularisation of higher education courses. The sub-division of courses into small units of curriculum content, has to an extent, made it much easier to introduce frequent and incremental changes to courses. The latter can be revised much more easily and quickly. It is no longer necessary to revise an entire course or programme of study, when minor changes can be made on a regular basis. This diversification of provision has also taken place in the public examination system at sixteen and eighteen years respectively. University admissions tutors are often faced with the complexity of a varied system, in much the same way that employers often find it difficult to evaluate the qualifications of university graduates. Not only this, but the sheer size of the public examination system now introduces risks in terms of the validity and reliability of the system. The increased flexibility and diversity of the educational system, thus has benefits, but also risks. Nevertheless, in the postmodern world, this increasing diversity shows no signs of diminishing, nor the pace of change slowing in any way.

It is perhaps rather tempting to view the postmodern social context in education as introducing an enormous degree of choice. With this choice, one might see the individual as possessing enhanced freedom, and moving within a world in which there is an almost unlimited array of potential. Within postmodernity however, this potential freedom is significantly limited by the nature of the market economy which is operating. There may well be the illusion of great freedom of action, but individuals are becoming increasingly aware of the larger scale pressures which are exercised by society. This is in a sense, the risk of the market system for education. There is greater choice, but this does not necessarily indicate that there is greater opportunity. The greater choice in society is mirrored by greater competition within postmodern capitalism, and it is at least debatable the extent to which this competition results in greater opportunity. The ultimate risk is of a society in which large numbers of people have invested in educational opportunities, and indeed invested considerably in time and money, and yet find that society is not able to deliver a commensurate range of opportunities. This could lead to individual disenchantment and the risk of a disengagement from the educational process.

Throughout this debate about education within postmodern capitalism, is the sense that education is being viewed very much as a commercial product and hence evaluated according to pragmatic criteria. Ultimately, this is functional within society as long as education can fulfil these pragmatic aspirations. On the other hand, the traditional way of viewing education was to justify it in more intrinsic terms. It was justified as an end in itself, rather than as a means to an end. Education was seen much more as a process whereby the individual could develop as a person, whereby one might enhance and expand ones view of the world, and ones perception of ones place in it. One might argue that to justify education in terms of being an end in itself is less subject to the vagaries of societal change, and generally likely to be a more stable assessment of the principles of education. A pragmatic, instrumental justification of education on the other hand, is more likely to depend upon, and relate to the wider economic forces in society.

The relationship between education and the broader concepts of culture in society also represents an interesting trend in contemporary society. Within modern society one might argue that definitions of culture, and of what constituted higher status culture as opposed to popular culture, was a social definition which was linked largely to the economic status of those who were in a position to make such definitions. For example, certain types of classical music might be defined as having a higher status than so-called pop music. Attempts at specifying defining criteria for higher status music and for other types of culture, might seek to distinguish different cultural forms. Ultimately however, one might seek to argue that different cultural forms were traditionally associated in modern society with certain economically-defined status groups, and therefore perhaps ultimately, with social class groupings. Such systems of cultural stratification were to some extent in modern society reinforced by the educational system. The latter defined and confirmed certain types of knowledge as being of significant worth, and these epistemological definitions were reinforced through the different school curricula, and ultimately through the public examination system. Equally well, certain types of knowledge were defined as being inappropriate for an academic curriculum, and were excluded from the relevant categories of knowledge.

During the transition to the postmodern world however, there have been numerous challenges to these curricular definitions, and in general there has been a broadening and loosening of the criteria used to define that which is acceptable as knowledge. Song lyrics have been analysed as poetry, and treated as contemporary literature, and avant garde works, whether in music or the visual arts, have become the subject of serious discussion. In the modern period, the intellectual heritage of Europe tended to be given pre-eminence as the subject for scholastic investigation. In the postmodern world, partly as a result of global communications, intellectual creativity is drawn from all parts of the world, in order to become the subject of analysis and discussion within our educational system. In intellectual terms, one might argue that the postmodern world is richer and more diversified, yet at the same time, there are raised the questions of how one might distinguish quality in terms of intellectual endeavour. The essential question is whether all forms of knowledge and of the intellectual life should be considered equal but different, or whether it remains possible to distinguish higher, and less higher, levels of creativity and understanding.

Postmodernity

One of the features of postmodernity discussed above, is that of the sheer variety of forms in contemporary society. One may see this as a fragmentation of society, and as in general a negative phenomenon which is dysfunctional and which undermines the cohesion of society. On the other hand, it may be viewed as a positive feature which enriches society, and perhaps more importantly, urges the social commentator to accept the broader complexity of social concepts.

With modernism, there was a tendency to seek fairly precise definitions for terms, and within a relatively structured scientific framework, to attempt to set precise parameters around the meaning and use of concepts. The role of the individual for example, might be viewed as being created at the intersection of several key macro social, economic and political forces. Within a postmodernist framework however, there tends to be the assumption that social life is much more complex than the individual being affected by a few key, large-scale social trends. Within modernism, the individual is to some extent seen as confined within a particular social role which is determined by a number of factors, not least of which are economic ones. Within postmodernism however the individual is often viewed as operating within a complex network of different social roles, from which the most relevant or appealing may be selected according to the perceived wishes or needs of the individual. The individual has the capacity to construct a social role, which may be unique, and which does not depend upon the roles of others. To that extent, society may be seen as consisting of as many different social roles as there are individuals. The latter convey information about their adopted social roles to others, partly by means of external signifiers which themselves may be the result of patterns of commercial consumption. The individual associates with a particular type of music, with particular modes of dress and personal decoration, and with particular patterns of cultural consumption. These represent choices by the individual, in terms of the methods selected by which the person will interact with society, and communicate the personal meanings and interpretations of societal norms.

A society with such a diffuse structure, can in some ways be viewed as functional for the individual, in terms of both risk and education. The individual can be viewed as free from the constraints of overbearing social forces, and able to self-define a series of roles in society which are both functional on the individual level, and also productive for society. One might view this as a societal model in which the individual has a greater possibility of self-fulfilment, and also indeed argue that although self-fulfilment is in a sense, an individual enterprise, it also has to some extent a socially-cohesive function. If everyone in society has the opportunity and potential for self-fulfilment, then this is arguably more conducive to a stable and less risk-inclined society than one in which people see themselves as reluctantly confined within the boundaries of economic and social imperatives. Equally well, one might well see as more constructive, an educational system in which individuals are free to create their own educational enterprise, and to develop along the lines of their evolving interests, rather than being confined within predetermined courses and curricula. Of course, it is difficult to imagine a structured educational system in which everyone would be free to create their own curriculum, but within the broad framework of a postmodern view of the world, there would appear to be not only a greater trend in this direction, but also that it need not be dysfunctional towards society at large. The issue of choice within a postmodern society is discussed in Morawski (1996, p. 9).

One of the key features of postmodernism is that it is associated with an unprecedented increase in global communications. Many consequences have developed from this, and no doubt many more will be gradually revealed as this phenomenon evolves. However, although one might argue that one of the effects of global electronic networks is to provide a medium within which the individual may become isolated from society, at the same time, one might equally argue that global networks also encourage the individual to have a sense of empathy with other human beings, and to have a feeling that the things which affect others, also affect oneself (see Griswold, 1994, p. 149).

In terms of risk, when there are problems with nuclear installations, when natural disasters occur, or airlines crash, or famines develop, then we can immediately see the consequences as they evolve, often in graphic details. Admittedly, there is the danger that we will become engrossed in the superficial image, and not completely register the scale of the disaster or the full human consequences. However, on the other hand, such images do have an immediacy. They can be transmitted and received in real time, and hence potentially have a major effect upon those receiving the images. There may well be a sense in which we are all elements in the same world, and subject to the same natural and technological forces. Such communication images may well encourage us to participate in, for example environmental policies, because we have come to understand that the influences which affect Africa, are the same influences which may well have consequences for us in the future.

In the world of education it can also help pupils and students to appreciate that the subject matter which they are learning, has consequences for distant parts of the planet, and for areas and countries which perhaps previously may have appeared to be somewhat irrelevant. Indeed, the issue of 'relevance' has always been a difficult one for teachers. At most levels in the educational system, but perhaps particularly during the secondary school years, teachers have sought many different strategies to illuminate the relevance of what they have taught. Global communications and in particular the internet, have to some extent remedied this difficulty. Students can very easily access the internet in different languages, and see very similar topics being discussed in a variety of world languages. They can see immediately that young people in Japan, France or Brazil are interested in just the same things as themselves. With this perhaps arises a wish to communicate, and perhaps to do so in the host language. One can also see the danger however, that just as say English became the lingua franca throughout the British Empire, and Latin in a previous era throughout the Roman Empire, so American English will rapidly become the lingua franca of electronic communication. In those areas of global communication where precision in rapidly-changing circumstances is essential (whether air traffic control or international finance) then there is a possibility that American English will gain the ascendency.

Postmodern society is also rapidly-changing. In the modern era, education originally drew upon the 'classics' in various spheres of human thought, and later this became somewhat amended. In the postmodern era however, there is a sense in which everything may be challenged. The new is forever being created and recreated, and one sometimes gets the feeling that there is no need to look back to classical authors or thinkers, or to received wisdom. This may in some ways be a good thing, since it encourages educationalists and students to reflect upon and challenge received wisdom. Indeed, received wisdom may not necessarily, in all circumstances, be wise. On the other hand, one of the assumptions of the functions of education was that a formal system existed at least partly to ensure the perpetuation of accumulated human culture. We did not want to lose the knowledge and understanding which we had gained. If we failed to transmit some elements of our knowledge to only one generation of students, then that knowledge would die out, except in printed documents. The danger on the one hand, of postmodernism, is that all knowledge may be, in effect, subject to challenge, and hence there will be nothing substantial to transmit. On the other hand, it may be seen as an advantage, that contemporary students and intellectuals subject all ideas to challenge, and hence usher in a more critical and analytic period, where no ideas are automatically accepted as valid without being subject to the most rigorous evaluation.

In the medieval world, it was frequently the case that people earned their livings either at home, or close to the place where they lived. This changed dramatically in the modern period, with large-scale industrialisation. Manufacturing tended to take place in locations which were devoted to the precise task of industrial production. They contained the technological equipment necessary for that production, and normally it was not easy to transfer that equipment. The production process was usually very labour-intensive, and it was frequently the case that large-scale migration of workers took place, in order to live nearby the place of production. There had developed a separation of the domicile and of the place of labour. In postmodernism however, there has been something of a reversion to the situation where people are able to unify their place of work and place of habitation. The computer and the internet have enabled people to work effectively from their habitation, and perhaps only occasionally to visit the office, the factory or the sales outlet. Patterns do differ of course, but this has become a realistic pattern of working. Postmodernism, as in many areas of life, has introduced many varied patterns of working. In medieval times, a typical pattern was perhaps that of the craft worker, working from home, and who passed on skills to the offspring. In the modern period, a typical pattern was perhaps that of the factory worker, with a precise division between the activities of the home and that of the workplace. Within postmodernism, we see a much greater proliferation of patterns of work.

Some people may still follow the modern work pattern, but in many other cases, there are combinations of home working and working in a specialized employment location. For some people, the location of the employer may be many miles from the home of the worker, who may only visit the head office once a week. In other cases, people may work at home, and travel to a number of different employment locations as necessary. In some cases, work may be primarily or even exclusively located at home. Such changes have created significant consequences for the legal basis of employment and of working, where in previous times, the legislative framework has been largely based upon a situation where people were assumed to work in a specific place, devoted to employment or manufacturing.

In education too, there have been parallel changes in postmodernity. During modernity there was the assumption that pupils or students travelled to specialized institutions of education in order to learn. They were assumed to learn largely in a face to face situation with a teacher or lecturer, and that transmission of knowledge and skills was regarded as central to the educational process. Within postmodernity however, has been witnessed the proliferation of many different models of teaching and learning. The internet and access to global information networks have resulted in many different sources of knowledge, and hence many different means by which students can access information. Students in contemporary society tend to learn and be taught in many different ways, and the parameters of potential learning have been extended almost infinitely.

References

Benton, T. and Craib, I. (2001), *Philosophy of Social Science*, Palgrave, Basingstoke.

Best, S. and Kellner, D. (1991), *Postmodern Theory: critical interrogations*, Macmillan, London.

Boyne, R. and Rattansi, A. (1990), 'The Theory and Politics of Postmodernism: By way of an introduction', in R. Boyne and A. Rattansi (eds), *Postmodernism and Society*, Macmillan, London, pp. 1–45.

Delanty, G. (1997), *Social Science: Beyond Constructivism and Realism*, Open University Press, Buckingham.

Delanty, G. (2000), *Modernity and Postmodernity: Knowledge, Power and the Self*, Sage, London.

Gergen, K.J. (1999), *An Invitation to Social Construction*, Sage, London.

Griswold, W. (1994), *Cultures and Societies in a Changing World*, Ca., Pine Forge, Thousand Oaks.

Harvey, D. (1990), *The Condition of Postmodernity*, Blackwell, Oxford.

Lyon, D. (1999), *Postmodernity,* 2nd edn., Open University Press, Buckingham.

Lyotard, J-F. (1984), *The Postmodern Condition*, Manchester University Press, Manchester.

Miles, S. (2001), *Social Theory in the Real World*, Sage, London.

Morawski, S. (1996), *The Troubles with Postmodernism*, Routledge, London.

Norris, C. (1990), 'Lost in the Funhouse: Baudrillard and the politics of Postmodernism', in R. Boyne and A. Rattansi (eds), *Postmodernism and Society*, Macmillan, London, pp. 119–153.

Wagner, P. (2001), *A History and Theory of the Social Sciences*, Sage, London.

PART II
CASE STUDIES IN RISK AND EDUCATION

Chapter 5

'Moral Panic', Internet Use and Risk Perspectives in Educational Organisations

Andrew Hope

Introduction

In recent years Internet provision has been introduced into over 30,000 schools in the United Kingdom (UK). This is primarily a result of the National Grid for Learning (NGfL), a £700 million government initiative aimed at ensuring that all schools in Britain were on-line by 2002 (DfEE, 1997). Additional government initiatives aimed at setting up on-line resources for schools, such as the Virtual Teacher Centre, have followed at regular intervals (Selwyn, 1999). The discussion of risks arising from school computer use has been sparse, with the UK government largely focusing on the potential benefits of the Internet at the expense of informed debate about the on-line risks to students (Moran-Ellis and Cooper, 2000, para 2.4). Media coverage of Internet risks in wider society has been labelled as exaggerated, sensationalistic, and inciting 'moral panic' (Akdeniz, 1997; Lawson & Comber, 2000).

In considering 'moral panic' and risk perspectives in educational organisations, several issues need to be addressed. These are the nature of risk perspectives, the validity of 'moral panic' as an analytical concept and the impact of 'moral panic' upon risk perspectives. Whilst there exist a variety of risks relating to school Internet use, including the accessibility of on-line pornography, racist websites and bomb / drug making sites, the focus of this chapter will be on a single issue, namely the use of chat–lines by children. Chat-lines (sometimes called chat rooms) allow individuals to converse in real time through short written messages (Britton, 1998, p. 154). The media has labelled chat-lines as the haunt of undesirables and a 'candystore for paedophiles'. Having briefly considered the nature of risk perspectives and how these relate to the concept of 'moral panic', the validity of the claim that media coverage of chat-lines is an example of 'moral panic', will be considered using the criteria suggested by Goode and Ben-Yehuda (1994). Drawing upon research data from a three-year project exploring school Internet risks the issue of whether risk perspectives in schools reflected media coverage will be considered. While there exist a variety of different parties involved in the discourse about Internet use in educational institutions, such as the government, Local Education Authorities, parents and students, the focus will be on staff risk perspectives. After examining staff risk perspectives concerning chat-lines and their use by students, the extent to which media discourse influenced staff risk perspectives will be considered. Before focusing upon the concept of 'moral panic', the writings of Ulrich Beck will be drawn upon to consider the nature of risk perceptions in late modernity, and explore their connection to the mass media.

Risk Perceptions and the Mass Media

Rather than being a natural occurrence perceptions of risk are built up through social processes. Therefore, such perceptions should not be seen as given 'truths' but rather as categories, which are the product of wider social processes of both negotiation and enforcement. Despite adopting aspects of a realist perspective in elements of his early writings on 'risk society', Beck recognises the importance of public perceptions of danger.

> [there exists] the risk itself and public perception of it. It is not clear whether it is the risks that have intensified, or our views of them. Both sides converge, condition each other, strengthen each other, and because risk are risks in knowledge, perspective of risks and risks are not different things, but one and the same (Beck, 1992, p. 55).

Despite there being an urgency in Beck's work to highlight the threat of certain global risks that are presented as 'objective dangers', such as acid rain, he recognises the role played by the scientific community, state and the mass media in selecting risks and focusing attention on them. Cottle (1998, p. 12) suggests that this can possibly be interpreted as Beck adopting a critical realist position. While this may be an over-simplification of the issue it nevertheless allows for a consideration that some 'risks' that are drawn into the public arena may be 'subjective creations'. Indeed Beck (1992, p. 22) readily recognises that knowledge about risks can be altered through being minimised, maximised or dramatised. In particular the selection and reporting of certain risks by the media can result in a wilful distortion of the representation of the exact nature and extent of hazards. If such arguments, clearly situated within a critical realist perspective, are readily accepted then questions of influence and power over risk knowledge become central. In this context risk perceptions are subjected to political as well as social influence. Indeed each society elevates some risks to a high point while depressing others out of sight. The choice of which risks to focus on relates to broader decisions about the social structure of society. In short, risk perceptions are inherently political. Moreover, if it is maintained that perceptions of certain risks may be dramatised and/or distorted then the motives for such manipulation may be seen to be political. As Beck notes:

Even in their highly mathematical or technical garb, statements on risks contain statements of the type that is how we want to live ... the growing awareness of risks must be reconstructed as a struggle among rationality claims, some competing and some overlapping (Beck, 1992, pp. 58–59).

Risk statements are an attempt to impose particular ways of seeing and living. Thus, different perspectives are often in competition and sometimes overlapping. Arguably those who can force their own risk perceptions on others, encouraging individuals against their own will to accept certain risks as 'naturally' the ones that should be focused upon are in a position of power. While allowing for the importance of scientific and legal systems in disseminating information, Beck privileges the mass media as a key agent in the formation of public risk perceptions (Cottle, 1998, p. 9). Insofar as various elements of the mass media are significant in creating public risk perceptions, they also have the potential to distort such viewpoints. Indeed, there is no reason why a rationality claim cannot be fabricated to serve wider social and political processes.

The media processes and mechanisms involved in the unveiling of risks to the wider public need to be understood with reference to social construction. This allows for a consideration of the possibility that the dangers highlighted in the media may be exaggerated or fabricated, providing a misrepresentation of a hazard. Indeed, if risk perceptions are constructed with reference to the mass media there is no necessary reason to presume that these views will be accurate in a strict realist sense. The concept of 'moral panic' offers a useful framework within which to consider how certain dangers may become exaggerated and sensationalised through media coverage. While there have been arguments over the computability of theories of 'risk society' and 'moral panic' (Ungar, 2001; Hier, 2003) it can nevertheless be recognised that in a society obsessed with danger there exists fertile ground for the creation of 'moral panics'.

Having considered Beck's reflections on the nature of risk perceptions, noted that the mass media are key agents in the formulation of public views, and posited that some of the reported risks may be exaggerated, it is now appropriate to consider in detail the concept of 'moral panic'.

'Moral Panics'

The field of study of 'moral panics' was originally developed by British sociologist, Stanley Cohen, drawing on American ideas of labelling and deviancy theory. Cohen's pioneering work on 'moral panics' focused on two youth subgroups, the Mods and Rockers and promoted an 'anxiety theory of 'moral panic', stressing popular concern arising from the perceived blurring of social boundaries as reported in the media. Cohen (1972) described how, during 1964, the media seized upon and exaggerated some minor scuffs in Clacton.

The media coverage was important because it was through this medium 'that most people received their pictures of both deviance and disasters' (Cohen, 1972, p. 30).

Cohen noted that news reports were exaggerated and distorted, misrepresenting the numbers involved and the amount of violence and damage. Of the ninety-seven arrests at Clacton, only one-tenth were charged with offences involving violence and twenty-four were charged with non-hooligan sort of offences, such as petty theft (Cohen, 1972, p. 37). Contributing to this exaggeration the reporting tended to be sensationalised, relying upon sensational headlines and melodramatic vocabulary. Words and phrases such as 'riot', 'siege', 'orgy of destruction' and 'hell-bent on destruction' were widely used (Cohen, 1972, p. 30). Another element of the media reporting was the tendency towards prediction that the event would be repeated. Thus, it was asserted that this was all part of a larger pattern, reflecting underlying causes that were gathering pace. Subsequently the media reported similar events during the 1964 Whitsun Holiday in Bournemouth, Brighton, and Margate, suggesting that the situation was getting worse, although all of these incidents were actually of smaller magnitude than Clacton. Furthermore, Cohen (1972) argued that the media coverage also entailed a form of 'symbolization' in which symbols were stripped of neutral meanings and used to evoke unfavourable responses. Such symbolisation was often part of the larger process of 'scapegoating', where certain groups perceived to be the cause of the problem had the public fears and fantasies projected onto them, becoming in Cohen's term 'folk devils'. Ultimately for Cohen the media and particular interest groups were central to the generation of 'moral panics'.

Since Cohen's original work the concept of 'moral panic' has been used in various reconstituted forms. The work of the Birmingham Centre for Contemporary Cultural Studies (Hall and Jefferson, 1976) introduced a critical theory perspective, emphasising the influence of socio-economic class and ideology. Although drawing on these British works American studies on 'moral panics' lost this theoretical cutting edge and the radical concern with issues of social control and ideology (Thompson, 1998, p. ix). Thus, American researchers were less inclined to look for society wide cultural and social structural explanations, such as crises of capitalism and cultural hegemony. Instead, an interest group theory of 'moral panics' was preferred, which stressed that such panics are more likely to emanate from middle rungs of the power hierarchy (Goode and Ben-Yehuda, 1994). This approach also utilised the concept of moral entrepreneur, a crusading individual who attempts to rouse the public and bring pressure on authorities to define particular behaviour as deviant and criminal. More recently, a 'grassroots theory' of 'moral panic' has emerged, which stresses that the state, interest groups and media cannot create concern where none exists. From this perspective 'moral panics' must be a reflection of genuine public concern. This grassroots theory has much in common with realist criminologists, such as Jones et al. (1986), who whilst not rejecting the concept of 'moral panic', perceive certain incidents to be examples of moral realism.

With current developments in information communication technology as well as the flourishing of niche and micro-medias it has been argued that the nature of 'moral panics' have changed somewhat. Considering 'moral panic' in the multi-mediated world McRobbie and Thornton argue that 'moral panics' have become the way in which daily events are brought to the attention of the media' (1995, p. 560). However, they also acknowledge that there is a tendency in contemporary British society to label a whole range of media events as 'moral panic'. Whereas Cohen conceptualised 'moral panics' as occurring infrequently, at times of cultural strain resulting from social change, it appears that there is currently less selectivity in applying the label to incidents of media misrepresentation. Importantly McRobbie and Thornton (1995) also maintain that so-called 'folk devils' can now produce their own media, and can attempt to resist or even incite their own 'moral panics'. Thus, the emergence of a 'moral panic' in contemporary society may be a more dynamic, contested, polyphonic process.

Critics of 'moral panic' have questioned the assumptions that their occur-rence is timeless and common to all societies, challenged the belief that they are seemingly embedded in collective consciousness and have drawn attention to the failure of the concept to provide an adequate explanation of the relationship between media and public opinion (Hunt, 1997, pp. 644–645). Indeed with regards to this last criticism it has been argued that the concept of 'moral panic' 'is a polemical rather than an analytical concept' (Waddington, 1986, p. 258). After all, it is entirely possible to panic about genuine problems so there exists a real difficulty asserting that certain public perceptions are instances of panic created by media exaggeration and sensationalism. The difficulty of comparing the scale of the response with that of the danger is a valid concern. Goode and Ben-Yehuda (1994) have addressed this problem of 'disproportionality' arguing that with regard to familiar, ongoing risks certain indicators can be used to check validity. Firstly, it is necessary to consider whether the figures used are exaggerated. Secondly, it should be asked whether the figures are fabricated. Thirdly, an assessment needs to be made of whether the attention paid to a condition is far greater than that given to another threat although the concrete danger is less. Fourthly, the issue needs to be addressed whether the attention paid to a given condition is far greater than during any other period of time without a corresponding increase in objective seriousness (Goode and Ben-Yehuda, 1994, pp. 43–45). However with some risks it is impossible to determine the nature of the objective threat (Ungar, 1992). In such cases, it would be difficult to assert that public risk perceptions were an example of 'moral panic'.

A further problem with the concept of 'moral panic' is measuring the actual influence it has on individual risk perceptions. If it is ascertained that a 'moral panic' has occurred, the assumption follows that individual opinions will reflect sensationalised and exaggerated media coverage. Yet this process itself might be merely correlation rather than causation. However, on a micro-level the source of an individual's view can be ascertained by questioning them about media influence and their exposure to such sources. Problematically if media influence is covert and subliminal then individuals may not be aware of it. Nevertheless, it would be possible to observe whether terms favoured in media reports or illustrative stories derived from media sources were used in discussing the perceived risk. Finally, it could be considered whether other sources have affected an individuals risk perception. Before addressing this issue in more detail, it is first necessary to ascertain whether the media coverage of Internet chat-lines can be regarded as a case of 'moral panic'.

Chat-lines, Media Coverage and the Concept of 'Moral Panic'

Concern in the media about young people using the Internet has tended to focus on two main issues, the accessing of pornographic images on-line and the activities of paedophiles in chat rooms. While anxiety about children and pornographic websites has tended to stress the 'corruption of innocent minds' (Daily Telegraph, 29.06.00), there has also been a recognition that youths might intentionally access such material for their own pleasure (BBC News On-Line, 10.10.99). However, media coverage of risks arising from chat-line use has been singularly focused on the activities of paedophiles, portraying both children and youths as simply being in danger. Thus news reports have stressed paedophiles' use of the Internet to communicate with one another, swap pictures of sex crimes and seduce children (Independent, 15.02.01).

It has been argued that public concern over Internet access represents a 'moral panic' (Lawson and Chomber 2000, Akdeniz 1997). Nevertheless, such claims are rarely backed up with evidence comparing the scale of the response with that of the danger. As Waddington (1986) notes without this association been made, the concept of 'moral panic' remains polemic rather than analytical. It is recognised that there have been recent high profile cases relating to on-line paedophile activity. However, the focus of this discussion will be on incidents and media coverage around the time of the research as the concern is to link media coverage with the staff risk perspectives.

Goode and Ben-Yehuda (1994) suggest media reporting of a particular issue might be regarded as 'moral panic' if it receives more coverage than another harmful condition with a greater threat. Thus, the question needs to be addressed of the extent of the threat posed by paedophiles using chat-lines. There have been a number of cases where male adults have used the Internet to seduce young girls and persuade them to meet off-line. During the year two thousand it was reported that a man aged thirty-three, 'lured' a thirteen year old girl to his home for sex after meeting her through an Internet chat room. He was jailed for five years in what was believed to be the first prosecution of its type in Britain (Daily Telegraph, 25.10.00). In another case around the same period a man aged twenty-eight, contacted a paedophile web site saying he was 'desperate' for underage girls. Police in the United States (US) who had set up the 'fake' Internet site, passed his details to Scotland Yard's paedophile squad. He was arrested and jailed for sixteen months after meeting up with undercover officers and paying £200, believing he was paying for sex with a child (Daily Telegraph, 23.05.00). In the US a girl age thirteen, developed an on-line romance with a man, who she believed was twenty-four. He turned out to be a forty-one year old, who was sentenced to eighteen months imprisonment in one of the first cases prosecuted under America's Communications Decency Act (Daily Telegraph, 07.08.00). Child abuse arising from chat-line use is a very real threat that should not be lightly dismissed. It would be difficult to argue that it receives more media attention than other issues that pose a greater threat. Indeed recently the National Children's Home and Charities Coalition for the Internet, have estimated that at least twenty-six cases in Britain of children being raped or abducted by paedophiles have been linked to Internet chat rooms. (Daily Telegraph, 24/09/03).

Media coverage of chat-line use could also be labelled as 'moral panic' if the attention paid to it was far greater than during any other period, without a corresponding increase in objective seriousness (Goode and Ben-Yehuda, 1994). The World Wide Web has only being widely accessible since the early 1990s. So it can be argued that there exists no sufficiently substantial previous historical period with which to compare the rise in media concern over widespread web based chat-line use. While child abuse, including child pornography, has a long history, it is not always directly comparable with the peculiar nature of Internet related sex crimes.

Media reporting of an issue can be seen as an example of 'moral panic' if the figures used are exaggerated or fabricated (Goode and Ben-Yehuda, 1994). Reporting a claim made by a senior police officer the Sunday Telegraph (03.12.00) ran a story with the headline 'Paedophiles calling a fifth of children on net'. The Internet allows individuals to conceal their age, so it would be spurious to assume that one fifth of children had communicating via the web with adults, let alone adults convicted of criminal sexual offences. It could therefore be argued that the figures are fabricated, as there is no objective way to test the validly of this assertion. Indeed the language used in reports about the dangers of on-line chat rooms can also be labelled as sensationalistic. It was argued on the *Tonight with Trevor McDonald* (25.10.00) television programme that the Internet had become a 'candystore for paedophiles' with children being 'targeted and groomed for abuse' (Daily Telegraph, 25.10.00). While the serious risk of Internet related child abuse should not be dismissed the analogy used is not valid. To label chat-lines as 'candystores for paedophiles' suggests that there is no on-line protection, that paedophiles can merely choose what they want and that indulgence is tacitly allowed. This is clearly an exaggeration of the situation. Insofar as such fabrication and exaggeration can be seen as typical of the media coverage of chat-lines then it can be asserted that this was an example of 'moral panic'. Using research data collected about Internet use in schools the impact that this 'moral panic' has had on the risk perspectives of educational staff will now be considered.

Research Background

The following data is drawn from a three-year research project into school
Internet use in eight educational institutions, which examined risk perceptions,
evaluated actual risks and described attempts by schools to alleviate on-line
dangers. Drawing upon theoretical sampling (Glaser and Strauss, 1967)
fieldsites were selected to produce a diversity of categories and information.
The resulting heterogenous multi-site study generated a diverse range of information, provided a firm basis for generalisation (Schofield, 1993; Kennedy,
1979), It was felt that student age might be an important factor in studying
staff Internet risk perceptions, so institutions within different age sectors were
chosen. Overall two primary schools (Avenue and Brooklands), two 11–16
schools (Canalside and Dalehouse), three 11–18 schools (Eastway, Forestfields
and Greenswold) and one post-16 college (Hightree) were selected as fieldsites.
Additionally an effort was made to approach schools that had long established
Internet use and those institutions where the Internet had been recently introduced. This represented an attempt to generate diverse information and allow
for the possibility that risk perceptions might change in schools as staff gained
more on-line experience. The research took the form of semi-structured interviews, non-participant observation and content analysis. Thirty staff and sixty
three students spread across the eight institutions were interviewed. The person
with primary responsibility for information communication technology (ICT)
in school served as an initial contact, but attempts were also made to interview
teachers who had no particular role to play with regard to Internet use.
In examining the impact that the 'moral panic' about chat-lines had on staff
risk perspectives it is first necessary to consider these views before assessing the
impact of media reporting on staff risk perceptions.

Staff Risk Perceptions and Chat-line Use in Schools

Spread across all eight schools in the research twenty-four of the thirty staff
interviewed expressed concern about students using the school Internet to
access on-line chat rooms. While ten staff were exclusively worried that
students were at risk from undesirable language and strangers, a further ten
tempered this concern with the view that students accessing chat-lines were
also abusing resources in a manner that could damage the school image. Four
staff discussed student use of chat-lines entirely in terms of the threat posed to
school image and resources. Notably the teachers interviewed in primary
schools described children in chat rooms as being at risk while three out of
four staff at the post-16 institution described the students' on-line 'chatting'
activities as a threat to the college. Reflecting this general concern chat-lines
were banned in all schools involved in the research, bar one. The ICT manager
at Dalehouse had allowed access to certain 'acceptable' chat rooms with the
aim of encouraging students to use the Internet. Indeed plans were afoot to

turn the main Internet suite, based in the Learning Resource Centre, into an after school cyber café.

In the primary schools chat rooms were seen as 'risky' insofar as they gave strangers access to impressionable young children. While noting that he felt it was a remote possibility, the Head of Avenue, expressed concern that students might be persuaded to meet with people who they'd chatted to on-line. Staff were worried that students who arranged to meet such strangers would be physically and / or psychologically abused. Although chat-line use was prohibited in the primary schools, there were organised activities when students were allowed to communicate with other schools on-line. The ICT co-ordinator at Brooklands related how some students had been invited to Local Education Authority technical centre for the launch of a government Internet initiative. They were taking part in an on-line 'chat' with other students and politicians. After a while a stranger illicitly gained access to the chat room and started to ask the children a variety of personal questions. The session ended and the children logged off the Internet without further incident. Reflecting upon the event the ICT co-ordinator related how she had been disturbed by the whole incident and was deeply worried by the ease with which a stranger had been able to communicate with the students. Notably this anxiety was not restricted to primary schools. Indeed, in Greenswold Secondary School the ICT manager remarked:

> It's going to happen somewhere eventually, it's going to happen isn't it. Some kid's going to get enticed out by the chat room whatever and something horrible is going to happen and the school will be blamed. I predict that now. I just hope it's not this one. But somewhere, sometime it will happen (ICT manager, Greenswold).

Although such fears focused primarily on the risk to students, there was also an awareness that incidents of child abuse would reflect negatively on the school involved. Within the fieldsite schools there were two occasions where students talked about meeting 'strangers' off-line. Two sixteen-year-old girls at Dalehouse, related how they regularly chatted with 'friends' on the Ministry of Sound website. The students appeared to know little about their on-line 'friends' who claimed to live in London and regularly go night clubbing. Nevertheless, these two students revealed that they were considering travelling to London to meet their on-line 'friends' and go clubbing. While it was difficult to assess how sincere the girls were in their intent, both their age and the financial cost would prove prohibitive. A year 10 student at Greenswold, told how he had met his girlfriend on-line. He said that they were both interested in motor racing and had started communicating via the Formula One motor racing website. They communicated on a regular basis for a month before deciding to meet up off-line. As the girl lived forty miles away, the student made the trip by train one weekend. Upon meeting up it was discovered that they were of the same age, shared similar interests and a relationship ensued. Strangely, neither of them had reportedly thought to communicate via the telephone before meeting. Incidents such as these might give staff cause for concern, possibly reinforcing risk perceptions prevalent in the mass media. However, staff were apparently not aware of either of the above cases.

Beyond anxiety about on-line paedophile activity, staff also expressed concern about the offensive or highly sexualised language sometimes used in chat rooms. In the primary schools staff concern focused solely on the negative effect such language might have on impressionable young minds. However, the ICT Head at Eastway jokingly remarked that while younger students might be exposed to unsuitable language it was probably the older ones who were the source of such conversations. Indeed this comment reflected a view evident in secondary schools that students' use of chat-lines was a source of danger for the institution, potentially tarnishing the school image.

In all post-primary schools, staff discussed instances where students used chat-lines to engage in explicit conversations. At Canalside the chat rooms attached to the World Wrestling Federation website was reportedly popular with students. Staff complained that while the website itself might appear innocuous the chat rooms were known to attract youths seeking to engage in sexual conversations. Indeed the Head of ICT at Canalside threatened to fine students for Internet misuse, though for legal reasons he was unable to carry out this punishment. This failure to enforce charges might have been fortuitous insofar as fining students for accessing unsuitable chat-lines could be seen as tantamount to forcing them to pay for on-line sex chats! The ICT manager at Greenswold argued that sixth form students were generally engaging in cyber-sex in chat rooms. Indeed one female sixth former, who was sat at a computer next to the ICT manager, started a conversation with the line 'hello sexy, want some fun?' before being told to log off. Nevertheless, although secondary school staff talked about students' unsuitable use of chat-lines this was still often tempered with concern that students using chat-lines were at risk.

Only in the post-sixteen college were students using chat-lines described largely in terms of the risk they posed. Three of the four staff interviewed saw student on-line chatting activities solely as a threat to the college reputation. The ICT manager at Hightree related that soon after they had installed widespread Internet access:

> We noticed what I would term very unsuitable language and very unsuitable topics of conversation. They were frankly obscene (ICT manager, Hightree).

According to the ICT manager, students were engaging in highly sexualised conversations with strangers using the school Internet. While this also reportedly occurred at all five secondary schools in the research the extent to which it occurred at Hightree caused alarm. The Head of Science related that in an attempt to stop the main ICT suite turning into a 'cyber-café' they had only installed Internet access on half the computers in the room. Indeed one member of staff at Hightree related how a female student had approached him complaining that chat-line access was restricted, she had reportedly insisted that using chat-lines at the college was a 'rite of passage'.

In summary, staff were concerned about risks posed by the activities of paedophiles in chat rooms as well as the adult nature of some of the language used. However, this concern in the post-primary schools was often tempered with anxiety that student misuse of the Internet through wilfully engaging in sexual on-line conversations might tarnish the school image whilst threatening staff authority. Interestingly this narrative of students as a source of danger was absent from media coverage of chat-line risks. This suggests that staff perceptions of the risks arising from chat-line use in schools might be at least partly based on experience. In exploring this issue further, the focus will now shift to a consideration of the links between media coverage and staff perceptions.

Linking Media Coverage to Staff Risk Perceptions

Two issues need to be addressed in examining the relationship between the media and staff risk perceptions. The first relates to the impact of media coverage on staff views of chat-line safety. Thus, the views of staff on the influence of the media will be considered before discussing non-conscious indicators such as their use of particular terms or stories. Secondly, the impact of other sources on staff risk perceptions needs to be explored. In particular the role of experience in the construction of staff risk discourse will be reflected upon.

All thirty staff who were interviewed were asked if they thought the media's representation of the Internet affected their view of on-line technology. Twelve staff responded that they believed it did and a further eight considered it a 'possibility'. The response given by a history teacher at Greenswold was typical of those who considered that the media might have an impact on perceptions.

Well I guess sometimes you read stuff, which you later forget but it still influences what you think, how you think about things (history teacher, Greenswold).

Of the remaining ten staff who believed that the mass media didn't influence their perception about the Internet, four remarked that they rarely read daily newspapers. Of course, this did not necessarily mean that other media, such as television, radio or books, didn't influence them. Conversely, the Head of ICT at Eastway, replied that she was the wrong person to ask about the impact of the media as she didn't have a television. All twenty staff who admitted the possibility that they were influenced by the media stated that 'undesirable others' on chat-lines were a risk. However, in this case correlation does not necessarily reflect causation.

There were only four unprompted instances where staff made reference to particular media stories to validate their viewpoint. An art teacher at Eastway backed up his assertion that unsupervised students would create mischief on-line by drawing upon media stories of Internet misuse in schools. However, when questioned further he couldn't recall whether the new stories gave particular examples of students misusing the Internet. The other three instances where staff made direct reference to stories in the media, related to the report about on-line paedophiles, which appeared on the *Tonight* television programme. Thus, a history teacher at Forestfields labelled the report as 'worrying', maintaining that it informed parents of the dangers that existed in chat rooms. All four of these staff maintained that they believed the media influenced their perceptions of on-line risks.

As previously mentioned media influence can potentially be measured through the usage of particular distinct terms or narratives used in media reports. Thus, all three staff who discussed the news item about the dangers of chat-lines referred to the phrase 'candystore for paedophiles', which was used in the report. Problematically few distinct terms stood out in the media coverage of chat-line risks. Rather the language used in the media tended to be commonplace. One exception to this was the term 'chicken hawking', the practice of paedophiles silently watching conversations in children's chat rooms. Yet, this phrase was infrequently utilised in the media. Another term used by the media when discussing the dangers of chat-lines was 'grooming', but as this word was also used in policy discussion, official documentation and research reports its usage could not be directly linked to media influence. During the research none of the staff interviewed mentioned the 'grooming' of children by paedophiles or 'chicken hawking'.

The majority of staff were aware of the dangers of children being abused through on-line chat rooms. Reportedly, no such incidents had occurred in the educational institutions involved in this research. Importantly staff appeared unaware of two incidents during the research where students discussed meeting 'strangers' off-line whom they had only communicated with previously via chat-lines. Arguably then, staff concern about paedophile activity in chat rooms could derive from media coverage. After all twelve staff maintained that they believed the media influenced their views about the Internet, while a further eight considered it a 'possibility'. So, it would seem likely that the 'moral panic' about chat-lines influenced to some degree certain staff risk perceptions. However, the data is far from conclusive. Nevertheless, what is evident is that staff views were also informed by other sources.

Although media discussion of on-line pornographic images suggested that children were both at risk and a source of danger, its discourse about chat-lines maintained that children were solely at risk. However, some staff described older students' use of the school Internet to access chat-lines 'dangerous' to the institutional image. Indeed of the twenty-four staff who identified chat-lines as a risk, ten said that students were both at risk and dangerous, whilst four discussed the issue entirely in terms of the threat posed to school image and resources. This suggests that staff risk perspectives were not merely constructed with reference to media coverage. Rather staff drew upon their own experience of chat-lines in schools in constructing their conclusions as to the possible negative outcomes. This indicates that the impact of a 'moral panic' on individuals is far from straight forward. Certainly, it would be difficult to deny that exaggerated and sensationalised media coverage does not have an impact on media consumers. Yet in the case of the 'moral panic' surrounding children accessing chat-lines, it would appear that some staff adapted their view derived from the media by drawing on their own experience. This may explain why of the thirty staff interviewed fourteen considered that to some extent chat-line use by students might threaten the institution. Indeed all fourteen of these staff referred to incidents where they had discovered students misusing the Internet. Interestingly ten staff believed they were not influenced by media coverage and of these six did not consider chat-lines a risk to the students or the institution. That six staff did not consider chat-lines to be a risk suggests that some individuals may not be effected by the media creation of ' moral panics'. Yet, the importance of media coverage should not be dismissed. Indeed the same twenty staff who considered they might be influenced by media coverage of Internet risk were anxious that students using chat-lines were at risk.

Conclusion

In summary, it can be argued that media coverage of the risks to children from on-line chat rooms is an example of 'moral panic'. That is not to deny that actual danger exists. The offences committed starkly illustrate the very real nature of the threat. Drawing upon Goode and Ben-Yehuda (1994) it is argued that the media coverage of this issue can be seen as 'moral panic' insofar as the figures used were exaggerated and in some cases apparently fabricated. Furthermore, the reporting of this issue was exaggerated and sensationalistic, with a tendency towards prediction. Cohen (1972) had identified all of these elements as being present in media coverage giving rise to 'moral panics'.

Having established that media coverage of chat-lines could be described as 'moral panic', the question was then asked as to how such reporting would impact upon staff risk perceptions. It was noted that twenty-four of the thirty staff interviewed saw chat-line use in schools as a risk. Of these twenty-four staff twelve believed the media influenced their views about the Internet, while a further eight considered it a 'possibility'. This suggests that the 'moral panic' over chat-lines may have effected the views of the majority of the staff interviewed. However, whereas media covered had merely focused on children being at risk, fourteen staff voiced concern that chat-line use in school threatened the institutional image while wasting resources. This suggests that staff risk perceptions relating to on-line chat rooms were not just a reflection of 'moral panic'. Rather a much more complex process was taking place. While some staff were accepting the views espoused in the media, others were ignoring them and some were adapting them.

Attempting to measure the impact of 'moral panic' on risk perceptions is a difficult process. If media influence acts in a subliminal and covert manner upon an individual, then they may be unaware of it. It has been suggested that looking for the use of distinct words, key phrases, or particular stories might be a way to measure the influence of the media upon individuals' risk perceptions. Future research needs to further explore the impact of media reporting on risk perspectives, whilst considering the power relations that dictate which views individuals come to privilege.

References

Akdeniz, Y. (1997), 'The regulation of pornography and child pornography on the internet', *The Journal of Information, Law and Technology (JILT)*, <http://elj.warwick.ac.uk/jilt/internet/97_1akdeniz.html>.

BBC News On-line (10.10.99) 'Net porn warning for pupils', <http://news.bbc.co.uk/hi/english/education/newsid_470000/470299.stm>.

Beck, U. (1992), *Risk Society: Towards a New Modernity*, Sage, London.

Britton, Z. (1998), *Safety Net*, Harvest House Publishers, Oregon.

Cottle, S. (1998), 'Ulrich Beck, "Risk Society" and the media: a catastrophic view?', *European Journal of Communication*, vol. 13(1), pp. 5–32.

Cohen, S. (1972), *Folk Devils and Moral Panics: The Creation of the Mods and Rockers*, MacGibbon & Kee, London.

Daily Telegraph (23.05.00), 'Judge demands law change to punish Internet paedophiles'.

Daily Telegraph (29.06.00), 'Porn risk to children'.

Daily Telegraph (07.08.00), 'Children at risk from net fiends'.

Daily Telegraph, (25.10.00), 'Why the net must be swept clean of paedophiles'.

Daily Telegraph (24.09.03), 'Microsoft closes all chatrooms to stop paedophiles'.

DfEE (1997), *Connecting the Learning Society*, Stationary Office, London.

Glaser, B. & Strauss, A. (1967), *The discovery of grounded theory*, Aldine, Chicago.

Goode, E. and Ben-Yehuda, N. (1994), *Moral Panics: The Social Construction of Deviance*, Blackwell, Oxford.

Hall, S. and Jefferson, T. (eds), *Resistance Through Rituals: Youth Sub-cultures in Post-War Britain*, Hutchinson, London.

Hier, S. P. (2003), 'Risk and panic in late modernity: Implications of the converging sites of social anxiety', *British Journal of Sociology*, vol. 54(1), pp. 3–20.

Hunt, A. (1997), '"Moral panic" and moral language in the media', *British Journal of Sociology*, vol. 48(4), pp. 629–648.

Independent (15.02.01), When just looking is no excuse.

Jones, T., MacLean, B. and Young, J. (1986), *The Islington Crime Survey: Crime Victimisation and Policing in Inner City London*, Aldershot, Gower.

Kennedy, M.M. (1979), 'Generalizing from single case studies', *Evaluation Quarterly*, vol. 3(4), pp. 661–678.

Lawson, T. and Comber, C. (2000), 'Censorship, the internet and schools: a new moral panic?' *The Curriculum Journal*, vol. 11(2), pp. 273–285.

McRobbie, A. and Thornton, S.L. (1995), 'Rethinking "moral panic" for mulyi-mediated social worlds', *British Journal of Sociology*, vol. 45(4), pp. 559–574.

Moran-Ellis, J. and Cooper, G. (2000), 'Making connections: children, technology, and the national grid for learning', *Sociological Research On-line*, vol. 5(3), <http://www.socresonline.org.uk/5/3/moran-ellis.html>.

Schofield, J.W. (1993), 'Increasing the generalizability of qualitative research', in M. Hammersley (ed), *Educational Research: Current issues, volume one*, Paul Chapman Publishing, London, pp. 91–113.

Selwyn, N. (1999), 'The discursive construction of the national grid for learning', *Oxford Review of Education*, vol. 26(1), pp. 63–79.

Sunday Telegraph (03.12.00), Paedophiles calling a fifth of children on net.

Thompson, K (1998), *Moral Panics*, Routledge, London.

Ungar, S. (1992), 'The rise and (relative) decline of global warming as a social problem', *The Sociological Quarterly*, vol. 33(4): 483–501.

Ungar, S. (2001), 'Moral panic versus risk society: The implications of the changing sites of social anxiety', *British Journal of Sociology*, vol. 52(2), pp. 271–291.

Waddington, P.A.J. (1986), 'Mugging as a moral panic: a question of proportion', *British Journal of Sociology*, vol. 37(2), pp. 245–259.

Chapter 6

Schooling, Actuarialism and Social Exclusion: Using the Education System to Serve the Broader Political Purposes of Law and Order

Simone Bull

Introduction

> Crime will be virtually abolished by transferring to the preventive processes of the school and education the problems of conduct which police, courts, and prisons now remedy when it is too late ([American] National Education Association, 1931, p. 43–44).

Compulsory schooling began quite openly as a means of imposing the habit of obedience to coercive authority, conformity to the state's ideological values and of suppressing insurgent ideas among the masses, rather than as a means of transmitting knowledge. To this day, it is argued that the essential function of free and compulsory government schooling is to protect society, to be a form of crime control (Botsford, 1993), although evidence to support the belief that an 'educated' child will be more law-abiding is ambivalent at best (Cowper, 1784; West, 1970). Key features of modern schooling – compulsory attendance, state-imposed curriculum, the imposition of conformist attitudes, values and behaviour – have been said to 'establish a despotism over the mind, leading by natural tendency to one over the body' (Mill, 1975, p. 130). This chapter argues that the rise of the 'risk society' (Beck, 1992) is extending and strengthening the law and order aspect of state schooling in Britain, the United States and beyond. It begins with an analysis of the liminal nature of 'youth' and goes on to argue that this liminality has brought about a significant increase in the use of closed circuit television (CCTV) and other forms of surveillance in British schools. Underlying ostensible motivations to protect staff, students and property is a fundamental government commitment to promoting actuarial stances towards crime control. Such an approach, it is argued, has the added advantage of devolving responsibility for a range of social ills onto communities. Further, it compounds the marginalisation of youth and in doing so exacerbates social exclusion.

Children have re-emerged as loci of risk anxiety (Jackson and Scott, 1999), often assuming panic-like proportions (Furedi, 1997). There have been many recent instances of such panics, notably the extensive coverage given to the murder of the Soham schoolgirls Holly Wells and Jessica Chapman in 2002. As Jackson and Scott note, 'childhood is increasingly being constructed as a precious realm under siege from those who would rob children of their child-hoods, and as being subverted from within by children who refuse to remain childlike' (Jackson and Scott, 1999, p. 86). Indeed, 'children are assumed to be at risk not only from abusing adults, but from bullies and abusers among their peers' (Furedi, 1997, p. 69), as in the highly publicised murder of James Bulger in Liverpool in 1993 (Furedi, 1997), the urban riots in Meadowell in 1991 (Campbell, 1993), and the Columbine High School shooting in the United States.

But while children are, on the one hand, hapless victims of an increasingly risky society (Smith, 2002) on the other they are the current 'folk devils'' of popular conception (Muncie, Coventry and Walters, 1995). Violence perpe-trated by seemingly 'ordinary' young people who come from 'ordinary' com-munities has highlighted a new source of danger, exacerbated by the 'historical amnesia' surrounding youthful offending (Newburn, 2002). Constructions of youth in the media, in popular writing, and in scientific treatises have charac-terized adolescents as outcasts, hormone-driven and morally deficient – essen-tially, dangerous (Giroux, 1996; Lesko, 2001). As Newburn notes, 'the most recurrent forms of moral panics in Britain since the War have been those surrounding youthful forms of deviance' (Newburn, 2002, p. 536). A survey of seventy-seven studies published between 1910 and 2000 on violence, youth (people under eighteen years of age), and race in the American media found that newspaper and television stories tended to portray youth as violent and connected with gangs, while at the same time underreporting their victimisation (Justice Policy Institute and Berkeley Media Studies Institute, 2001). Yet, in 1998, absolute levels of reported violent crime committed by youths were the lowest they had been in twenty-five years (Census Bureau, 1998).

Extreme fear of youth is an established media panic (Los Angeles Times, 21/04/02). Images of 'ordinary' teenagers 'going bad' can be found in a range of media products such as *Time* magazine, *The New York Times*, *60 Minutes II*, *MBC News*, *CNN* and *20/20*. Not surprisingly, polls show adults fear personal victimization by youths (Los Angeles Times, 21/04/02). Where, throughout the twentieth century, specific groups of youth were periodically constructed as 'folk devils', nowadays the threat posed by young people has become more generalised, though the threat posed by particularly 'risky' groups remains (Alexander, 2000; Pearson, 1983). The elasticity of the concept of youth, occupying an uncertain and therefore unpredictable liminal zone somewhere between childhood and adulthood, may help explain the dual construction of youth as being both at risk and a source of risk.

In 1994, President Bill Clinton told a Music Television audience that youths must change their ways to stop causing trouble for grownups. The Clinton administration was inaugurated in January 1993 promising to 'put children first'. Nonetheless, their health and welfare policies blamed teenagers for nearly all major social ills: poverty, welfare dependence, crime, gun violence, suicide, sexual promiscuity, unwed motherhood, Acquired Immune Deficiency Syndrome, school failure, broken families, child abuse, drug abuse, drunken driving, smoking and the breakdown of 'family values' (Males, 1996). Inspired by much of the campaigning that takes places in the United States (Pilger, 1998, p. 84), successive governments in England and Wales have expressed harshly punitive sentiments towards youth, the 'unpeople' (Pilger, 1998, p. 99):

> [British politicians] don't have any good news about young people. Or if they do, they make out it's absolutely amazing that a young person has done something good. Young people are meant to go around mugging people, or on drugs, aren't they? (interviewee quoted in Pilger, 1998, p. 103).

The Labour Party slogan 'tough on crime, tough on the causes of crime' is readily used to encourage the scapegoating of youth. The insecurities and fears that are now characteristic of contemporary British and American societies have influenced the identification of youth in general as a new source of threat.

This notion has become so embedded that in the Strathclyde town of Hamilton in Scotland, initiatives designed to reduce peoples' fear of crime have had the opposite effect. The 'Child Safety Initiative's' stated intention was to make all sections of the community safer, by imposing a curfew on those under the age of sixteen. Instead, the curfew reinforced the idea that youth pose a crime risk, institutionalised fears that different groups have of one another and widened the divisions between them. Popular images of young people as risky were not challenged. Rather, public suspicions were simply confirmed (Waiton, 2001).

Risk, Actuarialism and the 'Culture of Control'

The 'reification of risk' (Bradbury, 1989) characteristic of late modernity entails not only the introduction of new forms of danger, but the development of individual and collective 'calculative' attitudes (Giddens, 1991; Young, 1999), otherwise known as actuarialism, which is a major motif of social control.

> The actuarial stance is calculative of risk ... it is not concerned with causes but with probabilities, not with justice but with harm minimization ... The actuarial stance reflects the fact that risk both to individuals and collectivities has increased, crime has become a normalized part of everyday life ... the 'other' is everywhere and not

restricted to criminals and outsiders ... Both individuals and institutions face the problems of sorting out the safe from the risky and doing so in ways which are ... merely probabilistic (Young, 1999, p. 66).

In encouraging individual and collective calculative attitudes (actuarialism) in all kinds of interactions and situations, the 'risk society' has effectively broadened the sphere of influence of the criminal justice system and 'widened the net' of social exclusion.

The need for actuarialism is explained by Young's (1999) 'six components of risk', calling to mind what Garland (2001, p. 163) has termed the 'crime complex' of late modernity. The first of these is a 'real' rise in risk as evidenced by rises in crime across developed countries since World War Two, a penumbra of incivilities, and the increasingly internecine nature of crime. The second component is 'revelation'; wherein the public are informed of more crimes than ever before, and of an increasingly diverse character. Next come 'expectations'. The last several decades have seen greater demand for civilised behaviour toward one another. Fourth, is 'reserve'; greater mobility characteristic of modern society has led to a decline in direct knowledge of fellow citizens, neighbours and so on. When combined with living in a more heterogeneous society, this leads to unpredictability, making us more 'reserved', even abrasive, in our interactions with strangers. Fifth is 'reflexivity'. The new forms of danger introduced by late modernity carry with them uncertain and fluctuating levels of risk that cannot be agreed upon. The final component of risk is 'refraction'. This is where the mass media, through excessive use of atypical criminal imagery generate fear of crime disproportionate to risk.

To varying degrees, the cultural, sociological and governmental perspectives on risk all maintain that risk cannot simply be accepted as an unproblematic concept, a phenomenon that can be isolated from its social, cultural and historical contexts. Rather, what are identified as risks are the outcome of socio-cultural processes that tend to serve particular functions (Caplan, 2000; Lupton, 1999). Some of those functions include reinforcing or accentuating inequalities (Lyon, 2001). The designation, 'risky', often serves to reinforce the marginalised or powerless state of individuals. Special attention is directed at them, positioning them in a network of surveillance, monitoring and intervention (Lupton, 1999). Notions of 'otherness' thus remain central to ways of thinking and acting about risk. For Douglas, risk acts primarily as a locus of blame. Douglas also notes that, 'since the present distribution of risks reflects only the present distribution of power and status... Intuitively, giving more risks to those who carry more smacks of elementary injustice' (Douglas, 1985, p. 10). Such objections are difficult to uphold in the face of a risk rhetoric that has developed in such a way as to suggest that risk calculations are devoid of moral judgement and are mere objective facts. This facade of moral neutrality has been described by Zygmunt Bauman (1995, p. 133) as adiaphorization, or 'the stripping of human relationships of their moral significance, exempting them from moral evaluation, rendering them morally irrelevant'.

Actuarial 'calculations' form the basis for risk prediction instruments now used in a wide variety of social settings. In the last decades of the twentieth century, risk assessment strategies have been vigorously pursued by criminal justice systems across the globe. They have given official recognition to a logic that makes it natural to monitor youth in order to determine the probability that they will 'offend' in the future (Tonry, 1999; Tyler and Boeckmann, 1997). For example, in the United Kingdom, eight to thirteen-year-olds who display anti-social behaviour are to be targeted by Youth Inclusion and Support Panels (YISPs) before they commit a crime. These YISPs comprise personnel from local youth offending teams, police and representatives from health, social services and schools. One of their objectives is to identify young people who might be at risk of offending (The Guardian, 23/10/02).

Such strategies are seen as necessary because the usual criminal justice mechanisms of modern British society are largely reactive; the police do not generally investigate crimes until they are reported, and purported offenders cannot legally be detained unless they are charged with committing specific offences. From the victim's perspective these are essentially 'ambulances at the bottom of the cliff', which do not take effect until after the initial damage has occurred. In the 'risk society' this is no longer sufficient, society requires more systematic and subtle mechanisms for protection. Portents of danger need not be specifically linked to crime (Young, 1999). Thus, the climate of heightened risk awareness, coupled with nostalgia for bygone days of carefree childhood and the sense that threats nowadays arise from pervasive social ills has engendered a preoccupation with surveillance (Jackson and Scott, 1999), as an important tool in risk management. This is a new surveillance, not intended to replace special provisions for those already identified as at-risk, but a much more subtle means of exposing even more young people to scrutiny.

'Feeding' Risk through Closed Circuit Television Surveillance

CCTV is one form of surveillance that has become so routine in Britain and the United States that people have become blind to its presence (Lyon, 2001; National Institute of Justice, 2003). But, as Lyon notes, 'surveillance always has two faces' (Lyon, 2001, p. 152). The substitution of physical control for virtual control may seem equitable but the essence is exploitation (*cf.* Althuser and Gramsci). As with the social control function of schooling, the sorting process facilitated by surveillance continues to remain largely hidden, except to the marginalised age, class, gender and/or ethnic groups who bear the brunt of it, and the 'nanny state' that promulgates it. After all, successful coercive authority always rests to some extent on assent by the coerced (Gramsci, 1971). That assent is achieved through hegemony, understood as the perme-ation throughout society of an entire system of values, attitudes, beliefs and morality that has the effect of supporting the status quo in power relations. The 'risk society', coupled with the plausible justifications for surveillance as being in the interests of safety and comfort alongside alienation of those who question the motivations underlying the presence of CCTV (Lyon, 2001), thus increases willingness to comply with being monitored.

As Furedi notes, 'following a long-established practice in the USA, the management of British nurseries and schools is increasingly subject to the exigencies of security concerns' (Furedi, 1997, p. 113). Millions of pounds have already been spent on CCTV subsidies to British schools, to assist with the prevention of burglary and vandalism outside of school hours. School security grant allocations to Local Education Authorities across England and Wales have amounted to approximately twenty-two million pounds annually from 1997–98 to 2001–02. Pilot funding from alternate sources is also available. Eastbourne Comprehensive School in Darlington, for example, has been awarded two hundred and forty thousand pounds to carry out security improvements to make students and staff safer (Darlington Council, 2003). Given the pervasiveness of CCTV in Britain since it was first introduced in public space in 1985 (Loader and Sparks, 2002), it seems reasonable to suggest that a significant proportion of this security budget is likely to have been spent on CCTV, although a variety of measures have certainly been funded. One school in North-East England has even introduced iris scanning linked to the provision of school lunches. The system knows which children receive free lunches and charges the others to their accounts. The school believes this makes lunches easier to manage and minimises bullying – since it avoids children carrying cash, and conceals the stigma associated with receiving a free lunch.

Little of this investment has been directed at primary schools. This is surprising, since much policy tends to be incident-driven, and several notorious incidents, such as the Soham murders and the Dunblane massacre in Scotland, involved primary school children. It is worth noting that the peak age of offending is eighteen for males and fifteen for females, that is, among those attending secondary school and post-sixteen establishments (Newburn, 2002). This suggests that the motive for installing CCTV is less to protect a school population frequently perceived as 'at-risk', than to monitor the most 'risky' school population.

Numerous schools in the Newport area of Wales have their digital cameras connected to their broadband infrastructure after hours and send pictures back to a control centre at the council offices (BBC, 05/06/02).

Sensational advertising from the security industry would have us believe that violent crises in classrooms are a common occurrence and that their ideal solution is the installation of CCTV. Schools and colleges are enticed to install CCTV by guarantees of cost-effectiveness, multi-functionality and efficiency. As well as preventing vandalism, anti-social behaviour, burglaries and the like, CCTV can be used for instant videoconferencing. Further, remote surveillance software can run in the background on any designated computer, including a home computer, so that schools paying five thousand pounds per year for high-speed Internet connections can also monitor digital CCTV after hours, though this has raised some important data protection issues. Schools are assured that 'protecting' their environments from external threats is essential because of the daily volume of human traffic, and that their main areas of concern should be entrances and exits, computer rooms, bicycle sheds and locker rooms – gateways to students, staff and their property. It seems that schools, like youth, are subject to dissonant perceptions. On the one hand, schools are being redefined as signifiers of 'safe' space – safe from other people and even from those within its walls. But, at the same time, the very presence of heightened security measures could be interpreted as a subtle form of criminalisation (Morrison, 1995).

One of the new city academies has announced plans to install CCTV in every classroom to ease monitoring and control of bad behaviour, allegedly the first of its kind in Britain to do so. It is claimed that the cameras will protect teachers from unwarranted accusations of abuse by pupils and safeguard expensive computer equipment. At another college CCTV was initially installed only in the music rooms where pupils were taught by people not on the school's main staff.

Similarly, Manchester City Council has outlined their application for government funding to install CCTV cameras in five local schools, purportedly in order to convince parents of their children's bad behaviour (The Guardian, 24/02/03).

In 1999 a college installed CCTV in girls' and boys' toilets to try and prevent pupils from smoking in the toilets, to stop graffiti and to make them a 'safe' environment for younger children (as opposed to smoker's dens dominated by older pupils, girls in particular). The cameras are among a number which have been installed around the college. These particular camera lenses apparently focus on the 'circulation areas' of the toilets, not cubicles or urinals, and are observed by staff in the main school office (BBC, 05/11/99). Since 2002, Wrexham children travelling to school by bus have been monitored by CCTV. The initiative came after a review of school transport by the Wrexham Council in which contractors, parents, teachers and pupils raised concerns over safety involving the misbehaviour of pupils. All companies who provide large school buses had to install cameras if they wanted their contracts renewed (BBC, 17/04/02).

There appears to be a dearth of published research on either side of the Atlantic characterising the general purpose, extent of adoption and actual or potential impact of CCTV in schools. Nonetheless, there is much to suggest that the use of CCTV in schools is not restricted to policing external threats – evidence of the 'expandable mutability' of surveillance (Norris and Armstrong, 1999). That is, CCTV cameras installed for a single purpose end up being put to more and more uses. Likewise, Jacques Ellul's strand of surveillance theory holds that new technology is never sufficient. We always want it to do more and to put it to more uses. Indeed, it appears that the *diagnostic and directive* functions of schooling, which determine social roles on the basis of 'permanent records' (Inglis, 1918) could now be facilitated by increased use of systematic surveillance, notably in the form of CCTV. This, in turn, facilitates the assignment of students to one of several risk categories – high, medium, or low (for example) in order that the e:*selective* function (Inglis, 1918) can operate to exclude the 'inferior'.

Research Background

The sections that follow outline the results of exploratory inductive research into the perceived impact of CCTV in educational institutions in the north of England. Semi-structured interviews were held with a Security Service Manager from one of the regions local councils (hereafter known as Alan), the Deputy Head of an eleven to sixteen co-educational establishment with nearly thirty years teaching experience (hereafter known as Barry), the Estates Manager of a primary school (hereafter known as Colin), the Vice Principal of another eleven to sixteen co-educational establishment (hereafter known as Dan) and a School Improvement Officer attached to a City Learning Centre with responsibility for information technology across one hundred and thirty schools (hereafter known as Edward). Inquiries were made as to the extent, distribution, and purpose of CCTV coverage in each of the participants' institutions, examples of its use, the impact of CCTV on teaching and learning as well as opinions regarding the introduction of video surveillance into classrooms.

Data Analysis

According to Gatto, Albert and Moore (2002), public schooling in America imparts a 'hidden curriculum' of seven lessons; confusion, class position, indifference, emotional dependency, intellectual dependency, provisional self-esteem, and that 'one can't hide'. Surveillance in schools is an integral part of the final lesson; students are now tacitly taught that they are constantly being watched, both by teaching staff and new technological means. The following quotes give an insight into the extent of CCTV use in secondary schools in the north of England:

> ... perhaps forty or fifty per cent have got a CCTV system of some sort or another ... a number of cameras in corridors that have been there for some years ... We have quite a number of ... motion activated systems ... in school grounds ... linked back to a centre; the operator will interrogate the system with the cameras to see what's going on ... (Alan)

> ... In the school office we've got a split screen monitor and that's linked to four or five camera units around the school. Three of those cameras are multi-directional, focus/zoom, which we control centrally ... we have one mini camera which we can use within school in case of trouble spots ... (Barry)

... four cameras covering the 'street'. This is an arcade with open access that provides a hub for community services, IT suite, cafeteria, classrooms etc. This arcade ends at a security door which gives access to the primary school itself. There is one camera above this door, with the three remaining pointing up and down the street so that the main thoroughfare is covered. There are also two external cameras, one covering the main entrance and one covering the playground, nature area ... there's a fence round it [the nature area]. But that won't stop the older ones getting over and vandalising the garden. So it's to stop that ... They're going to be recorded at reception ... (Colin)

If you look over there in the top corner, that is what we call our security camera. We've put these into every room and any member of the team can go onto any desktop and they can monitor any room. So if I'm sitting in my office along there I can split the screen into four, five, whatever, and I can monitor what's going on in any classroom at any time ... (Dan)

While the threat posed by youth is posited as general and no longer recognisable by markers of ethnicity, gender, religion or social status alone, the very nature of visual surveillance readily lends itself to superficial profiling of youth. After the Columbine shooting, black trench coats were considered an important indicator of dangerous youths. It is likely that popular cultural representations of gender, race and class will always remain indicators of danger (Hall, 1996). Youth are identified as dangerous depending on aspects of their history and social makeup, their popular culture, class, accent, race, abilities and placement in school, their friends, gender, clothing, headgear, physique and even style of walking. The acceptability of profiling from CCTV footage, as a means by which 'problem' students are identified, is indicative of the persistence of popular cultural markers:

A lot of students have got different walks, mannerisms ... which you can see when you watch them on the camera. You've only got to ID one of a group and then you can normally by association work out who the others in the group are ... (Dan)

... we can often say, oh that's so and so, 'cos you know the kids, but for somebody else to be able to identify them it would be difficult ... (Barry)

CCTV is being put to some additional uses in secondary schools in the region:

... we've tracked down 3 or 4 in the last 15 months pupils who've set off fire alarms. We're not directly linked to the Fire Brigade but if we were it would cost us £600 a shot ... It has helped us to identify intruders ... drug dealers hanging around at the gates ... (Barry)

... It was vandalism in the sense they were writing on the walls. It makes the place look untidy. They might have been smoking, they might have been sitting on the stairs chatting. Well they should not have been there; they should not have been doing what they were doing. Part of the program is to increase that so we can monitor what they're getting up to ... (Dan)

We were getting problems with vandalism in the girls toilets so we put the camera in the corridor, not inside the toilets ... keep a track of who was going in and out ... it's used every 3 or 4 months ... (Barry)

... just to make sure that there are no pupils doing what they shouldn't being doing. We have a lot of devices that could easily go into pockets in here ... (Edward)

It is my conjecture that the state has lost confidence in the ability of parents and teachers to regulate the behaviour of young people 'appropriately'. As one participant pointed out:

Children are getting a lot more difficult to control in a classroom. Teaching has become much harder and a fair proportion of teaching time is taking up really in just trying to contain the children ... (Edward)

Risk, 'Responsibilisation' and Social Exclusion

The systematic use of surveillance systems is diffusing less overt means of segregation and exclusion through society (Norris and Armstrong, 1999). Since the 1970s, crime prevention policy has shifted dramatically from an exclusive emphasis on traditional criminal justice agencies through to the currently popular idea of partnership (Loader and Sparks, 2002). This general trend has held for all foci of activity (offenders, victims, communities) and styles of implementation (top-down, bottom-up). What distinguishes crime prevention policy today from past regimes is the emphasis on safety, both in public and in private. Hence, the flagship term 'community safety', given credence in the Morgan Report (1991, p. 3):

The term 'crime prevention' is often narrowly interpreted and this reinforces the view that it is solely the responsibility of the police. On the other hand, the term 'community safety' is open to wider interpretation and could encourage greater participation from all sections of the community in the fight against crime.

The elevation of the concept of 'community' to centre stage in policy formulation is part of the process of 'responsibilisation' in which we are all encouraged to share actively the increasing burden posed by crime. Schools are key targets in this process.

New surveillance initiatives form part of 'a spreading transcarceral complex designed to keep troublesome populations in their place' (Carlen, Gleeson, and Wardhaugh, 1992, p. 7). This message, necessitated by the 'responsibilisation' agenda inherent in risk society, entails a shift from an Orwellian scheme where the state watches over citizens, to one where all vested interests engage in surveillance activities.

> ... governmental decarceration discourses have not been predicated upon any diminution of punitive rhetoric. Rather, the phenomenal costs of imprisonment and residential care are to be reduced by transcarceral policies designed to ensure that the pains of imprisonment are brought into – and sometimes enforced by – the 'community' (Carlen, Gleeson and Wardhaugh, 1992, p. 8).

Despite the appearance of minimal state interference and community autonomy promoted by the 'responsibilisation' agenda, it is important to recognise that the underlying premise of state schooling is that the government is the true parent of all children, the state is sovereign over the family. Thus, just as it wrested the role of educating young people from their families back in the nineteenth century, the nanny state has assumed responsibility for regulating the behaviour of young people and it is using schooling to do so. And what better way to lower the cost of controlling a population than by using state schooling as a mechanism (Lott, 1990).

The rise of actuarialism in educational settings needs to be considered part of a broader discourse of community safety and law and order, that seeks to anticipate trouble and to exclude and isolate the deviant – an exclusive philosophy that, in the long term, may significantly increase risk (Young, 1999). Tackling social exclusion in Britain rests in part on neighbourhood renewal, addressing 'problems' in the most deprived areas. CCTV is an important element in this crusade. Ironically, as this chapter has argued, specifically in relation to the educational system, CCTV has the potential to exacerbate tendencies to exclude people. It does this by facilitating greater surveillance on the basis of the social characteristics of the people under its gaze, whose presence or behaviour is deemed unacceptable.

It is far from certain that the expansion of surveillance measures in schools will have the desired effect. For Presdee, 'school – the site where the State and adult society have the most effect and influence on young people's lives – and the streets that surround it, have become central to the violent carnival performances of young people' (Presdee, 2000, p. 145–6). This is evidenced by the number of illegal fires lit in schools by young people every year and the stabbing of Head Teacher Philip Lawrence, in December 1995 (Presdee, 2000). Just as policies emanating from the United States regarding CCTV in schools are driven by high profile school shootings, the Secretary of State for Education and Employment in the United Kingdom set up the Working Group on School Security following the fatal stabbing of Philip Lawrence. Even so, people are more likely to cite the Dunblane massacre in Scotland as the driving force behind heightened security measures in schools. Presdee's (2000) work would suggest that if controls on the school environment increase, it would be expected that ever more extreme performances would be generated by way of relief. CCTV provides disruptive students with a counter-productive opportunity to 'perform' for the cameras (*cf.* Lyon, 2001).

Conclusion

Education is a form of social control. As such, it is ideally placed to meet the demands of the 'risk society' for pre-emptive protection from crime. It does this through actuarialism, which in turn is fed through surveillance. CCTV is one such surveillance device increasingly used throughout the education system as the surveillance revolution sweeps across the world. The importance of such surveillance lies in the social construction of youth as both 'at-risk' and a source of risk. Surveillance in schools therefore allows pre-emptive social controls on a key target. There is a dearth of research on the purpose, extent of adoption and actual or potential impact of CCTV in schools. Accounts in the media and preliminary interviews in the North of England indicate that CCTV is common in secondary schools, due to extensive government funding. Other technologies are also used. A wide range of motives are cited including protecting gateways to staff, students and their property; providing evidence of pupil ill-discipline; making school toilets a 'safe' environment for younger students; protecting teachers from unwarranted accusations of abuse by pupils. However, from the perspective of the funding state, this approach allows responsibility to be placed on the community, rather than directly on the government. It might indicate a loss of confidence in parents' and schools' ability to exert control by existing methods. It criminalises youth, possibly by design, and it is consistent that most of the funding appears to be directed at the 'risky' age group, not the 'at-risk' group. Pre-emptive surveillance based on existing stereotypes may actively direct youth toward a criminal class, and in doing so increase rather than reduce social exclusion. If teenage rebellion is a carnival performance, tightening up controls might also exacerbate the situation.

References

Alexander, C. (2000), *The Asian Gang: Ethnicity, Identity, Masculinity*, Berg, Oxford.

Bauman, Z. (1995), *Life in Fragments*, Blackwell, Oxford.

BBC (05/11/99), 'School puts spy cameras in toilets', http://news.bbc.co.uk/1/hi/education/506140.stm.

BBC (17/04/02), 'CCTV monitors school bus behaviour', http://news.bbc.co.uk/1/hi/wales/1935285.stm.

BBC (05/06/02), 'Spy cameras target school vandals'. http://news.bbc.co.uk/1/hi/sci/tech/2016772.stm.

Beck, U. (1992), *Risk Society – Towards a New Modernity*, Sage Publications, London.

Botsford, D. (1993), 'The Calvinist Roots', *Educational Notes*, 15, Libertarian Alliance, London.

Bradbury, J.A. (1989), 'The Policy Implications of Differing Concepts of Risk', *Science, Technology and Human Values*, vol. 14(4), pp. 380–399.

Caplan, P. (ed) (2000), *Risk Revisited*, Pluto Press, London.

Census Bureau (1998), *National Crime Victimization Survey*, U.S. Department of Justice, Bureau of Justice Statistics, Washington.

Campbell, B. (1993), *Goliath: Britain's Dangerous Places*, Methuen, London.

Carlen, P., Gleeson, D. and Wardhaugh, J. (1992), *Truancy: The Politics of Compulsory Schooling*, Open University Press, Buckingham.

Cowper, W. (1784), 'Tirocinium: Or, a Review of Schools', in W. Cowper (1817), *Table Talk and Other Poems*, John Sharpe, London.

Darlington Council (2003), www.darlington.gov.uk.

Douglas, M. (1985), *Risk Acceptability According to the Social Sciences*, Routledge and Kegan Paul, London.

Furedi, F. (1997), *Culture of Fear – Risk-taking and the Morality of Low Expectation*, Cassell, London.

Garland, D. (2001), *The Culture of Control: Crime and Social Order in Contemporary Society*, Clarendon, Oxford.

Gatto, J.T., Albert, D. and Moore, T. (2002), *Dumbing Us Down: The Hidden Curriculum of Compulsory Schooling*, New Society Publishers, Philadelphia.

Giddens, A. (1991), *Modernity and Self-Identity*, Polity, Cambridge.

Giroux, H. (1996), 'Hollywood, Race, and the Demonization of Youth: The "Kids" are not "Alright"', *Educational Researcher*, vol. 25, pp. 31–35.

Gramsci, A. (1971), *Selections from the Prison Notebooks of Antonio Gramsci*. International Publishers, New York.

Guardian (24/02/03), 'Classroom CCTV Alarms Teachers'.

Guardian (23/10/03), 'Fears Over Youth Crime Crackdown'.

Hall, S. (1996), 'Who Needs Identity?' in S. Hall and P. du Gay (eds), *Questions of Cultural Identity*, Sage, London.

Inglis, A. (1918), *Principles of Secondary Education*, Houghton Mifflin, Boston.

Jackson, S. and Scott, S. (1999), 'Risk Anxiety and the Social Construction of Childhood', in D. Lupton (ed), *Risk and Sociocultural Theory – New Directions and Perspectives*, Cambridge University Press, Cambridge.

Justice Policy Institute and Berkeley Media Studies Institute (2001), *Off Balance: Youth, Race and Crime in the News*, http://www.buildingblocksforyouth/media.

Lesko, N. (2001), *Act Your Age! A Cultural Construction of Adolescence*, Routledge, New York.

Loader, I. and Sparks, T. (2002), 'Contemporary Landscapes of Crime, Order, and Control: Governance, Risk and Globalization', in M. Maguire, R. Morgan, and R. Reiner (eds) (2002), *The Oxford Handbook of Criminology*, 3rd ed, Oxford University Press, Oxford, pp. 83–111.

Los Angeles Times (21/04/02) 'The New Demons: Ordinary Teens'.

Lott, J.R. (1990), 'An Explanation for Public Provision of Schooling: The Importance of Indoctrination', *Journal of Law and Economics*, vol. 33, p. 199.

Lupton, D. (ed) (1999), *Risk and Sociocultural Theory – New Directions and Perspectives*, Cambridge University Press, Cambridge.

Lyon, D. (ed) (2001), *Surveillance Society: Monitoring Everyday Life*, Open University Press, Buckingham.

Males, M. (1996), *The Scapegoat Generation: America's War on Adolescents*, Common Courage Press, Maine.

Mill, J.S. (1975), *Three Essays*, Oxford University Press, Oxford.

Morgan, Report (1991), *Safer Communities: The Local Delivery of Crime Prevention Through the Partnership Approach*, Home Office, London.

Muncie, J., Coventry, G. and Walters, R. (1995), 'The Politics of Youth Crime Prevention: Developments in Australia and England and Wales', in L. Noaks, M. Levi, and M. Maguire (eds), *Issues in Contemporary Criminology*, University of Wales Press, Cardiff.

National Education Association (1931), 'What We Shall Be Like in 1950', *Literary Digest*, January 10, pp. 43–44.

National Institute of Justice (2003), 'CCTV: Constant Cameras Track Violators', *National Institute of Justice Journal*, vol. 249, pp. 16–23.

Newburn, T. (2002), 'Young People, Crime, and Youth Justice', in M. Maguire, R. Morgan, and R. Reiner (eds) (2002), *The Oxford Handbook of Criminology*, 3rd ed, Oxford University Press, Oxford.

Norris, C. and Armstrong, G. (1999), *The Maximum Surveillance Society: The Rise of CCTV*, Berg, Oxford.

Pearson, G. (1983), *Hooligan: A History of Respectable Fears*, Macmillan, Basingstoke.

Pilger, J. (1998), *Hidden Agendas*, Vintage, London.

Presdee, M. (2000), *Cultural Criminology and the Carnival of Crime*, Routledge, London.

Smith, M. (2002), 'Fear of Youth', *The International Child and Youth Care Network*, vol. 41, June 2002.

Tonry, M. (1999), 'Why are U.S. Incarceration Rates so High?' *Crime and Delinquency*, vol. 45, pp. 419–437.

Tyler, T. and Boeckmann, R. (1997), 'Three Strikes and You're Out, But Why?' *Law and Society Review*, vol. 31, pp. 237–265.

Waiton, S. (2001), *Scared of the Kids: Curfews, Crime and the Regulation of Young People*, Sheffield Hallam University Press, England.

West, E.G. (1970), *Education and the State*, Institute of Economic Affairs, London.

Chapter 7

Young People's Attitudes to Drug Education

Matthew Pearson

Introduction

It is widely acknowledged that schools have a responsibility to educate their pupils to lead responsible lives and that young people should be given the skills and knowledge to become full participants in society and therefore to create identities which synchronise them with the economic requirements of the world in which they live. Education about substances which are, or can be harmful to health specifically drugs, alcohol and tobacco, is a statutory requirement in England, and the Department for Education and Skills in its latest consultation on this matter advocates that the issue of drugs education is best dealt with 'through well-planned Personal, Social and Health Education (PSHE) and Citizenship provision and should take a whole-school approach' (DfES 2003: 5)

This chapter examines a specific drugs education project in relation to the 'risk society'. In particular I am concerned here with showing how discourses related to risk are already operating tacitly within drug education programmes, and the ways in which young people are being encouraged to evaluate personal and social risks related to substance use and abuse. But a cautionary note is also struck here as I outline how schools and government agencies are hampered from implementing educational strategies based on risk because of social and cultural pressures. These social and cultural pressures require schools to 'play safe' in this arena and stress prohibition and complete abstinence instead of exploring approaches which construct substance education as a more provisional project, and which draw on conflicting evidence to present a complex picture of how self-identity and substances are inextricably linked especially in relation to the lives of young people.

The chapter draws on several theoretical foundations. Beck's formulation of modern post-industrial society as a 'risk society' is central to the development of the argument. Beck points out that risks proliferate in modern societies multiplying beyond our attempts to control and limit them. Toxic pesticides, chemical spillages, nuclear war, penicillin resistant strains of infection are just some of the nascent horrors Beck unleashes on his readership. But these threats which place us, either as individuals or as a species, on the brink of extinction, have been created by the very process of scientific and technical rationality which promised to deliver society from the vagaries of the natural world. In Beck's work we read that the more the scientists fight to rid us of these evils, the more that new evils are created, and so the important question is not about identifying courses of action which have any associated risk, since nearly all human activities have degrees of risk attached, but which courses of action are the least risky and possibly injurious to health or social and economic well being.

Drugs, alcohol and tobacco are all substances closely associated with personal and social risk. For instance, smoking is directly and unequivocally linked to cancer, but the risks of developing the disease are not evenly distributed amongst smokers and some people may smoke heavily for many years without contracting the disease or appearing to suffer ill-health. These people become walking counter claims to the arguments of science and provide smokers with a justification to continue a habit which is entirely irrational. Similarly alcohol abuse is also a prodigious killer, with numbers of annual deaths in the UK running four times higher than those linked with the use of illegal drugs. As well as considering long term health implications, the consumption of drugs and alcohol can cause death and injury in the short term and many accidents are created or exacerbated by excessive alcohol consumption. But again we find that many people appear to drink heavily all of their lives without suffering any visible signs of ill-health or injury. The human body does not always behave as medical science predicts it will. This means that as individuals we are constantly making choices about what to put into or leave out of our bodies, and these choices are often tangled in a web of rational and irrational decisions about what risks are attached to a particular behaviour. If it were possible to inject heroin with no risk of being addicted, no short, medium or long term health issues, and no chance of being prosecuted, then many people would see the drug differently. Dwyer and Wyn (2001) in a landmark text about the pressures of growing up in a post-industrial society, demonstrate how young people have to negotiate complex and often conflicting arenas of risk. The desire to conform and meet school and parental expectations is strong in many young people but so is the need to assert individuality and build self-identity. In the complexities of the risk society, where no courses of action are rarely un-problematically good or bad, this is especially difficult. The research on which this chapter is based has confirmed that drugs education programmes which make explicit reference to these identity forming pressures and allow young people to reflect on their identity in relation to how and what they consume are likely to be more effective than programmes which concentrate solely on communicating the facts about drugs and substances and which do not make references to the complex psycho-dynamic processes of growing up in today.

This work also draws on the social theories of Anthony Giddens and Zygmunt Baumann who have written extensively on the nature of the individual and self-identity in late- or post-modern society. Giddens posits the notion of the self as a 'reflexive project' (Giddens, 1991: 32). The reflexive project of the self requires individuals to continually construct their own identity and engage in psychic processes of identity maintenance. This situation is peculiar to late-modernity because society no longer, as it did in the past, creates trajectories of development and ready-made rites of passage for subjects. Instead we are constantly having to turn our gaze inward, looking around us to assemble resources and put in place strategies with which to fashion these identities. Baumann's concept of 'liquid modernity' (2000) broadly charts this same development and gives us a trope of peculiar power with which to describe the rapid changes in self and identity which are occurring in late capitalist societies. Solid modernity, the necessary precedent to liquid modernity, is characterised by Baumann as a situation where people are inserted quite rigidly into social structures, and where subject positions were defined primarily in relation to overarching social and institutional constraints. In contrast to the fixed certainties of solid modernity, liquid modernity sees these bonds melting away and the individual floats free of the institution and a diffuse and shifting network of social relations takes its place. Negotiating these complex networks, which necessitates the construction of an identity with which to 'front' the world, becomes the key project of the individual.

A key constituent of this self-identity is the material goods we buy and consume and the lifestyles which are linked to particular patterns of consumption. The marketing apparatus of late-capitalist society and multi-national corporations with enormous budgets for advertising, have achieved unprecedented levels of sophistication and almost every commodity is now sold as a necessary accessory to a particular life-style or set of life-choices. This chapter draws on the ideas of Giddens and Baumann to illuminate the ways in which young people are presented with substances as another life-style choice where to partake is to create a particular identity for oneself and conversely, to abstain is also to create an identity.

Background

This chapter's empirical base is an evaluation of a drugs and substance education programme which ran in a local education authority in the North of England between 2000 and 2003. The programme was funded by the New Opportunities Fund in conjunction with the LEA drugs action team. A professional puppet theatre[1] was commissioned to write a production about drugs, alcohol and tobacco and perform this to all of the secondary schools within the LEA. The show, titled *A Shot in the Dark* played predominantly to year 9 pupils (14 years of age), although shows for parents in the evenings proved very popular and ensured the show gained a high profile in local communities. The show lasted around 45 minutes and was followed by a workshop where the puppeteers, all experienced actors and youth workers, used their dramatic skills to facilitate further work on themes raised in the show. The show itself was a highly sophisticated production, and although young people seeing the show for the first time often complained before seeing the show that puppet shows were for young children, the adult content and realistic storylines, as well as the topical humour and some excellently observed characterisation, ensured that the show was universally popular. The use of puppets was especially powerful in the context of drugs education as the dramatic context of a puppet show worked as a distancing mechanism. This distance allowed the actors to use the puppets to raise issues which would have been difficult to broach in conventional performances. As Steve Wright, who wrote the show and played many of the key characters explained: 'when you have a puppet on the end of your arm, you can say just about anything you want!'

The evaluation investigated the impact of *Shot in the Dark* on young people's thinking about drugs, alcohol and tobacco. All young people who saw the show (6125 in total) over the three years completed two questionnaires. One was related to the show itself and asked questions about favourite scenes, which characters the young people most closely identified with, and what messages they thought the show was conveying. The second questionnaire, administered in advance of the show to literally thousands, asked young people about their knowledge of substances; what they had tried and their motivations; where their knowledge of drugs had come from; and how they would prefer to be educated about substance use and abuse. In addition to the questionnaires, I conducted focus groups with 5 groups of young people in different schools who had recently seen the show. These were semi-structured group interviews and generated a wealth of qualitative data to set against the quantitative data from the questionnaires.

There is a growing literature on the use of theatre in education (often abbreviated to TIE), particularly its use in dealing with social and personal issues. Macdonald and Nehammer (2003) reported on an education project in South Wales where children of 10 had written their own drama piece on drugs which was performed by professional actors. Both teachers and pupils viewed the show favourably and 'choice' emerged as a principle theme identified by a significant number of respondents and perhaps echoing, albeit in a weak way, the exercise of agency and the splicing of rational decision-making with concomitant social and cultural pressures which characterises a risk based approach to drug education. Douglas and others (2000), evaluated a theatre in education project where young people took control of the dramatic and artistic process and reported gains in confidence, self-esteem and social skills as a result of this intervention. The *Shot in the Dark* programme combined features of a scripted performance with a workshop format to give young people a range of educational experiences. The performance itself sparked off considerable interest amongst the young people and the subsequent workshops allowed issues to be explored in more intimate groups drawing on the expertise of the performers in facilitating discussion and debate. From a methodological perspective, *Shot in the Dark* operated within a paradigm of social and personal education which is often called 'harm reduction'. This paradigm seeks to minimise social and personal harm from taking drugs by stressing pragmatic and practical knowledge about the details of drug use. Workshop slots delivered by the actors from the company centred on real-life scenarios and educated young people in the best courses of action. For instance the practicalities of comforting and caring for a panicky drug user were covered. Later follow up work in focus groups revealed that the young people retained a great deal of the knowledge and skills from this segment of the programme.

Discourses of Risk and Education

Beck's seminal writings on the 'risk society' are now over 10 years old and have created great interest in sociology, and have created a powerful arm of the discipline which sets out to give a different account of the development of modern societies to that of the post modernists. Yet the application of the risk society, primarily as an epistemological tool for understanding why the world is like it is, is not often evoked in debates about education. Writings which theorise educational settings from the perspective of where a society is constantly locked into a struggle to understand, limit and control the circulation of risks (defined sometimes glibly as 'bads') as well as material progress – we should term this generically 'goods' so that the synecdochical construction works – are few and far between. Analyses which involve formal schooling and link modern schooling to advances in sociological knowledge are particularly rare. This lack of writing about risk and education may be a result of both the inherently conservative nature of schooling, and the prevailing political agenda which has effectively locked all debate about compulsory schooling into increasingly arid spirals of adumbration about results and performance, predicated always on narrow conceptions of the curriculum as a body of facts or knowledge to be absorbed in a seemingly transparent and unproblematic way by young people.

Some work on risk and education has been done in the sphere of adult education; commentators, such as Johnston (1999), have advocated models of andragogy which take account of the 'risk society', and where more complex models of citizenship are developed in contrast to the rather simplistic notion of being a 'good citizen', which is sometimes evoked in discussions of school based citizenship. The problem when discussing substance use is that the whole field shifts uneasily between a number of conflicting and competing curriculum areas and arenas of school activity. Science has traditionally staked its claim here, aiming to link a rational-technical account of how drugs work on the body sometimes peppered with cautionary tales to scare young people into abstinence. But cutting across science claims to ownership of the substance education agenda is the influence of PSHCE (personal, social, health and citizenship education), where this complex topic is seen as something to be linked holistically to teaching about young people's identities. Science is less important in this instance than an understanding of why people do what they do, and PSHCE, as practiced in many secondary schools in the UK, often feels more like a combination of sociology and psychology than the traditional hard sciences of chemistry, biology and physics.

The literature on young people's engagements with drugs, alcohol and tobacco is extensive and many studies into habits of consumption have been conducted. For instance, Macmillan and Conner (2002), examined young people's drug use and cognitions when they went to university. Using questionnaires they discovered that an increasingly liberal attitude to drugs was displayed as university careers progressed, and this liberalisation was particularly marked in the transition between years 1 and 2 of university careers. This suggests that the lifestyle of university encourages some to take illegal drugs (ecstasy was a very popular choice), and the existence of a large peer group to confirm one's own belief in consumption could also be very influential. Peer pressure is often evoked by commentators in this field as a powerful persuasive source acting on young people.

The pressure to 'fit in' with a certain group or to not be seen as 'square' is undoubtedly a factor in experimentation with drinking, drugs and smoking, and many school based education programmes offer young people techniques and strategies for resisting peer pressure or at least understanding how it operates. *Shot in the Dark*, as a dramatic production, was able to demonstrate in concrete terms, how peer pressure operates. The protagonist, a young person named Joe, is initially resistant to taking drugs and pays attention to his overbearing father who states 'drugs are muck, if I catch you with them, you'll be out of this house'. But as the result of visiting a night club, and with his natural defences lowered by the consumption of alcohol, Joe does take an unspecified pill and suffers a black out as a result. When asked why Joe decided to take drugs, the focus groups all identified the peer group as being significant, although many comments were qualified by an acknowledgement that ultimately the decision was Joe's and he had to bear responsibility for what happened. But most groups were also keen to point out the hypocrisy of the father, who delivers his stern warnings about drugs from an armchair with a can of beer in one hand and a cigarette in the other. Later in the show we see the beleaguered mother of Joe complaining about her husband's spending on smoking, most of which is taken surreptitiously from her purse. At the beginning of the show, Joe is out of the house and his mother delivers a monologue full of grim imaginings about him coming to harm because of drugs. Her hyperbolic musings – she imagines him lying dead in an alley – set up a perfect comedy moment as Joe enters the house unscathed and she promptly tells him off anyway. The plot of *Shot in the Dark* was constructed to fully acknowledge the conflicts inherent in taking up moral positions on drugs, and as the story proceeds, the audience get to appreciate how absolute judgements about substances are often problematic.

Research which charts young people's substance 'careers' is of particular interest when evaluating behaviour from a risk perspective as these studies provide data on how young people's habits develop over time and the influences which impact on patterns of consumption. Howard and Egginton (2002) conducted a longitudinal study of young Britons between the ages of 13 and 18 and found a distinct group who they argue seek out 'psycho-active' lifestyles. These lifestyles are associated with heavy, often binge drinking, smoking and associated drug usage. Egginton and Parker also asked young people where their information about substances had come from, and found that they tend to rely on 'informal sources of information' (p. 427). These sources of information are of dubious quality, consisting of stories and rumours about drug usage which are laid down in a sedimentary fashion among groups of substance-using young people, and which can often be misleading, misguided or just factually incorrect. Howard and Egginton report how direct observations of people suffering the consequences (both good and bad) of drug use are then converted into anecdote and re-circulated. This process of informal drug education as uncovered by Egginton and Parker, reveals the extent to which young people are minded to ignore the advice given at institutional levels, such as that emanating from schools. The risk trajectories for the consumption of substances, particularly in combinatory form, are therefore defined by the consumers themselves and scientific knowledge about these matters is not used when some young people make calculations about whether or not to consume. I found some evidence to support Egginton and Parker's findings although a high percentage of young people at the age of 14 still do value the information on drugs and substances given to them at school. Seventy-two per cent reported that they had received useful information from teachers and school, but when asked whether schools are a good place to learn about drugs, 25 per cent answered yes. Although this is an apparently modest level of approval for school based drugs education, it was still the largest single category of response. Eleven per cent identified parents as a good source of information, but 17 per cent stated that the media was a useful way of learning about drugs, drinking and smoking. The results of the questionnaire concerning young people's attitudes to the drugs education they are receiving and their identification of good sources of information show a varied picture. Further analysis by ethnic group and gender and school, which is too detailed to include here, revealed that these variables had a significant effect on young people's attitudes to drugs education.

The Risk Society and Substance Consumption

I outlined earlier in this chapter the ways in which substance consumption, in both legal and illegal forms, is always bound up with risk assessments. Individuals engaging in substance use constantly weigh up the risk factors associated with their consumption habits and arrive at personal constructions of what they find acceptable. The research and evaluation conducted for this paper revealed that young people have an acutely developed sense of the risks associated with particular patterns of consumption, and the focus groups revealed instances of young people explaining in detail how they reach decisions about which risks to take. Perhaps the most common theme was the issue of smoking at school. Sixteen per cent of young people surveyed admitted to being smokers, that is they smoke at least once a week, and 60 per cent of these smoked between 1 and 5 cigarettes a day. Focus group work revealed gender differences in attitudes to smoking. Girls could be characterised as social smokers and many reported their main reason for smoking was as a part of a group activity with friends. Cigarettes were often shared and few girls in the focus groups reported that they smoked alone. Boys also reported social smoking as a factor, but a noticeable number did admit to smoking on their own and told me that their smoking was not motivated by social consider-ations. As a result, twice the number of girls reported being smokers than boys (20 per cent of girls are smokers, 10 per cent of boys), but boys were far more likely to be heavy smokers, smoke alone and spend significant sums of their money on cigarettes. Many of these young people bring cigarettes and smoking material to school and engage in subtle subterfuges to prevent detection. The old cliché of the schoolboy smoking behind the bike-sheds still holds true in many cases, and pupils were able to explain in detail how their strategies for avoiding being caught smoking at school. *Shot in the Dark* contained plotlines concerning smoking – Joe's father was a heavy smoker and fails to see how his habit conflicts with his pronouncements on drugs – and the workshop which followed the performance also dealt with smoking. The workshop facilitators adopted a range of procedures to educate young people about smoking, with a popular approach being a calculation of how much smokers spend in a lifetime. This long-term economic calculation of the disbenefits of smoking appealed to the maturity of the young people and when questioned in focus groups about the impact of the workshop, many remembered the sums involved and admitted to being surprised about how the costs of even a casual smoking habit can mount up.

A new development, and one which underlines the complex trajectories of risk and risk assessment which are being undertaken by young people, concerns the use of cannabis. Teachers involved in the drug education project reported an alarming increase in the numbers of pupils bringing cannabis into school. These pupils had picked up on stories in the media about the reclassi-fication of the drug and rather than understanding the full implications of reclassification (which was not law at the time of the research), had evaluated the drug as being legal and therefore acceptable to bring to school. They reasoned that punishments for bringing the drug into school would only be commensurate with those for bringing tobacco in. This behaviour left schools who caught pupils with cannabis in complex legal and institutional dilemmas and the drugs advisers at the LEA were constantly working to clarify posi-tions, liaise with the police and give advice to schools on how best to tackle this growing problem. From the relative safety of the position of evaluator, I was able to see how complex decisions about risks were being made by young people, but a failure to understand the intricacies of the law placed them in risk positions, with possible exclusion and expulsion from school and the involvement of the police.

When questioned about cannabis use, which is rare among 14 year olds with frequent users accounting for only 3 per cent of the sample, debates about the relative harm of the drug compared to alcohol and tobacco were common. Young people had realised that cannabis was not a killer drug, and many had a range of anecdotes and personalised pseudo-scientific evidence to justify the legalisation of the drug. The debate about cannabis legalisation is a society wide issue and it neatly demonstrates how Beck's theorisation of risk turns on the competing claims of various rational frameworks:

> The growing awareness of risks must be reconstructed as a struggle among rational-
> ity claims, some competing and some overlapping. One cannot impute a hierarchy
> of credibility and rationality, but must ask how, in the example of risk perception,
> 'rationality' *arises socially*, that is how it is believed, becomes dubious, is defined,
> refined, acquired and frittered away (Beck, 1992: 59).

Beck argues here that rationality is not an absolute or a given, and it cannot fall back on scientific or technical know how and evidence in order to justify itself. Rationality is instead a negotiated product arising from social interactions, and like all socially constructed knowledge it can be rendered provisional or deconstructed. Claims and counter claims about the relative harm done by smoking cannabis illustrate this complex web of risk perceptions in modern society very well, and interviewing with young people about the drugs use and status revealed that they were well aware of these developments. Furthermore, amongst the small number of young people who did use the drug regularly (defined as consuming it more than once a month), it was far more likely to hear arguments in favour of cannabis supported by information and anecdote which had not been imparted in school. The evaluation project revealed that a small number of 14 year olds had effectively rejected the drugs education laid on for them by schools and other agencies; they evinced deeply sceptical viewpoints about the veracity of the information emanating from institutions and built instead, risk profiles for the drug based on personal knowledge and peer interactions. Reaching these young people with the impor-tant messages about substance use and abuse is extremely difficult for schools because of a predisposition which many displayed to treat formal knowledge about drugs as being overly negative, exaggerated or untrue.

Discussions with other young people in focus groups who had never used cannabis were similarly interesting. In 3 of the 5 focus groups where none of the pupils had used cannabis (excepting a single puff on a joint), young people tended to overemphasise the personal and health risks of the drug. Key messages about cannabis as a gateway drug, that is a drug which is not particularly harmful in itself but which leads users into an escalation of their drug habits involving more damaging drugs, had reached these young people and they were able to express clearly their ideas about how cannabis use could be damaging. One young person of 14 explained it this way:

Smoking pot you see, well it's not that bad, my brother's done it, and some of my friends have tried it. But, erm, you need to hang round with certain people to get hold of it, and they can be well dodgy, you could get into other stuff, stuff which is like really bad ...

This assessment of the risks associated with the drug is sophisticated and shows a sound understanding of the peer networks and influences which characterise drug experimentation in young people. The people who are described as 'well dodgy' (*well* acts as an intensifier in this utterance) are necessary to procure access to the drug, but this young person has articulated how these people could also lead you further into a drug culture. This statement was greeted with almost universal agreement amongst the other eight members of the group.

Any discussion of drugs and substance usage will turn inevitably back to the body as the site of consumption. Giddens' exploration of the reflexive self in late modernity has led him to write about the body and explore the complex meanings which surround corporeal presence:

'The body' sounds a simple notion, particularly as compared to concepts like 'self' or 'identity'. The body is an object in which we are all privileged, or doomed, to dwell, the source of feelings of well-being and pleasure, but also the site of illnesses and strains. However, as has been emphasised, the body is not just a physical entity which we 'possess', it is an action-system, a mode of praxis, and its practical immersion in the interactions of day-to-day life, is an essential part of the sustaining of a coherent sense of self-identity (Giddens, 1991: 99).

Theorising the body as an 'action-system' allows us to see how the pressure on young people to engage with substances is considerable. Using substances is not simply a matter of consumption, it is a symbolic act which has ramifications for social status and self-identity. Media coverage has in recent years centred on the aggressive selling of alcopops to teenagers and young people. Alcopops use sugar and flavourings to disguise the taste of their often potent alcoholic content and come in a variety of colours and designer inspired modes. Traditional choices for teenage drinking; particularly lager, and cider based drinks have been replaced by alcopops which are based on spirits, and when asked to name drinks they consumed regularly, young people identified alcopops as the most popular drink. The marketing of alcopops fuses image and content to create new types of drink which are easy to consume and which turn the body into a site of fashion. Clothes and fashion are essential items for young people's identities but alcopops extend this designer and fashion conscious approach into the realm of alcohol consumption.

And what of the young people who do not drink, smoke or use illegal drugs on a regular basis? These were by far the largest single group in the survey. Can we chalk these results up as a great success for preventative education and rest easy that messages are getting through and that not all young people seek out danger and thrills to further their social standing? Certainly not, these young people are only 14 and have many years to go before they reach a state of what could provisionally be called adult maturity, and many certainly will try smoking and drinking, and some will become long-term smokers and heavy drinkers. From a statistical perspective, the fate of some of them at least is sealed. Bringing discussion back to the young people's lives at this point, we found in our research, primarily in the focus groups, that abstinence has a dynamic all of its own. The young person who decides not to drink or smoke is doing more than simply complying with the wishes of the school and possibly their parents, they are engaged in a coherent statement of their own identity in relation to these substances. Furthermore they realise that their abstinence will have social consequences, and whether the motivation for abstinence is moral, religious or simply the result of close parental control, these young people will be judged by peers and their identities will develop accordingly.

Conclusion

I have argued here that an approach to drugs education which takes seriously the theoretical perspectives of the risk society would be of benefit to many young people. Current teaching about drugs and substances in schools largely ignores the role of consumption or the rejection of consumption in identity formation and maintenance, and therefore ignores the complex cultural and social factors which affect young people's sense of who they are and what they will become. Empirical work has suggested that programmes of education founded broadly in what is termed the 'harm reduction' paradigm are effective in imparting useful practical information to young people, but more work needs to be done to develop educational strategies where young people can explore their identities in relation to the products, both legal and illegal, which they come into contact with. Giddens' analysis of the rapid institutional changes which characterise late-modernity and the subsequent untethering of individuals from social bonds which would have sustained them in the past, points to the increasing importance of educational strategies which confront the challenges which young people face in creating and maintaining self-identity and gives them pragmatic tools for evaluating the risks inherent in substance consumption.

Note

1. *Shot in the Dark* was written by Steve Wright, who founded the Wright Stuff Theatre of Puppets to explore the uses of puppetry in personal and social education. Wendy Thelwell processed the questionnaire data for the evaluation and her hard work is duly acknowledged here.

References

Adams, P. (2003), 'Health education: part or all of the PSHE and citizenship framework'? *Health Education*, vol. 103(5), pp. 272–277.

Baumann, Z. (2000b), *Liquid Modernity*, Polity Press, Cambridge.

Beck, U. (1992), *Risk Society: towards a new modernity*, Sage, London.

Department for Education and Skills (2003), *Drugs: Guidance for Schools*, [consultation document issued April 2003). [online]. Available: www.dfes.gov.uk/consultations/ docs/227_2.pdf. Date accessed: 24/12/2003.

Douglas, N., Warwick, I., Whitty, G. and Aggleton, P. (2000), 'Vital Youth: evaluating a theatre in health education project', *Health Education*, vol. 100(5), pp. 207–215.

Dwyer, P. and Wyn, J. (2001), *Youth, Education and Risk: Facing the Future*, Routledge, London.

Giddens, A. (1990), *The Consequences of Modernity*, Polity Press, Cambridge.

Giddens, A. (1991), *Modernity and Self-Identity: Self and Society in the Late Modern Age*, Stanford University Press, Stanford USA.

Howard, P. & Egginton, R. (2002), 'Adolescent recreational alcohol and drugs careers gone wrong: developing a strategy for reducing risks and harms', *International Journal of Drug Policy*, vol. 13, pp. 419–432.

Johnston, R. (1999), 'Adult learning for citizenship: towards a reconstruction of the social purpose tradition', *International journal of lifelong education*, vol. 18(3), pp. 175–190.

Macdonald, G. and Nehammer, S. (2003), 'An evaluation of a drug education play for schools in south Wales', *Health Education*, vol. 103(2), pp. 83–87.

McMillan, B. and Conner, M. (2002), 'Drug Use and Cognitions About Drug Use Amongst Students: Changes Over the University Career', *Journal of Youth and Adolescence*, vol. 31(3), pp. 221–229.

Quicke, J. (2001), 'The science curriculum and education for Democracy in the risk society', *Journal of Curriculum Studies*, vol. 33(1), pp. 113–127.

Chapter 8

Risks and Uncertainties in Vocational Education in Africa

Nkongho Arrey Arrey-Ndip

Introduction

Vocational and technical education has been variously defined, depending on the country involved. The Australian National Training Authority (ANTA) (2003) has given alternative terms used for vocational and technical education internationally. These include technical and vocational education and training (TVET), vocational and technical education and training (VTET), technical and vocational education (TVE), and further education and training (FET). In this chapter, the term Vocational and Technical Education (VTE) has largely been adopted. However, other terms may be used as required.

In spite of the different terminology and the nuances that have characterised its definition, the central mission of VTE has been universally recognised. Generally, VTE focuses on imparting individuals with occupational and work-related knowledge and skills, within the framework of scientific or general education. Vocational and technical education is recognised as a 'source of skill training for many individuals prior to employment and afterwards on the job'. This form of education 'is delivered by schools, public and private training centres, non-governmental agencies and employers' (Adams et al., 1992, abstracted in The Forum, 1993, p. 6).

The National Policy on Education (for Nigeria) (1977, revised 1981, cited in Ajeyalemi, 1990), views technical education as 'technical, commercial, and other vocational courses' (p. 83), designed to train students to apply scientific knowledge in tackling society's numerous problems, which are practical or technical in nature. The policy recognised that for students to remain competitive, the training they receive should go beyond the mere provision of manual and technical skills. UNESCO (1989) defined technical and vocational education as 'all forms and levels of educational process involving, in addition to general knowledge, the study of technologies and related sciences and the acquisition of practical skills, know-how, attitudes and understanding relating to occupations in the various sectors of economic and social life' (no page number).

Vocational and technical education in Africa can appear to be a rather incoherent system, full of risks and uncertainties, such that it can sometimes be 'difficult to predict exactly what is going to happen at any given time be it in the present or the (near) future' (Lorenzen, 2002, p. 1). It is hard to ascertain what the best delivery system of courses for any given student may be in the face of extreme inadequacy of teaching-learning resources and a gloomy labour market situation.

Lorenzen (p. 1) quoted Gollub and Solomon (1996) to have defined a chaotic system:

> as one that shows sensitivity to initial conditions. That is, any uncertainty in the initial state of the given system, no matter how small, will lead to rapidly growing errors in any effort to predict the future behaviour ...

Irrespective of the apparently chaotic nature of some education in the world, each system constantly strives to remain in a state of equilibrium by removing those elements in it that may, otherwise, affect this state. Vocational and technical education in Africa is no exception. It faces the challenge of eradicating these negative aspects in its system so as to balance it and return it to equilibrium. Many forces are responsible for the risks and uncertainties in VTE as would be seen in this chapter.

An activity is risky when it promises little or no returns to the individual engaged in it. As an activity area, VTE in Africa reflects this character; an individual who offers programmes in this field takes a risk because the consequences may be unpleasant. He/she may not gain employment upon graduation, first, because of his/her insufficient job entry knowledge and skills, and second, because the labour market does not provide for any such jobs.

VTE in Africa is not only risky, but also uncertain. Those who enrol in its programmes are never sure of what the future holds for them; for they are constantly in doubt as to the capability of the programme providers to deliver effective training – i.e. provide skills that guarantee a paid job. Very few people in Africa today depend on VTE for jobs because of this uncertainty. The future of VTE in Africa is, undoubtedly, uncertain, especially in the face of perennial political instability in the continent and rapid global transformations, such as industrialisation, globalisation, and modernisation.

This chapter is approached from two perspectives. The first will look at the subject from the historical context of risks and uncertainties in education in the continent, and analyse the nature of risks and uncertainties that were part of VTE in the period and show how these still influence the present day system. The second will look specifically at the elements in its management, both external and internal, that expose the system to risks and uncertainties. These will be treated as sources of risks and uncertainties in VTE system in Africa. The chapter will close with a conclusion, suggesting the way forward.

Historical Context of Risks and Uncertainties in Vocational and Technical Education in Africa

In his 'exploratory paper', Sifuna (2001) argued that current African problems 'have their origins in the colonial period' when education was not a 'developmental process', but a 'mechanism of exploitation'. According to Sifuna, colonial education 'was designed and implemented to serve the needs of the colonial state, which was to produce a low level educated cadre of labour force to facilitate economic production' (p. 21). This set the stage for the current problems VTE is facing in recent times, with its concomitant effects. The author stressed that African independence did not change the status quo, as it 'failed to alter the colonial economic structure, their educational systems continuing along the western models and paradigms that have little relevance to African development' (p. 21). For instance, VTE, especially in the British colonies 'followed the pattern in Britain with regard to curriculum and certification', but it did not follow 'the trend in the area of organization and administration', which would have improved its offerings, and thus reduce some of the risks inherent in the programmes (Ajeyalemi & Baiyelo, 1990; Collinson & Aidoo-Taylor, 1990, p. 28).

In spite of the inadequacy in the education system inherited by African countries (Rwambulla, 2002), this did not in any way affect the subsequent expansion of education in Sub-Saharan African countries, in the 1960s and 1970s, when most of these countries had political independence. By this time, the economies of African countries were experiencing rapid growth (through cash crop production, extraction of forest products and minerals and other commodities) and majority of the countries realized that it would be gainful to plough back the fallout from their economies in the development of their citizens. The visions of these leaders were consequently 'translated into rapid expansion of educational institutions including (vocational and technical education)' (p. 1). However, Ajeyalemi and Baiyelo (1990), presenting the case of Nigeria maintained that this expansion led to quantitative expansion at all levels of education, while the quality of education provided continued to receive criticism. This situation was not only peculiar to Nigeria alone.

Nevertheless, the support the governments gave to VTE 'ranked high on the national budgetary provisions', as the focus 'was on creating a critical mass of professionals and skilled labour force, essential for (rapid) economic growth and development' (Rwambulla, 2002, p. 2). The governments were also concerned with providing an environment that encourages industrialisation. They argued that the substantial investment would result in the attainment of industrial growth by their countries, as well as lead to increased school enrolment. This has not happened, at least as far as industrialisation is concerned.

However, the 1980s and 1990s saw Sub-Saharan African countries, for example, recording significant growth in their economies, which subsequently resulted in the rise of individual personal income. But this was not to last long. As Rwambulla puts it, 'by the dawn of the new century, the gains made were in decline, as the performance of the economies was sliding into recession' (p. 2). This had a maximum impact on VTE in the nations concerned. Vocational and technical education in such countries suffers more from any internal structural adjustment taking place in the education sector, because of its capital-intensive nature. There is evidence to show that whenever African governments are facing serious financial crisis, and have to decide on which level of the educational system to cut back on financing, the axe had often fallen on the VTE system, because of its expensive nature (see Collinson & Aidoo-Taylor, 1990). The consequences of such decisions have often been heavy absence of facilities and infrastructures in schools, which leads to poorly motivated teachers, the production of low quality graduates and an atmosphere of mistrust between stakeholders and the schools, among other things.

The future of vocational and technical education has been, and still is, a regular subject for debate in many parts of the world. Some experts have even predicted its demise, 'because it has been considered as obsolescent and not sufficiently cost-effective' (Atchoarena & Cailods 1999, p. 1). Further commenting on this, Atchoarena and Cailods argued:

> Of course, this concern is not new, but since the early nineties, the collapse of planned economies and the emergence of globalization have put it at the centre of reflection on some society's greatest challenges: unemployment, modernization, competitiveness, and the struggle against poverty and exclusion (p. 1).

Undoubtedly, VTE in Africa has a share of its own challenges in this turbulent global education milieu. As a dependent system, 'linked' to a giant network of global educational systems, albeit indirectly, it is affected by what transpires in this network. However, VTE in Africa has its peculiarities, most of which are the result of the way and manner the system is planned and managed. These open the system, as a whole, to risks and uncertainties, which result from inappropriate educational reforms, social representation, inflexible course offerings, and lack of access to higher education, among others. The uncertainty surrounding the system has made it difficult to predict exactly what can happen at any given time be it in the present or the near future. For instance, it is nearly impossible to ascertain whether the graduates who are churned out of VTE institutions and programmes each year do have a future, or whether those currently in school would follow their programmes to the end. Sometimes, it is difficult to see immediately, how these risks and uncertainties manifest themselves in the system; while at other times, it is immediately evident. Elements that may contribute in opening the system to risks and uncertainties have been reviewed later.

Inappropriate Educational Reforms and Inadequate Curricula Provisions

African countries have recognised the importance of VTE in their development endeavours. Consequently, they have embarked on the opening of secondary

technical schools, institutes of technology and polytechnics to provide middle-
and high-level technical courses for national development. Some have even
made technology as part of general education and compulsory for every
secondary school student irrespective of their future careers. To demonstrate
their support for VTE, countries have been reforming vocational education
curricula, designing teaching manuals, promoting initial and in-service teacher
training, among others. How appropriate and effective have been these
reforms? Do they help in reducing the risks and uncertainties in the
programmes or do they instead help in increasing them? What implications do
they have for the growth and development of VTE in Africa? Although these
efforts have been substantial, they remained, nonetheless, quantitatively and
qualitatively inadequate. There still exist certain lingering shortcomings, which
must at all costs be remedied, to ensure that Africa competes equally with the
other regions of the world (UNESCO, 1982; Ajayelemi, 1990; Okoye, 2002).
Further reacting to this, UNESCO (1982) lamented:

> Technical and vocational education has not been sufficiently developed, ... The
> teaching of (technology), the prerequisite for (industrial growth), comes late in
> school curricula and is only seldom provided for adults in the context of out-
> of-school education ... In educational content, which is usually devised with refer-
> ence to other cultures, the characteristics, experience and rich cultural heritage of
> Africa and the values that are capable of ensuring the continuity, cohesion and
> progress of African societies are too often neglected. The methods and the very style
> of teaching are often ill adapted to the true spirit of these societies ... (p. 40).

There are accounts of educational reforms in a number of African countries
in the 1970s and 1980s. Most of the reforms during this time have been
on vocationalisation because it was believed that it held the magic wand of
economic development (Sifuna, 2001). Wide-ranging reforms in the late 1980s
brought the structure of the education system in Ghana closer to the American
model, aiming to make education more responsive to the nation's economic
needs. A similar idea was also tried in Nigeria, in the 1960s, with the introduction of the comprehensive high school. But these experiments failed due partly
to the capital-intensive nature of the project, which implies that those who
adopted the model failed to imagine the financial implications and other
parameters. As Castro (1993) noted 'the comprehensive high school model
is difficult to transfer to countries where there are large status differences
between manual and non-manual occupations. In such cases, few students or
parents choose training in manual skills' (p. 12). These failures are, however,
not uncommon in the field of vocational and technical education in Africa.
The secondary modern school, which was also tried in some states in Nigeria
persisted until the early 1970s, and later disappeared, without any trace, from
the educational system, due largely to its declining status and the paucity of
funds (Ajeyalemi & Baiyelo, 1990; Collinson & Ajdoo-Taylor 1990).

It is yet unclear why curriculum reforms from other countries, which have failed to accelerate the growth and development of the countries from which they were borrowed, are adopted sometimes entirely, or with minor modifications by African countries. It is doubtful if these borrowed ideas, which are most often improperly modified, would be able to develop transferable skills in students to enable them cope with the challenges of modern technology (UNESCO, 1983).

Atchoarena and Delluc (2001), speaking on the same subject, argued that the reforms process carried out by English-speaking African countries as opposed to French-speaking ones tend to adopt 'more 'radical' lines of intervention, including greater attention for skill development and employment in the informal sector' (p. 15). It also promotes 'entrepreneurship and self-employment training' (ibid.), among other things. This suggests that the VTE system in French-speaking African countries lack some of these interventions.

In the area of financing, Durango (2002) showed that some countries such as South Africa, Zimbabwe and Tanzania have chosen to introduce a levy to support initial vocational training, following the experience of many Latin American Countries. But the question remains as to whether these imported reforms have always been sufficiently modified, or even implemented. If not they risk creating unproductive institutions and training systems, which will in turn produce ill-adapted school leavers and trainees, who would be a burden to their families, societies and the economy. Incidentally, Castro (1993, p. 13) has maintained that 'education and training systems cannot simply be imported into a country and expected to operate as they do in their country of origin'. According to him, differences in societies affect the type of institution or training model that can succeed; and importantly, any identifiable limitations in the model, which can be handled in the country of origin, could become serious, and out of hand, in other countries. Unarguably, the importation of reforms from other cultures and adopting them with little modifications is pregnant with a lot of risks and uncertainties.

Reasons could be proffered why reforms are usually insufficiently modified in Africa. It has been argued that the type of education acquired by a majority of senior government officials in Africa had made them strangers in their own lands, making them instead conversant with the situation in the developed world. 'As a result, there is a strong temptation for them to follow a path of slavish imitation, which leads straight to failure, because the real problems are neglected, whereas straightforward insight would have brought ample rewards' (M'Bow, 1982, pp. 49–50). So many reforms have failed because their designers disregarded the conditions and the context for which they were intended, as noted by Castro (1993) above. Vocational and technical education in particular, have suffered tremendously from these shortcomings, in spite of the fact that it has a role in the training of skilled workers, middle-level technicians and other categories of employees important to the socioeconomic life of countries.

The following are pertinent questions often taken for granted, relating to curriculum reform or development that have the potential for making the environment of the vocational and technical education system in Africa unpredictable and risky.

- Have curriculum planners in vocational and technical education 'made the right selection from (the) culture pool of importation, critical things that should be learnt in' vocational and technical education programmes?
- 'Do their selections agree with ... the goals and aspirations' of their people?
- Have the curriculum planners selected too many things for learning in vocational and technical education programmes from the culture pool of importation that are not necessarily priorities?
- Have they left too many things in the culture unselected?
- 'Are all parties likely to be involved in the implementation process', such as administrators, educators, and teachers, 'fully consulted at the stage of curriculum planning ...?' (Ojiji, 1987, p. 132).

The issues raised above deserve being examined critically by individuals whose responsibility is to plan instructional programmes.

Curriculum Reform Implementation

African countries have many ambitious curriculum reform plans, but implementation has remained the critical issue, at all levels, thus opening a floodgate of challenges and problems, which are underlined with numerous risks and uncertainties. For instance, a new system of education was created for Ghana, giving new impetus to technology education. The integrated approach to teaching was suggested as the recommended method of teaching, ' because the aim was to predispose the pupils to the industrial world and for them to be given the basic skills that will familiarize them with technology, science and various vocations'. In spite of all these efforts the programme still had implementation problems. There were no qualified and properly motivated teachers to teach the new technical courses. There was also a marked absence of technical support personnel, technical workshops and other facilities. And worst of all, 'many people still saw the academic education as the best vehicle for upward mobility in the society and, as such, the idea received less approval from the majority of the people, especially those of the higher socio-economic status'. The Ghana example is a reflection of the global continental picture. This has often put VTE programmes in a very difficult situation (Collinson & Aidoo-Taylor, 1990, p. 27).

Inflexible Courses

As the society changes, the needs of individuals also change. New aspects of knowledge and skills should be brought into the curricula to take care of these changes. In short, as new technologies and processes are discovered, schools should teach this new knowledge and skills so as to obtain new development objectives and ensure that graduates of the programmes secure employment upon graduation. Teachers also need to be re-trained to meet the challenges of technological changes (UNESCO, 1983; Okoro, 1991; Mathis & Jackson, 1997). This is necessary because, as M'Bow (1982) noted:

> ... in a world characterised by extremely rapid changes in every sphere of life and by the constantly growing impact of science and technology on all human activities, the paths of progress inevitably entail a command of the highest forms of knowledge and know-how (p. 46).

Ideally, VTE 'curricula should be based on analysis of tasks to be carried out on the job' (p. 6), since the potency of such curricula is judged by the extent to which trainees can use their skills at their places of work (Adams et al., 1992, abstracted in The Forum, 1993). According to Muller and Funnel (1991), the quality of curricula provision depends on 'providing the right type of learning opportunities to whom we are obliged to provide' (p. 14). The absence of these may not be helpful for the programmes.

   In fact, confidence in VTE programmes has been undermined by the perennial unemployment problem of school leavers, 'weak skill-based training and quality teaching, and limited relevance of programmes' (Stevens, undated, no page number) to the needs of businesses and industries, as well as to those of graduates for self-employment. Again the inflexible nature of the curriculum does not encourage the participation of women in some key technical areas. Deeply held social attitudes, even within the VTE system itself, continue to limit women to traditional female subjects such as Secretarial Studies and Home Economics (Ajeyalemi & Baiyelo, 1990; Gray et al., 1993; Bachu, nd; Stevens, undated).

The Type of Curricula in Use

According to Ajeyalemi & Baiyelo (1990) 'the quality of instruction cannot be divorced from the quality of the curriculum' (p. 93). A major problem facing all areas of VTE in Africa (Okoro, 1993) 'is how to develop suitable curricula that are relevant to the needs of students, the society and employers of labour' (p. 67). The type of curricula emphasized in most African countries is predominantly the 'conceptual or thematic approach', which is more theoretically based. Citing Yager (1989), Ajeyalemi & Baiyelo maintained that:

> There is evidence that such an approach merely encourages students to master the concepts and processes, which they can recall for oral recitation or for examination, but which they cannot use for anything else ... Such memorized knowledge has little transfer value to new situations outside the school context and neither does it

promote curiosity and creativity skills nor prepare students to grapple successfully with science and technology issues in real life context (p. 93).

This approach seldom leads to the production of graduates who are well grounded in the knowledge and skills of their specialisations, which is the major goal of vocational and technical education. This calls for the VTE curriculum to progress beyond the thematic structure and incorporate instructional strategies that provide students with a real world context for studies in the field. This should make the programmes interesting to the students, and thus enhancing their chances of succeeding in life.

Lack of Access to Higher Education

One obvious constraint on VTE programmes in most African countries, which makes them uncertain and even risky to pursue, is the fact that they do not guarantee smooth access to higher education. Many students would normally be interested in an education programme that ensures continuity. Desai and Whitesite (2000) support this in their study of vocational education graduates in the State of Gujarat, in India. In the study, the graduates were asked to indicate the three factors that they felt would improve the quality of vocational education in the state. One of the factors they mentioned was the need for 'the provision of more opportunities for higher education' (p. 57).

Some countries, however, have pathways to give vocational and technical school graduates access to further education. Generally, in most countries of Sub-Saharan Africa, pupils who opt for these schools will find little progression as far as higher education is concerned. This has helped to contribute to the negative image accorded VTE in Africa. It should be pointed out that any educational programme that lacks apparent destinations for its entrants stands the risk of being looked upon as inferior. Consequently, an educational institution or programme that has an inferiority label attached to it cannot flourish. To prevent the implantation of this negative label, equal opportunities should be provided for all persons who desire further education; since the right to aspire and to achieve should be limited only by natural endowment and not by any artificial restrictions, as has been the practice in some African countries. To show the extent of the problem, many educational reforms taking place in Africa today have taken the challenge to make the system open by demolishing all blocks to further education for those who are capable (Atchoarena & Delluc, 2001; Oranu, 1996).

This problem has its roots in the colonial system of education inherited by many African countries. Before technical examinations were nationalised in most countries of Africa, examination bodies such as the Royal Society of Arts (RSA) and the City and Guilds of London Institute (CGLI) were very instrumental to the future of technical college graduates. These examination bodies still influence systems in some countries.

The problem here was that trainees under this system were not given broad-based education to supplement their chosen occupations. Unfortunately, after the take-over by local bodies in some countries, practices were not significantly altered. This led to the graduates of technical colleges not being able to secure admission into tertiary institutions. Largely because these local examination bodies did not see the need to introduce more general education into the curriculum of the colleges. 'For this reason, the image of vocational and technical education remained tarnished as a programme for academically weak students' (Oranu, 1996, p. 19). This led technical school graduates to be despised because of their insufficient general education background. This also closed the door to many jobs which, otherwise, would have been opened to them, if they have backed their technical skills with general education subjects. It is only recently that these shortcomings are being addressed in some countries through the reforms they have undertaken. For instance, Oranu has shown that in reforming the Nigerian education system in 1985, the country made general education courses in 'English Language' and 'mathematics', among others, 'mandatory components of the technical curriculum'. Gray et al. (1993) support this reform when they cited the World Bank as having emphasized the need for 'a strong basis of literacy, numeracy and problem-solving skills as a foundation for effective technical and vocational education' (para. 7).

But on the whole, it would seem, there is as yet no popular response, in many countries, to the low esteem accorded to the graduates of technical colleges, resulting from the kind of educational programmes they are exposed to. Satisfactory individual performance of a few countries, as may be observed, does not contradict the global picture.

Teaching of VTE Courses

There appears to be relatively poor teaching of vocational and technical education courses in many African countries today. According to Eyibe (1990), 'one urgent problem … in (VTE) is how to make … teaching effective in the classrooms (and laboratories) so that students will derive full benefits from their studies' (p. 3). The teaching going on in VTE programmes emphasizes more rote learning than experimentation. The practice in most of the schools and programmes today is for teachers to load students with information for them to memorize, which they will later regurgitate in answer to test or examination questions. It is not surprising, therefore, that 'most of the graduates from the system can only read and memorize scientific and technological information, but may not be able to think in, do, or use science and technology as their counterparts in developed countries' (Ajeyalemi, 1990, p. 12). The emphasis placed on certificates/examinations in implementing the curricula content of most vocational education programmes poses a great risk to the programmes. Schools today hardly stress the acquisition of practical skills as a final outcome. This puts the graduates at a disadvantage as far as jobs are concerned.

While visiting some technical institutions in Africa, Bennett (2001) observed a precarious teaching situation in most of them. In fact he was dismayed to discover that 'vocational training, whether in traditional crafts such as carpentry, or modern crafts such as refrigeration or computer repair, is carried out on the (chalkboard), in front of fifty or more students' (p. 9). According to Bennett, VTE is

> one area of education system where both the students and their parents are totally cheated. It is the one area where students graduate 'qualified' in a certain specialism, unable ever to get a job in that area, without informal training through apprenticeship (p. 9).

Again, VTE is unfortunately one area where the concern of donors is mainly on how to sell machines and equipment that will never be put to use. A visit to technical workshops of most colleges in Africa will elucidate this point.

Furthermore, the dearth of textbooks in most VTE systems leads to teachers using 'their time dictating or writing on the (chalkboard) notes for their students to copy down' (Gray et al., 1993, para. 41). This contributes to the poor teaching going on in VTE programmes, with its obvious consequences.

Social Representation and Image of VTE

The pattern of development in formal education on the continent and the society's perceptions of the purpose of education has affected adversely the development of vocational and technical education before the majority of the countries ever gained independence and these factors continue to do so. This system of education has had a chequered history on the continent. Given its humble beginnings in most of these countries, therefore, it was misunderstood by educators and other stakeholders and society as a whole (Collison & Aidoo-Taylor, 1990; Oranu, 1996).

Historically, VTE has not enjoyed the same status as other disciplines. There has been a dichotomy in status between VTE and other disciplines especially those in the liberal arts and even science. As a result, VTE has been treated as a second-rate discipline- offered for the under-privileged masses, the have-nots- and shunned by the elite, the cream of the society.

It has been argued that when a formal type of education replaced the traditional African type of education, the poor image of technical education in the West was transplanted into the African education systems. This led to technical education and manual work in most of these countries being despised and reserved for the dropouts from the formal education system until this day, even as the image has long changed in the West. The disdain for vocational and technical education is further fueled by the prestige accorded to secondary (general) education, the type of education through which upward mobility into office jobs is guaranteed (Ajeyalemi, 1990).

According to Echu (2000), people (in Cameroon) generally prefer programmes leading to white-collar jobs because they are misled into thinking that technical professions are reserved for dropouts. This viewpoint is encouraged by 'some parents who tend to send their children to technical schools or get them to learn a trade only after the latter have failed to progress normally in a secondary grammar school' (p. 26). 'School-leavers consider (VTE) as an inferior òption for learning because of its low, informal status and little official recognition, and because they view it as a way of closing the door to further study' (Stevens, undated). According to a school proprietor in Nigeria, who was worried that his country has 'never really given due priority to technical education as an economic mainstay', with the above bias, 'in favour of white-collar jobs, even the few polytechnics and technical schools set up by government have not been able to change these misplaced attitudes' (Opus Dei Information Office on the Internet, 2003, no page number).

Conflicting Government Policies

African governments have never lacked education policies. However, in relation to vocational and technical education, these policies have often been unclear. It is as if these countries do not actually know what they expect from the system. In a study of technical colleges in South Africa, Lumby (2000) found out that there is an incoherent relationship between national and regional policies. These seemingly unclear and conflicting policies and procedures have often led to delays in executing programme plans, which have had a negative impact on the VTE system.

Lumby reported the findings of research she carried out in which vocational training administrators were frustrated by failure of the government 'to set out clear and long-term regional and national plans, and by the frequent changes in direction' (p. 105). The situation in South Africa is just a reflection of the overall picture, especially, considering the fact that the country is one of the most advanced in the continent. Again, some of the quoted comments from the same survey conducted by Lumby expose the turbulent nature of the environment in which vocational and technical education operates in Africa:

> Long term planning is basically impossible with an Education Department that is not capable of setting out the rules of the game clearly. Because of the uncertainty in our education system it is not possible to plan effectively. We try to survive from year to year, currently, we survive and try to do the best we can with our limited resources. Government must wake up! (p. 105).

In their concluding remarks, Collinson & Aidoo-Taylor (1990) pointed out that policies intended to improve on the provision of vocational and technical education in Ghana have been ill-considered, not specifying 'direction, organisation and financing'. Only clearly defined policies and programmes of technical education can save the system in Africa. Stressing their point further, the authors showed that 'significant and meaningful expansion and development in technology in many advanced nations were only achieved with clearly defined policies and programmes through Acts and Statutes' (p. 32). They cited several examples of such Acts and Statutes, a few of which include the British White Paper on Technical Education of 1956; the Canadian Technical and Vocational Education Act of 1961, among others. They maintained that these Acts and Statutes had as a goal the resolution of problems being faced by technical and vocational education; consequently, they were broad-based-covering 'institutional arrangements, staffing, programme levels and linkages'. The Acts and Statutes also addressed 'issues of funding, practical training and employment and planning based on the economic needs and the stage of development of the country' (ibid.). Perhaps, it could have been helpful if vocational and technical education policies in Africa were as comprehensive as these, thus unambiguously specifying the direction, among other things, that the programmes should follow.

Involvement of Industry in Vocational and Technical Education

It would require the participation of industry and businesses in the process of vocational and technical education for its instructional quality and relevance to the society to be assured. What seems fashionable in recent times is the movement 'towards a global village with a single economy'. This will evidently force 'countries to redesign their VTE system in order to produce a well adaptive workforce' (Gurbuz, 2001, no page number). Effective vocational and technical education will depend upon establishing a relationship between the 'education and training providers and industries which consequently or concurrently, employ the trainees ...' (Gray et al., 1993, par. 84).

'The informal sector in African countries accounts for more than 60 per cent of urban employment and this trend is set to continue' (Stevens, undated). Yet in some of these countries Micro and Small Enterprises (MSEs) are not given the encouragement to play their part in the development of these countries. In some cases, the taxation system tends to inhibit private initiative. According to Stevens, 'micro and small enterprise' growth and development is central to the life of African countries, 'because of its potential to enhance technological capacities and contribute to the diversification of production and exports' (no page number). This presupposes that VTE needs to cooperate fully with the private sector so as to enable it to work towards meeting the major challenges African countries currently face. These include 'to prepare for jobs that exist at the present time, to build capacities to adjust, compete ... and most crucial, to enhance abilities to create jobs and employment for oneself and for others' (no page number).

Still on the relationship between technical and vocational colleges and industry, Lumby (2000) quoted a principal of a technical college in South Africa as saying:

> I feel there is a very sad discrepancy between what is required by industry and what is happening in the institutions ... I feel there needs to be a closer liaison between industry and education authorities and the people who draw up the courses and perhaps the institutions which are able to steer their courses within the framework of the curriculum towards what is actually needed (p. 107).

This feeling permeates VTE systems in much of Africa. VTE systems in the French-speaking Sub-Saharan African countries are fraught with numerous setbacks. One of which is the fact that they 'ignore the informal sector, especially the artisans' micro-enterprises' (p. 11). The reasons for this weakness are not far-fetched. The VTE systems in these countries were, by design, modelled on the school system, with its bias against traditional apprenticeships. This lack of serious attitude on the part of French-speaking Sub-Saharan African countries towards traditional apprenticeships seems to continue, in spite of the important role this sector is expected to play in ensuring the growth of a vibrant economy; as well as for adult and youth employment. Such scenarios create uncertain environments for graduates from VTE systems in such countries. However, support for dual training is now well acknowledged in some countries, which are now participating in complementary training of apprentices. This support needs to be encouraged, although it may not be easy to convince training centres and their trainers to accept this category of students; moreover, the apprentices themselves may find it abnormal to go back to a formal school environment again (Atchoarena & Delluc, 2001).

Importantly, absence of a reinforced role of industry and businesses in the training programmes of vocational and technical education institutions in Africa opens the system as a whole to great risks. Vocational and technical education institutions are preparing its graduates for the job market, which comprises enterprises and businesses. If industries do not know what is happening in schools and schools do not know what is happening in them, then there is something inherently wrong. It would then mean that the schools are preparing students for jobs that are unavailable (see Okoro, 1991).

Another noticeable feature is that a great majority of training centres in Africa lacks units in charge of relations with enterprises; such units would have served as mechanisms for the registering of data concerning the local enterprises, including their activities, as well as their needs. They could also have as function the targeting 'of continuing-education activities, the organisation of work-experience programmes, the provision of labour market assistance to graduates and, later on, their follow-up would also come under its responsibility' (Atchoarena & Delluc, 2001, p. 11). For her part, Lumby (2000) noted that colleges just produce graduates; no attempts are made to gather information on employment, so as to evaluate the efficiency of producing the numbers of students they turn out each year. The collection of these data would, no doubt, increase the effectiveness of the local supply of training.

Absence of Basic Technology Concepts in Primary Schools

Basic technological concepts should form part of the curriculum at the primary level. This will foster the culture of technology at an early stage. However, very little in terms of technical education exist in the primary schools in most countries of Africa, especially those in sub-Saharan Africa. What could be described as rudiments of technology education in some of these countries are pupils' involvement in indigenous arts and crafts; basket weaving, needlework, and domestic science being the commonest ones (Ajeyalemi & Baiyelo, 1990; Collison & Aidoo-Taylor, 1990). So children get into vocational and technical colleges without previous knowledge of the rudiments of technology. This has contributed to the negative attitude society has for most technical professions, especially those at the craft and technician levels. Some scholars even argue that introducing technology may be ineffective at this level, because at this stage children are incapable of making any meaningful vocational choices, since vocational and technical education assumes that a choice has been made of an occupation (see, for example, Okoro, 1993).

Conclusions and Suggestions

The role and contribution of VTE in socioeconomic development is unques-tionable. Consequently, for vocational and technical education to develop, African planners should begin to be progressive in their thinking. They should direct their resources towards the development of the system.

Despite all the reforms undertaken by African countries things have not changed very much in real terms. Available studies carried out on the voca-tionalisation of the school curriculum show that things have hardly changed in the way the school system is structured, as well as in people's perceptions of education. Western education remains the main attraction, acting as a vehicle through which access into the elite status is attained. Problems identified as obstructing the total implementation of the VTE model in most countries include 'high unit costs; an absence of clarity in aims and objectives; shortage of qualified teachers to teach vocational subjects; and the low status as viewed by the students and the community' (Sifuna, 2001, pp. 27–28).

Not withstanding these problems and challenges, VTE in Africa can improve. As a way forward, it would be prudent to examine some of the recom-mendations made at the convention on vocational and technical education that was held in Paris in 1989. These recommendations should serve as yardsticks for individual country self-evaluation of the extent to which they are successfully planning and organising vocational and technical education, whether or not they were attracting members to the convention. This may help in minimising the factors of risk and uncertainty that may result from a poorly planned and organised VTE system.

In conclusion, some very constructive recommendations with regard to VTE can be found in article 2, sections 2, 3 & 4 and article 3, sections 1, 2, 3 & 5, of the convention document (UNESCO, 1989, no page number).

References

Adams, A., Middleton, J. and Ziderman, A. (1992), 'The World Bank's Policy Paper on Vocational and Technical Education and Training', *Prospects, Vol. XXII: 2 (82)* [Abstracted in The Forum for Advancing Basic Education and Literacy, vol. 3(1), Nov. 1993, pp. 6–7.

Ajeyalemi, D. (1990), 'Introduction', in D. Ajeyalemi (ed.), *Science and Technology Education in Africa: Focus on Seven Sub-Saharan Countries*, University of Lagos Press, Lagos, Nigeria, pp. 1–4.

Ajeyalemi, D. and Baiyelo, T.D. (1990), 'Nigeria', in D. Ajeyalemi (ed.), *Science and Technology Education in Africa: Focus on Seven Sub-Saharan Countries*, University of Lagos Press, Lagos, Nigeria, pp. 59–95.

Atchoarena, D. and Cailods, F. (1999), 'Can Technical Education be reformed?' *IIEP Newsletter*, vol. XVII(1), January–March, pp. 1–3.

Atchoarena, D. and Delluc, A.M. (2001), 'Revisiting Technical and Vocational Education in Sub-Saharan Africa: An update on Trends, Innovations and Challenges (Final Report)', *IIEP/Prg. DA/01.320 Rev.*, Paris, November.

Australian National Training Authority (ANTA) (2003), *Glossary of VET Terms U-Z*, WebPages: http://www.anta.gov.au/gloUtoZ.asp, Retrieved, 14/11/03.

Bachu, Y. (nd), 'Challenges of Skills Development and Entrepreneurship Education in Uganda, WebPages: http://nnuc.evtek.fi/tvet_seminar_02/Bachu%20-%20Uganda %20CHALLENGES%20OF%20SKILLS%20DEVELOPMENT%20AND%20EE.pdf

Bennett, N. (2001), 'Corruption in Education Systems in Developing Countries: What it is doing to the Young', *Paper delivered at the 10th International Anti-corruption Conference*, WebPages: http://www.10iacc.org/download/workshops/cs34a.pdf, Retrieved 3/10/03.

Castro, C. (1993), 'Models of Vocational Education and Training', *The Forum for Advancing Basic Education and Literacy*, vol. 3(1), pp. 12–13.

Collison, G.O. and Aidoo-Taylor, N. (1990), 'Ghana', in D. Ajeyalemi (ed.), *Science and Technology Education in Africa: Focus on Seven Sub-Saharan Countries*, University of Lagos Press, Lagos, Nigeria, pp. 18–35.

Desai, G. and Whitesite, T. (2000), 'Vocational Higher Secondary Education Graduates in the State of Gujarat', *Journal of Vocational Education & Training*, vol. 52(1), pp. 49–61.

Durango, L. (2002), 'The Financing of Technical and Vocational Education and Training (TVET): Options and Challenges for Sub-Saharan Africa', *Paper Presented at the Nordic UNEVOC Network Workshop on Training for Survival and Development in South Africa*, Oslo, Norway, 14–15 Nov., pp. 2–7.

Echu, G. (2000), 'The Quest for Education in Cameroon', *Mpokofu Echoes*, 1, pp. 25–27.

Eyibe, S.C. (1990), 'Effective Teaching in Technological Education as a Research Activity', *Journal of Technical Education Review*, vol. 2(2), pp. 3–12.

Gray, L., Fletcher, M., Foster, P., King, M. and Warrender, A. (1993), 'Reducing the Cost of Technical and Vocational Education', *Education Research Paper No. 03*.

Gurbuz, R. (2001), 'Designing and Developing VET Curricula of Two Year Colleges for Turkish and Global Industry, A Case Study in Turkey', *International Conference on Engineering Education*, August 6–10, Oslo, Norway.

Lorenzen, M. (2002), *Chaos Theory and Education*, WebPages: http://www.libraryreference.org/chaos.html; Retrieved 17/09/03.

Lumby, J. (2000), 'Technical Colleges in South Africa: Planning for the Future', *Journal of Vocational Education and Training*, vol. 52(1), pp. 101–118.

M'Bow, A. (1982), 'Address', in UNESCO (ed.), Conference of Ministers of Education and those Responsible for Economic Planning in African Member States *Final Report*, Harare, 28 June–3 July 1982, Organised by UNESCO with Cooperation of ECA and OAU.

Mathis, R.L. and Jackson, J.H. (1979), *Human Resource Management*, West Publishing Company, U.S.A.

Middleton, P. (1990), 'Lesotho', in D. Ajeyalemi (ed.), *Science and Technology Education in Africa: Focus on Seven Sub-Saharan Countries*, University of Lagos Press, Lagos, Nigeria, pp. 36–58.

Mugabe, R.G. (1982), 'Address', in UNESCO (ed.), Conference of Ministers of Education and those Responsible for Economic Planning in African Member States *Final Report*, Harare, 28 June–3 July 1982, Organised by UNESCO with Cooperation of ECA and OAU.

Muller, D. and Funnel, P. (1991), 'Quality in Vocational Education and Training', in D. Muller and P. Funnel (series eds.), *Delivering Quality in Vocational Education*, Kogan Page Limited.

Ojiji, C.O. (1987), 'Publishers, Curriculum and Public Examinations', in A. Dada (ed.), *Mass Failure in Public Examinations (Causes and Problems)*, Heinemann Educational Books, Ibadan, Nigeria, pp. 125–135.

Okoro, O.M. (1991), *Programme Evaluation in Education*, Pacific Publishers, Uruowulu-Obosi, Anambra State, Nigeria.

Okoro, O.M. (1993), *Principles and Methods in Vocational & Technical Education*, University Trust Publishers, Nsukka, Enugu, Nigeria.

Okoye, O.I. (2002), 'Business Education in the Democratic Nigeria: Emerging Issues for National Integration', *The African Symposium: An on-line African Educational Journal*, vol. 2(4), WebPages: http://www2.ncsu.edu/ncsu/aern/decembjnl.html, Retrieved, 18/09/2003.

Opus Dei Information Office on the Internet (2003), 'Institute for Industrial Technology in Lagos, Nigeria', WebPages: http://www.opusdei.org/art.php?w=32&p=1700, Retrieved, 02/04/2003.

Oranu, R.N. (1996), *Vocational and Technical Education in Nigeria*, WebPages: http://www.ibe.unesco.org/Regional/AfricanProjects/AfricaPdf/lago2ora.pdf, Retrieved 18/10/2003.

Rwambulla, W. (2002), 'The Failures and Successes of Technical, Vocational Education and Training Interventions in Developing Countries', *Paper Presented at the 2nd World Congress of Colleges and Polytechnics*, Melbourne, Australia.

Sifuna, D.N. (2001), 'African Education in the twenty-first Century: The Challenge for Change', *Hiroshima University Journal of International Cooperation in Education*, vol. 4(1), pp. 21–38.

Stevens,Y, (undated), 'Education for Durable Peace and Sustainable Development', *Issues Paper, OSCAL/DESA, United Nations*.

UNESCO (1982), 'Conference of Ministers of Education and those Responsible for Economic Planning in African Member States', *Final Report*, Harare, 28 June–3 July 1982, Organised by UNESCO with Cooperation of ECA and OAU.

UNESCO (1989), *Convention on Technical and Vocational Education*, UNESCO-UNEVOC International Project on Technical and Vocational Education, Web Pages: http://www.unevoc.unesco.org/publications/pdf/conv-e.pdf.

Chapter 9

Risk Management in School Based Design and Technology

Jeff Knox

Introduction

In this chapter I intend to explore how the combined effects of legislation, assessment policy, funding and attitude have modified three different aspects of risk within Design and Technology departments in the secondary sector of United Kingdom (UK) education.

Health and Safety

The first and perhaps most obvious area to address, relates to the risk of injury and illness. The foundations for the present working environment were largely set in place as a result of the 1974 Health and Safety at Work act. This was the single most important piece of legislation to set the course of change. During the early 1990s, the Workplace Health and Safety Regulations were introduced. These built on and strengthened the 1974 act, introducing amongst other things, a requirement for 'risk assessment' to be carried out and documented before undertaking any hazardous activities.

Schools were for the most part slow to respond to these new requirements. They were already engaged in a period of almost constant change with repeated modifications to the National Curriculum being imposed even before existing schemes had been evaluated. Teachers faced a near impossible workload, having to assimilate new requirements, re-write schemes of work and re-plan lesson delivery whilst at the same time continuing to teach with full timetables. With little or no time allocated to plan and implement these fundamental changes to curriculum structure, it is hardly surprising that new regulations, which did not have an immediate impact on day to day teaching, were placed further down the list of priorities. These new requirements were introduced during a 'difficult' political climate. One where market forces were seen as the 'holy grail' towards which all organisations had to be directed.

The instruments for change within schools had traditionally been the Local Education Authority (LEA) teams of advisers – experienced teachers at the forefront of their subject. They were the drivers of curriculum development and staff training and would normally have been the catalysts for such change. Their role had traditionally been to visit, advise, train and support staff within the schools of 'their' LEA. However, during the late 1980s and early 1990s this role had been undergoing an enforced change from 'advisory support' towards 'inspection'. These changes were as a direct result of the 'market force' rationale imposed by the Conservative government of that time.

This commercial ethos dictated that more and more of the education budget went direct to schools, by-passing the strategic control that the LEA's had previously enjoyed. This of course brought numerous benefits for schools, removing the perceived 'dead hand of bureaucracy', but the losses were more subtle and unforeseen – until the damage was done. The Local Education Authorities were prevented from top slicing income to fund the advisory services as they had done in the past and the schools were free to buy in specialist support from whatever agencies they chose, based on the 'best value for money'. Sadly, these high ideals were introduced during a period of sustained budget cuts. There was, at that time, a political dogma which followed the theme:

If we reduce funding and increase expectations year on year, organisations will be forced to become ever more 'efficient'.

This of course presumed that all organisations were 'inefficient' at the outset and the new direction was usually accompanied by stomach turning platitudes such as 'cutting out the fat' and becoming 'lean and fit'. Many schools facing year on year resource reductions were forced to choose between building maintenance, staff development and staff. First and foremost, pupils need teachers, so the outcomes were reasonably predictable. Building maintenance was cut, staff development was cut and finally, the most experienced (and most expensive) teachers were cut. Any teacher in front of a class was better than no teacher! Advisers had no market to purchase their courses and had little choice but to become OFSTED (Office for Standards in Education) inspectors to pay their way. By 1995, most LEA advisory services had all but disintegrated.

The National Association of Advisors and Inspectors in Design and Technology (NAAIDT) had traditionally awarded certificates based on local skill based health and safety programmes set up by these LEA Advisors. This operated in the specialist areas of design and technology such as welding, milling, circular saws and the like, but in many areas, these in-service courses had now ceased due to the lack of any central organisation. Concurrent to this loss, schools had already been experiencing difficulty in recruiting and retaining suitably trained and qualified staff because the political direction had for a number of years been depressing both salaries and working conditions for teachers. This difficulty included design and technology staff. (Brierley, 1991, p. 10). Classes were, in some cases, being taught by non-specialists who through no fault of their own, did not know how to operate equipment competently and safely. Such staff either continued, with the possibility of injury, damage to equipment, or both, or, (preferably), they simply avoided using the equipment and failed to meet the National Curriculum requirements in some areas.

As early as 1991, Brierly had highlighted that the overall level of risk in schools was rising. (Brierley, 1991, pp. 93–95) and by 1998 this growing problem was well recognised by all interested parties. These findings were repeatedly confirmed in OFSTED reports over the following ten years. For example, the 1997/98 annual report stated that in relation to design and technology:

> ... the large size of an increasing number of teaching groups also limits access and poses health and safety risks (OFSTED, 1998).

By 2000/01, there was some cause for optimism but the situation was still far from good and again, the OFSTED annual report made the following observations about design and technology provision:

> Despite improvements, particularly in specialist technology colleges, resources and accommodation for design and technology are poor in one fifth of schools (OFSTED, 2001).

> The average group size has stabilised this year but is still too high. This imposes additional health and safety risks (OFSTED, 2001).

Local education authorities had initially been invited to set up and run a new national scheme of health and safety certification for design and technology staff. Unfortunately, whilst being very supportive of the initiative, they were no longer in a position to do so, due to the lack of available advisory staff that were now needed for implementation. This was during a period when head teachers were finding themselves in the increasingly difficult position of engaging design and technology staff without having any real knowledge (via certification) about their minimum competencies in the subject area. Of course this was not a problem if the applicants were trained design and technology staff (DFEE circular 4/98). But for many applicants, they had perhaps been trained in other curricular areas and after gaining some experience of teaching design and technology they were seeking career development or promotion into a shortage area. It is an accepted tenet that;

> Teachers are not qualified to teach unless they clearly demonstrate appropriate knowledge and understanding of Health and Safety issues (Raymond and Twyford, 1999, p. 64).

Local education authorities were in a similarly difficult position. They were the employer and they therefore carried the responsibility for health and safety, yet they were powerless to implement the long overdue revisions to working practices called for by the act. Schools were the budget holders; they decided priorities. League tables, which only report on academic performance, simply added to the pressures with increasing numbers of uncertified staff and deteriorating buildings and plant Eventually it fell to DATA, the Design And Technology Association, to take the lead. This body is the professional association for design and technology teachers. Over a two-year period, DATA collaborated with the Health and Safety Executive (HSE), the Department for Education and Employment (DfEE), the teacher training agency (TTA), the National Association of Advisors and Inspectors in Design and Technology (NAAIDT), the Local Education Authorities (LEAs) and the British Standards Institution (BSI). This latter body was concurrently revising the British Standards publication BS4163, which was the health and safety standards for design and technology in schools and similar establishments. Eventually, an agreement on format and content was reached by all parties. The result, in 2000, was a new nationally based health and safety certification scheme for design and technology teachers. This scheme was given the quasi-legal status of an Agreed Code Of Practice (ACOP). Its existence was recognised in the curriculum order laid before Parliament in 2000 which, amongst other things, removed any statutory requirements for health and safety in design and technology and replaced them with an agreed code of practice.

This certification, to which all new and existing design and technology teachers were expected to subscribe, consisted of three parts. First were the four specialist areas of food, textiles, materials and control systems. All teachers were expected to gain certification in one or more of these specialist fields. Secondly, there were eight endorsement certificates for materials specialists. These endorsement certificates were optional and covered areas such as casting, turning, milling and welding. They are only needed if the teacher is actually carrying out that particular process. The third area was the 'core'. All design and technology teachers are expected to gain the core certification, which amongst other things, crucially addresses the long overdue issues of risk assessment.

Risk Assessment

One of the main aims of this new certification scheme has been to raise awareness of risk and liability and thereby bring about change to the existing culture. The objective being a paradigm shift of attitude from the 'yes we should, but …', to the 'how can we'. It was recognised that such a shift may require the reallocation of resource priorities and in some instances it would even be necessary to eliminate desirable activities completely. However, these are necessary consequences of risk management.

The area of risk assessment often opens up major dilemmas for design and technology teachers as their awareness is raised. Staff often arrive with vague perceptions that they should have some form of risk assessment for the circular saw or the food processor or similar specific items of equipment. Unfortunately, this is just the tip of the iceberg within education. First, we have the issue of experience. The risk levels associated with fifteen year-old pupils who are familiar with items of equipment such as the soldering iron, are quite different to those of a younger group who are being introduced to the equipment for the first time. Teachers therefore need to take account of this experience when assessing the risk. Although industry is often subjected to much more rigorous enforcement, it does have the benefit of predictable repeatable processes. Indeed, quality and profitability depend upon trained and competent staff working with modern well-maintained equipment to produce large numbers of identical high quality outcomes. While within education some may see this as the ideal, the reality is the very antithesis of this description.

Teachers may attempt to repeat the process of national curriculum delivery, but education does not work like a sausage machine. As any teacher will confirm, no two lessons ever planned to cover the same material, turn out to be the same. All pupils are different with needs that differ from day to day. Predictability is the missing element and this is down to the variable nature of the students. Even in classes with similar experience, there are still issues to consider. Some groups are able, motivated and socially integrated, whereas others are perhaps less so and more disaffected or more disruptive. Account must therefore also be taken of both attitude and pupil ability when assessing the risks of using equipment.

Then there are issues of disability to consider. Are there any pupils in the group who are particularly at risk? Extra care needs to be taken if an asthmatic pupil is carrying out a process in the workshop where dust is created. Similarly, additional control measures are needed for a pupil who is a celiac and in a food room when flour is being used, or for the child in the textile area suffering from dermatitis when working with certain fabrics or dyes.

Teachers also need to take account of the room size and shape. Can all remaining pupils still be adequately supervised from any part of the room during demonstrations to a small group? Does the number of children in the group make a particular practical activity unsafe due to overcrowding or lack of sufficient protective equipment?

Gradually, a depressing realisation comes to dawn, that it is not just one risk assessment per process that is needed, but multiple assessments of each process for each teaching group. Furthermore these assessments will be dynamic; they will change year-on-year as the nature and size of each pupil group changes. This may be just about manageable if it is incorporated into the thinking process needed for lesson planning, but this is simply not enough! The Health and Safety at Work Act explicitly requires that these risk assessments be recorded in a retrievable form. Visions flash by of no time to teach due to the administrative burden, of wheelbarrows filled to overflowing with risk assessments, moving from one room to another with each teacher.

Clearly, such a situation is untenable. Individual risk assessment for all activities in the education field is impracticable. But what are the alternatives? The best solution seems to be a mix and match approach. Basic generic risk assessments can be completed for individual items of equipment. Considerable guidance in the form of model design and technology risk assessments is available from the Consortium of Local Education Authorities for the Provision of Science Subjects (CLEAPSS). Further guidance is also available from BS4163-2000. These specific, but generic risk assessments for each item may be supplemented by further generic assessments for each classroom or workshop. Finally, the issues and control measures arising from the nature and size of the pupil groups can be recorded within the lesson plans with schemes of work that are specific to each individual member of staff. Although the generic elements are onerous in the early stages, they do have the advantage of remaining relatively stable. Such a system can be just about manageable.

Staffing Issues

Another problem area that needs to be addressed is the level of risk when staff absence occurs. Ideally, cover by a competent qualified design and technology supply teacher will be purchased on a daily basis. However, it is rare to find this ideal in operation. More common is to find a school providing its own cover for the first two or three days of absence. This may mean that staff from other subject areas lose marking time to cover the classes (which removes the possibility of practical work), or staff within the department reorganise internally to ensure that key classes are covered. Accidents are often seen to occur when an unusual set of circumstances have disrupted an established work pattern, so clearly there is an increase in the level of risk at these times. Accidents can happen in the class where cover is being undertaken, but these are just as likely to be within the classes of the other teachers who are trying to provide work or check progress whilst simultaneously coping with their own teaching. Children cannot be stacked up in an 'in tray' and dealt with when time allows, like live broadcasts, the action has to take place there and then. Extra care is needed during these times.

Even when a supply teacher is found to cover the design and technology classes of an absent colleague, the head of department still has the task of induction and concern about competency with machines. Temporary replacement staff are an unknown quantity and initially need careful monitoring. Hopefully though, this level of risk will recede somewhat as the new DATA certification scheme becomes more firmly established.

It should be noted that all Newly Qualified Teachers (NQTs) of design and technology were expected to gain this certification from the summer of 2001 onward. It was also anticipated that there would be a three-year transition period, during which all existing design and technology teachers would transfer over to the new scheme. At the time of writing these targets have only been partially met.

Newly qualified teachers (NQTs) of design and technology, who have attended traditional university-based programmes where both undergraduate and Post Graduate Certificate in Education (PGCE) provision are co-existing, seem to fare best. PGCE provision is more difficult to service due to the shortages of time and equipment. Those NQTs emerging from 'new initiative' schemes such as School Centred Initial Teacher Training (SCITT) and Graduate Training Programmes (GTP) often have the least opportunities for such certification.

A similar piecemeal picture is repeated with the transfer of existing staff. The three-year transition target has already been extended to four years. However, the few LEAs that have been fortunate enough to retain advisory staff in design and technology tend to have good systematic programmes of staff development in place with the certification of existing staff progressing well. Similarly in denominational schools, (which for the most part means grant aided Catholic schools) there often exist partnership groupings which are significantly more proactive than their counterparts in the LEA sector. Schools in partnership with Initial Teacher Training (ITT) providers again show higher than average adoption of the new scheme. It is easy to discern a trend. Those enjoying support and advice from the wider education community are moving forward whilst those working in isolation are generally not! One is forced to reflect on the losses that have resulted from this competition based market forces model.

Risk and Recent Trends in Design and Technology Education

So how is the current somewhat sporadic Health and Safety certification affecting education? Are we seeing a change in the culture? Are design and technology staff becoming more averse to risk as they gain greater awareness through the DATA core certification? Do they embrace it and actively manage the process?

Certainly in my work visiting schools, both in a supervisory role for students undertaking Initial Teacher Training and in my work as a registered design and technology health and safety consultant, delivering courses and awarding DATA accreditation to established staff, I see great variation, but there is a trend. Years ago, design and technology teachers would complain bitterly about the increasing numbers of pupils in practical classes. Perhaps because they were unaware of the legal position or possibly because teaching was seen as a vocation rather than a career, they would then often continue with a sigh of resignation and commence practical activities in overcrowded conditions. This of course, was on the clear understanding that it was just to make sure the pupils had 'the best possible chance'! I will leave the reader to ponder whether this was to be the best possible chance of education or injury.

Thankfully, this is changing. In the face of these continuing problems, breadth of pupil experience is being abandoned and curricular delivery modified. Optimism is being replaced by pragmatism. If a school does not have enough space or equipment for safe teaching, it is not uncommon for pupils to end up watching a video or reading about a process rather than actually doing it. There is an emerging base line recognition that the health and safety of the pupil is more important than the range of educational experience. To the outside observer, the temptation will be to say ;and why not?' Surely, this is no different to many other areas of the school curriculum. It also has the added bonus of being cheaper and safer as well. Such an approach however, destroys the very soul of the subject. It is akin to developing the artist by looking at pictures, or developing the musician by listening to music. In some areas it is not enough to just 'know about' a subject, there is also the need to be able 'to do'. This is of intrinsic and fundamental importance.

What about the teachers themselves? What do they perceive as the real risks to the health and safety of the children in the care? Two themes emerge more strongly than any other. The first is the unpredictable nature of the children and the risks thereby created by dangerous tools and equipment. The progressive removal of effective teacher sanctions, such as the abolition of corporal punishment and the imposition of targets to reduce exclusions, result in children having little to fear from inappropriate behaviour. I must add at this point, that I have no desire to either defend or deprecate either of these control measure examples. My wish is to draw attention to the fact that, without alternatives being provided, the imposed restrictions on teacher control have indirect consequences. The second and equally significant issue for the design and technology teachers is the overcrowded workroom. Teaching practical classes of twenty-two to twenty-four pupils can be unsafe even in adequately sized rooms. But when attempted in rooms designed for eighteen, the risk usually becomes unacceptable. It is interesting to note that the 1918 Education Act limited practical classes to a maximum of twenty children per adult, yet nearly a hundred years on, the issue of class size and workroom overcrowding has become worse rather than better! Two distinct problems exist here that should not be confused. The overcrowded workroom with more pupils than its design capacity is intrinsically an unsafe environment, but separate to this is the actual number of pupils present. A workshop the size of a factory would be large enough for perhaps two hundred pupils but it would not be safe to attempt to supervise this number. This was the point that the 1918 Education Act was highlighting, and the considered view then was that twenty was the most that could be safely supervised by one person. While it is difficult to firmly establish the significance of these issues I do not think it would be too great an exaggeration to say that they probably account for ninety per cent of the stress and mental energy expended by teachers in attempting to meet their statutory requirements to provide a safe and secure learning environment for the pupils in their care.

If the problem could be addressed by the simple purchase of extra workbenches or extra tools for the larger groups I am sure that funding would be found. But even if it could be found, it would not solve the basic problem of not having anywhere to put the additional resources. Workshops are not concertina boxes that can be stretched at will, and, being in the middle of a major structure with other teaching rooms adjoining, it is often impossible to extend a room with new building work. These problems can become even worse for teachers teaching classes with, for example, a wheelchair bound disabled pupil. We are told that as more and more special schools are phased out, and pupils with special needs are integrated into mainstream education, the funding to support their needs follows them to the mainstream schools. This is true and this extra funding would typically pay for the special height adjustable workbenches and specially adapted tools for such pupils. What it fails to address though is the fact that a wheelchair bound pupil has the same space requirement as four able bodied pupils to ensure adequate mobility. Schools cannot just 'lose' three pupils from a class to accommodate such a pupil and cannot just build an extra bit onto the workshop to increase the physical space. Equally, they cannot and should not discriminate against the disabled pupil, and so find themselves in an impossible safety dilemma. I can clearly remember one such teacher approaching me during an 'in service' course. He was at his wits end with worry about the unsafe conditions in his overcrowded 'specially adapted' workshop when the wheelchair pupil was present and implored me for advice on what to do next.

Even though at the time of writing, the political climate currently favours education, with new school building programmes being funded in almost every part of the country, this 'new build' is still designed for classes of up to twenty-one pupils. This is still above the 1918 Education Act limits and not a great deal of help to the teacher who continues to be allocated classes with pupil numbers in the low to mid twenties. To minimise risk to an acceptable level, something has to give! For many schools, the only solution to the issue of space shortages is the removal of the larger machines and equipment. The transition to a narrower educational experience in order to gain a safer environment is now often seen as the only realistic solution. Almost all practical activities are now primarily determined by the equipment needed and size of the physical outcome, rather than by the range of designing and making skills exercised.

Risk in Product Development

Some may argue that the examination results in the General Certificate in Secondary Education (GCSE) in design and technology contradict this rather bleak picture. This leads us into the second area of risk in education that I wish to explore. It is indeed true that examination results for design and technology continue to rise and are currently improving at a greater rate than all other subjects bar one (OFSTED, 2001). Paradoxically, this improvement in design and technology examination results may not be a reliable indicator of improvements in either design skills or the use of innovative and appropriate technology. Indeed, it is simply an indication that schools and pupils are becoming ever more skilled at meeting the examination requirements. There is no doubt that this improvement is happening as a result of hard work by both pupils and teachers, but this is missing the point. If we look at the aims of design and technology, then map these against its assessment, they show a rather poor correlation. We are not, in general, assessing what we say we are aiming to achieve!

The fundamental ethos of design and technology is to create an environment that improves the quality of life for the user. Most commonly, this is achieved through the creation of artefacts that are of higher quality, of lower cost, that last longer or are more pleasing to work with. 'Making something better' is not achieved through 'copying'. 'Making something better' will not be achieved by selecting the safe material process that is known to work. 'Making something better' can only be achieved through experimenting, exploration, innovation and synthesis. This means taking risk! Not the risk to life and limb, but the risk that the outcome will not be a success. Unfortunately, we seem as yet unable to design an examination system that rewards the process when the outcome itself is not a success. Importantly failure is an essential element of progression in the design process. Pupils and teachers are aware that examination success is better achieved through known safe routes. I would therefore argue that the examination statistics and the league tables are in fact currently poor instruments of assessment. They are acting as levers of change to the nature of the subject that they are attempting to assess. Assessment becomes the master, the dictator of activity, rather than the servant of its aims. Those familiar with quantum physics will immediately recognise the similarity to Heisenberg's uncertainty principle, whereby the act of observing the particle causes it to alter its state and thereby invalidates the very observation being made.

Essentially, our present examination structure is altering the ethos of design and technology. The subject is undergoing a subtle but steady change whereby 'risk' in product development is avoided. Reliable product outcomes equate with reliable examination outcomes. This looks good in the school league tables and contributes significantly to the government's long term education improvement targets, but the products themselves are often bland, standardised and predictable. They are the very antithesis of the aims of the subject!

The Future of Design and Technology in the UK

The final area that I would like to briefly explore relates to the risk that some pupils may be receiving an inappropriate technology education. Design and technology has for many years carried with it the millstone of the 'craft' courses from which it emerged. These craft courses were originally seen as suitable non-academic programmes for the less able. Indeed, the rather pejorative term 'craft for the daft' sums up former and, to some extent, current views of the subject. In an attempt to gain respectability and academic standing, the design aspect was emphasised. Design carried value. Product designers, architects, advertising consultants and similar design based professionals had common experiences, they had graduate status, they were members of the managerial and professional social classes and they enjoyed good remuneration and working conditions. The traditional woodwork, metalwork, cookery and needlework titles did not map well against future development for the subject. Initially, these craft classes moved under the umbrella of Craft, Design and Technology (CDT). However, within a few short years, design had become the jewel in the subject crown with the craft element of the title being quietly dropped to leave us with the present title of Design and Technology.

Even the technology element has now been relegated to an item of secondary value. It is used simply as a vehicle to demonstrate design skills. Pick up any academic or educational journal with a design and technology contribution and the main theme will be about the value and development of design skills. The type of person contributing to such journals is more likely to have risen through a design based route rather than a craft focussed one. They tend to be more articulate by the very nature of the design background from which they have developed. Craft based staff, used to working and writing in a more technical language often find it difficult to contribute work of a similar eloquence and in the main, tend not to do so. This leaves the design side with ownership of the academic high ground.

For pupils that are more able the higher order thinking skills of design, offer a challenge and can inspire them to future study in the field. Unfortunately, for those pupils who find it difficult to cope with the more abstract and lateral thinking demands of the design process, they are rarely offered a vocational alternative. This situation is slowly improving in some schools with the introduction of the Vocational Certificates in Education (VCEs) and their advanced counterparts, the AVCEs. It must be recognised however that administering two contrasting assessment programmes within a department is difficult and adequately funding such programmes remains a major problem. Practical skill based courses consume materials and need expensive equipment that academic programmes do not. Designing is always cheaper than making. Financial difficulties tend to be cyclical and during such times of strain, the most expensive courses are usually the first casualties of any cost cutting exercise. As previously discussed, the teaching environment with large class sizes and small workshops tend to act as further disincentive to the introduction of more practical 'skill based' educational programmes in many schools.

Design and technology is in many ways a microcosm of the traditional English educational system. We have academic design based programmes most suited to the top twenty per cent of pupils being delivered to the majority of the school population. This almost universal subservience of technological skills to the design process is I feel, not really in the best interests of the nation or many pupils.

Most people would accept that supply and demand should be the primary determinant of income. There are for example, very few individuals, who have the ability to play football at the highest level, but for those who can, they can quite rightly command high levels of remuneration. Yet, in Britain today, there are many plumbers in the London area earning twice the salary of university lecturers. The balance of probability would suggest that there are more lecturers who would be able to successfully complete apprenticeships in plumbing than there are plumbers who would successfully complete doctorate level degrees, and carry out research and teaching. Whilst all individuals are of value to society, and our society would rapidly become dysfunctional if either element was removed, one is forced to question the values that allow the creation of such inversion of monetary worth. Despite this growing imbalance, the emphasis, the direction and the development in design and technology remains focused on the academic, that is.the design aspects of the subject. The present UK Government has set a target of fifty per cent of young people entering Higher Education by 2010. Entry to higher education is, realistically, only through the 'academic' door. In this respect, design and technology is positively helping to meet these government targets, but despite this, there is still a question in the minds of many. The question is not new, but it needs to be asked and re-asked. Are we in education, properly meeting the needs of the nation and its young people?

Conclusion

In this chapter I have attempted to highlight the three main areas of risk that teachers, pupils and design and technology as a subject faces. The greatest areas of concern in terms of health and safety are the large group sizes and overcrowded workrooms, followed by the unpredictable and inappropriate behaviour of pupils and lack of effective sanctions. Teacher attitudes are changing and, with such unsatisfactory conditions pertaining, the breadth of pupil experience is now being restricted. This is not resulting in worse examination results, which begs the question why? I have attempted to demonstrate how within our assessment system, we are currently failing to properly assess the activity of pupils against the aims of the subject. Consequently, there is an increasing risk that teachers are teaching pupils to pass exams rather than to engage them with the subject. The physical and organisational problems highlighted previously only serve to exacerbate this trend. Finally, I have examined the appropriateness of a design ethos in a design and technology curriculum that is meted out to all pupils. As a country, we continue to implore all to 'reach for the sky', a process that guarantees failure for the majority. Yet at the same time, we are failing to provide a suitable environment to develop the practical day to day skills that we as a nation will always need no matter how technologically advanced we become. We perhaps need to stop trying to take everyone to the top of the same ladder and concentrate more on taking everyone up to a point which is appropriate to them and for society as a whole. It is here that they can genuinely meet the true aims of design and technology by creating a better living environment for other people. I fear at present, that we may be risking our future prosperity by sacrificing the balance of need to the ideals of aspiration.

References

Brierley, D. (1991), *Health and Safety in Schools*, Chapman, London.
British Standards Institution (2000), *Health and Safety Standards for Design and Technology in Schools and Similar Establishments*, HMSO, London.
Health and Safety Executive (1992), *The Health and Safety at Work Regulations*, HMSO, London.
OFSTED (1998), *Annual report*, HMSO, London.
OFSTED (2001), *Annual report*, HMSO, London.
Raymond, C. and Twyford, J. (1999), *Safety Across the Curriculum*, Falmer, London.

Chapter 10

Higher Education in Further Education: A Risky Business or Too Good to Miss

Freda Bridge

Introduction

The education system in England has undergone, and continues to undergo, substantial change. The major issue facing further education (FE) and higher education (HE) is the imperative for substantial growth of higher education. In order to meet the current government's target for such growth it is clear that some HE will need to be delivered in further education colleges. This brings an important dimension to the relationship between FE and HE. In many areas there are excellent collaborative links that can be extended and developed. In other areas it provides opportunities to develop new and innovative arrangements. The Learning and Skills Development Agency (LSDA), formerly the Further Education Development Agency, together with HEFCE's interest in FE, has resulted in some contribution to the debate of delivering HE in FE. For those embarking on introducing HE into FE it is desirable that risk factors are taken into account.

This chapter outlines the national policy context and the contemporary position of HE in FE and in doing so considers the historical background, current policy trends and development, the interface between HEFCE and the LSC and ways in which this could be developed to deliver HE. In considering these issues I shall focus on the implications for both HE and FE following current trends.

A Historical Perspective

In order to assist in the understanding of HE in FE a consideration of the historical background would be useful in order to identify any trends. Up to the 1970s, HE had been perceived as elitist with a take up of less than 5 per cent of school leavers opting to undertake study in higher education. Secondary education increased after the Second World War, providing a suitable time for

policy makers to consider expansion of higher education. Therefore, a spate
of growth was seen in higher education. Some of this was in already existing
institutions but there was the opportunity for the creation of new HEIs including the Open University (Parry and Thompson, 2002). The system allowed for
three types of HEIs – universities, polytechnics and colleges of higher education. The 1992 Further and Higher Education Act enabled polytechnics to
become universities, thus resulting in two types of HEI – the universities and
the colleges of higher education.

In reviewing the uptake of higher education following on from this growth
it is clear that HE students are predominantly from the same social class
background (Field, 2002). Another feature of the expansion was that the 'old'
universities (pre-1992) had the lowest proportions of students from the lower
socio-economic groups (op cit).

There has been a tradition, since the 1960s, of delivering HE within FE
prior to the latest governmental imperative linked to increase participation in
HE. However, Parry and Thompson (2001) argue that this had not such a high
profile in FE colleges as it was:

> overshadowed by the rise of polytechnics and other large colleges as national
> institutions during the 1980s (p. 1).

Funding arrangements have contributed to some of the confusion around
the delivery of HE programmes in FE colleges. After the 1988 Education Act,
funding for HE in FE colleges was divided into two areas. One area was
funded by the funding council for polytechnics and HEIs. The other funded
from local authorities for 'non-prescribed' HE. In 1992 the HE sector was
brought into one system with the polytechnics being redesignated universities.
Prescribed courses included higher and first degrees, diplomas in higher education, diplomas in management studies and other advanced provision such as
the training of teachers. Non–prescribed courses were non-advanced further
education but included some advanced programmes, for example, higher
national certificates (HNC). The Further Education Funding Council (FEFC)
took over the funding for non-prescribed courses from the local authorities in
1993. when considering new developments, risks associated with funding must
be a consideration along with other risk factors.

Parry and Thompson (2001) describe the way the FEFC operated 'a policy
of no policy' with regard to non-prescribed higher education. In 1999 FEFC
transferred funding responsibility to the Higher Education Funding Council
(HEFC) for a considerable amount of this type of HE but leaving some HE
provision within FE. The move towards a much higher take up of HE in
England in the 1980s also made the issue of HE in FE particularly significant.
The result of this was a growth in cross-sector collaboration, particularly as
HE was becoming more extensive. One difference for FE colleges was that they
were increasingly becoming the deliverers of HE programmes.

Another consequence of the massive growth in HE was the development of
franchise arrangements. These arrangements were usually for undergraduate

provision and provided several advantages to both the FE and HE institutions. They provided the opportunity for expansion for both parties. They also provided a more regional focus on HE delivery as well as providing the opportunity for staff in FE to teach on new HE programmes. Other advantages were the progression routes provided for students. Staff within FE colleges were able to contribute to curriculum development of HE programmes thus providing professional development opportunities that would have not otherwise been available. An interesting risk here is the way in which staff in FE could then become interested in HE as a career. Franchise programmes also provide the risk of having to take on board additional quality assurance procedures of the validating institution.

In 1994 when approximately one in eight HE students were studying in FE colleges (Parry and Thompson, 2001) the government decided it was timely to stop the expansion of full-time higher education. Of the one in eight students previously referred to, one sixth were studying on a franchise basis. FE colleges offered most of their HE provision on a part- time basis with qualifications below first-degree level. Because of this, the FE colleges at this time were not caught up in the expansion of HE in the same way as HE institutions. Parry and Thompson (2001) refer to the role of FE as 'auxiliary and ancillary' in the move to mass higher education. They describe FE colleges as having a useful role in ensuring the availability of a wide range of students ready for entry into HE.

In 2001 The Learning and Skills Council (LSC) took over from FEFC the responsibility for FE provision and found that it had responsibility for work that was not considered part of its remit, i.e. HE.

National Policy Perspectives

Background to the Policy Context

The areas of further and higher education in the United Kingdom have undergone, and will continue to undergo, a period of rapid modification (Weil, 1999). Failure to keep pace with the changes at public, governmental, and economic levels can lead to significant difficulties for institutions which are otherwise committed to delivering quality education (op cit). In this context, a major concern has been the role of academic staff delivering HE programmes in both further education colleges and higher education institutions. Their work has been affected by several government initiatives such as Kennedy (1997) and Dearing (1997).

The Kennedy Report

The Kennedy Report was a timely report for FE as it was developed during a period of change and rapid growth for FE. The following review of the report

highlights the crucial role of FE in education, the benefits of further education
delivery, the economic perspective and the role of academic staff.

In 1997 Helena Kennedy QC, chair of the Further Education Funding
Council (FEFC), produced a major report entitled '*Learning Works: Widening
Participation in Further Education*'. Defining FE as 'everything that does not
happen in schools or universities' (Kennedy, 1997, p. 1), she goes on to claim
that FE is crucial nationally in terms of economic renewal and social cohesion.
FE has always had, as a strength, the fact that it can deliver on a local and
sometimes regional basis in a cost-effective way, thus enabling individual
students to have dedicated programmes often vocationally work related. FE
holds this central position by offering opportunities to people who would
otherwise be excluded from further or higher education: the unemployed and
low-skilled workers, ex-offenders, refugees and members of immigrant groups,
underachievers, to name some fitting into this category. One of the main
thrusts of the Kennedy Report involves a blurring of the boundary between
FE and HE. Indeed, much degree level education has already been franchised
to FE institutions, and much of the increase in HE is expected to take place in
colleges of further education (Pring, 1999). This illustrates the wide variation
of provision that is available within FE. Therefore, can FE take the risk of
such diversified provision?

Kennedy argues that for FE to function effectively it is important for institutions to perform successfully with regard to (1) the quality of education provided
(2) the amount of funding available and (3) the range of students attracted to
learning. The report expresses a concern that in a competitive market where
other organisations vie for the same resources, a 'business-like' mentality has
arisen in which rivalry takes precedence over the 'public service ethos of the
colleges' (Kennedy, 1997, p. 5). Rather, a good balance between market forces
and public provision is required which is similar to the modern NHS. This
implies that there needs to be a basis of sound principles and good management
employed to ensure both widening participation (new students from an even
wider, diverse background) and financial survival in the latter-day climate.

Clearly an important role in achieving such an ideal is that of teaching in
FE and HE. With regard to the former, however, Kennedy (1997) does not
explicitly address the issue of academic staff and how they should be supported
in an ever-changing working environment. This is disappointing considering
the emphasis on the vast range of provision illustrating the need for supportive
professional development. Indeed, Kennedy is not alone in this regard. As the
teaching of HE in FE institutions is a very recent phenomenon for some
providers of FE (Pring, 1999), it currently lacks much in the way of an analytic
literature. Indeed most, if not all research in this area focuses on HE.

The Dearing Report: The National Committee of Inquiry into Higher Education

The 'Dearing Report' is, in fact, a comprehensive publication by The National
Committee of Inquiry into Higher Education. In terms of employees it states

that academic organisations, 'should be able to recruit, retain and motivate staff of the highest calibre' (Dearing Report, 1997, p. 220). According to Dearing, academic staff play an important part in the nation's economy, as they constitute 1.8 per cent of the entire workforce. This report is the only one to acknowledge the crucial role of staff in HE or indeed any staff delivering HE programmes. One of the report's main recommendations is in regard to professional development. At present, one of the main pre-requisites for most lecturing/teaching jobs is the award of a good degree and/or research qualification. Although this ensures staff are of a high academic standing paradoxically it does not necessarily ensure they are suited to the teaching responsibilities of a lecturer. It is interesting to note that there is no expectation for HE staff to gain a teaching qualification, even though this is now possible. As such, there is a significant amount of on-the-job training in all modern universities with some HEIs offering accredited teaching qualifications. Despite the necessity and time consuming nature of such training, opportunities for promotion are generally based on the agenda of individual institutions in which research is commonly privileged over teaching Indeed, in a survey, only 3 per cent of academic staff believed that achievements in teaching would lead to promotion (op.cit.). This inevitably leads to some staff concentrating on their research as crucial to professional development and career enhancement even though a significant proportion of their time is spent teaching. Such an emphasis can lead to a reduced focus on teaching quality.

It can be claimed, therefore, that there is inadequate recognition of teaching for staff in HE. In this context, the high value placed on research can clearly have consequences for FE staff working on HE programmes as they operate in an environment where teaching, not research, is central, although some FE colleges are now considering how staff can be involved in research, particularly through studying for higher degrees. The Dearing Report asserts that more focus is required on the ways in which teaching is supported. The focus is on issues such as teaching support materials, for example, information technology, staff development policies and sources of funding, to highlight some. It was this report that advocated the creation of The Institute for Learning and Teaching in Higher Education (ILT) which could offer accreditation for teaching abilities, skills and knowledge. This, of course, has now been established and considered by ILT to be a huge success. It does provide a professional support in relation to teaching and learning in higher education through a variety of means such as web sites, conferences and a professional journal. All higher education staff involved in teaching are urged to become associate members though there is a stark difference in uptake on this between the 'old' and 'new' universities (ILT, 2002).

The Dearing report shows how contemporary policy for HE in FE can be supported and developed. It is embodied in five of the recommendations:

1.   Renewed growth in HE should be focused initially on sub-degree levels.

FE colleges have traditionally delivered sub-degree work and are well placed to do so considering their excellent track record in this area. This method of uptake of HE is helpful to non-traditional students who would otherwise not be able to study at HE level.

2. That priority in this growth should be accorded to FE colleges.

This again links to the success of FE colleges in this area as localised provision can be seen as appropriate here.

3. That the bodies responsible for funding further and higher education should collaborate and fund projects designed to promote progression to higher education.

This is indeed a sensible suggestion although the practicalities will be significant. The LSC and HEFCE have currently started to do this and produced a useful discussion document Partnerships for Progression (2002). This will be considered later.

4. In support of a local and regional role for higher education, the FEFC regional committees should include a member from HE.

5. The quality assurance criteria for franchising arrangements should be specified which include a normal presumption that colleges should have only one HE partner.

Franchising requires a significant amount of quality assurance especially when more than one franchise.partner is used, which is often the case. A set of criteria can only be helpful to higher education institutions (HEIs) and further education colleges (FECs) in establishing good quality assurance for franchised programmes. The presumption that a college should only have one HE partner is one which colleges find restrictive. This is often due to curriculum issues and the FE colleges not always finding the coverage they need with one HE partner. The approach of using one HE partner is sensible in that HEIs can have different systems and procedures that the FE colleges must follow. In reality, the FE colleges will build on their strengths for HE provision and will need to ascertain the HEI or HEIs that they can work with.

This was an unanticipated outcome of the Dearing Report as indicated by Parry and Thompson (2001), particularly in giving FE colleges a leading role in the expansion of HE. The reason why this was so surprising was that the Kennedy Report had taken the view that HE was not significant to the mission of FE. The Dearing Report highlighted many issues facing HE and in its deliberations considered the delivery of HE in FE. The report also highlights the pressure staff face in deciding on the importance of teaching and/or research to their promotion opportunities. Again, this can be seen as a risk factor in determining whether or not a FE institution should embark on delivering HE programmes.

Criticisms of the Dearing Report

Following the publication of the Dearing Report there has been inevitable commentary and criticism from academics and HE analysts (Parry, 1999; Robertson, 1999; Weil, 1999). Much of this criticism has focused on a perceived bureaucratic tendency in Dearing with staff seeing the Dearing Report as being critical of the way they work and the report trying to establish some kind of agreed working procedures. In considering HE staff, many perceive themselves to be afforded a certain amount of academic freedom and see bureaucratic procedures as anathema to them. As this study is considering the professional development needs of staff teaching HE programmes in FE it has been important to look at the working conditions of both education sectors. This critique of the Dearing Report highlights the staffing issues faced within HE but acknowledges that this is important in trying to establish a way forward for determining the needs of those members of staff in FE teaching HE programmes.

In short, many of its solutions to current academic problems involve an ethos of control in which standardised procedures and bureaucratic structures are created. Weil (1999) argues that such tendencies maintain the illusion of stability, while, in fact, stifling the creative diversity of staff, and missing new forms of social organisation which are inevitably 'unstable'. HE staff would consider any way of trying to establish control that stifles creativity or gets in the way of academic freedom as unacceptable. It is claimed that the measures enacted to develop teaching and learning must take into account the pressures for new kinds of knowledge, and that the recommendations of the Dearing Report largely fail to achieve this (op.cit.). This illustrates the debate and dichotomy about research and teaching by HE staff. Many HE staff see themselves as researchers and do not see the need to develop their teaching skills (Dearing, 1997).

There are several ways of considering the subject divisions in HE that can be the subject of debate with academic staff. However, despite their frequent inter- and intra-disciplinary divisions, academics have traditionally regarded themselves as part of a single community (Becher, 1989). They are considered the 'intellectuals of society' (Weil, 1999) and maintain rather stringent allegiances to the profession. So the risks of challenging these values are substantial for people whose livelihood depends upon success within the system (Gergen, 1994). Nevertheless, from within and outside institutions, new voices in the form of social and technological change and the shift to mass FE and HE now threaten taken-for-granted academic positions (Weil, 1999). This could lead to the generation of creative dialogue among academics (Gregory, 1996), though all too often there is only the formation of groupings that guard against what can be seen as 'dilution' (Weil, 1999).

For HE this can be seen in relation to their teaching and to the changing nature of the student population. This can be through the development of new knowledge in their specialist field or indeed in developments in teaching and learning. New knowledge in an academic discipline is straightforward, but the innovation in teaching and learning can provide quite a challenge for some academic staff. Examples of this include the use of information and communications technology, the growth of e-learning and supporting students with different needs. One of the problems appears to be how this vision should be realised, particularly in relation to how academic staff see their working conditions.

The Dearing Report is one such proposal designed to recommend strategies for academic development through the professional development of staff. It aimed to outline a plan for the future of HE, and yet many have argued that it failed to fully appreciate the 'mess' of existing organisations (Barnett, 1997). It was also a disappointment that there was no congruence with the Kennedy Report especially as Dearing had considered the delivery of HE in FE colleges. In this context it has been argued that the Dearing Report puts forward structural – or bureaucratic – solutions to issues that are not inherently structural in nature (Weil, 1999). The main problem with these solutions is that they cannot touch deep cultural barriers to change within a system that has developed over time and has, therefore, a defined culture. The Dearing Report is an attempt to reduce perceived 'mess' in academic organisations such as HEIs, and not to reduce such barriers. Its central assumption is that by making HE more orderly, it will become more efficient (Weil, 1999).

A way of looking at this is to take the example of the Institute for Learning and Teaching. This was set up as a vehicle to accredit professional development in the managing of learning and teaching, to help institutions exploit the potential of communications and information technology, and to stimulate innovation. (ILT, 2002). However, what it has actually produced is an emphasis on information technology as a way of improving efficiency with little attention being given to how this might facilitate new forms of learning (Weil, 1999). Indeed, as Capra (1996) states:

> The use of IT is based on an outmoded model of humans as information processors; information is presented as the basis of thinking, whereas the human mind thinks with ideas (p. 176).

It is unclear also what 'innovation' might mean. As Weil (1999) states:

> How will increased ... quality control and standard setting ... generate the risk-taking that is integral to maintaining a responsive and innovative system? (p. 177).

A further criticism is that Dearing does not fully come to terms with the new kinds of learning that are needed in the 21st century and does not go any way to identifying strategies to enable the future students to meet the needs of employers. Employers seek people who can deal with a variety of complex and shifting predicaments (Jarvis, 2000), yet the Dearing Report treats these issues in a way that subscribes to deeply embedded, mechanistic perceptions of knowledge and learning (Weil, 1999). A focus away from passive information processing models of human intelligence to the active construction of knowledge by the learner (and this includes the professional development of teachers) is gaining significant currency in pedagogic research (Postman, 1992).

This is especially the case in the existing hierarchies of academic 'tribes' (Becher, 1989). How might moves to introduce 'learning conversations' (Ainscough, 1997) be undermined by traditional practices and power relationships in HE? There are implications here in the development of teaching and learning strategies that require a radical reconsideration of existing methodologies assuming that academic staff are basing their present work on such. This illustrates the need for some radical re-thinking for some academic staff in HE and how they operate. The debate becomes even more complex when the situation regarding HE teaching with FE is considered.

Resource issues cannot be taken away from the discussion as they are crucial, particularly in a time of change when additional resources could be required. This was also a feature of the Bett report. Such tensions are inevitably heightened should they appear at a time of scarce resources. The technological solutions that are promoted by the Dearing Report (1997) cannot remove these problems by themselves (Blatt et al., 1999). This approach acknowledges that new forms of knowledge generation and communication are required in order to improve service delivery. As Schon (1995) states:

> Most of the knowledge essential to professional practice is not what the research university calls fundamental knowledge ... We should think about practice as a setting not only for the application of knowledge but for its generation ... Perhaps there is an epistemology of practice that takes fuller account of the competence practitioners sometimes display in situations of uncertainty, complexity, uniqueness and conflict (1995– cited in Weil, 1999, p. 29).

There is a debate to be had following the Dearing Report regarding the recreation of knowledge and where this should be developed. If staff teaching on HE programmes are to be allowed or expected to do this what are the implications for staff within FE who teach HE?

Widening participation is a central focus of both the Kennedy (1997) and the Dearing (1997) Reports. In the latter case, Weil (1999) has argued that by focusing at a rhetorical level, rather than by proposing better forms of funding for such individuals, the review unwittingly colludes in the 'iconisation' of HE, and perpetuates patterns of social exclusion. This was surely not an intended outcome of the Dearing report and is not in line with current governmental policy geared specifically towards social inclusion.

Trends and Policy Development

In the previous section a consideration of the historical development of HE in FE was given. The government and others can see how FE can contribute significantly to this growth in HE through the provision of more localised courses building on existing provision. Smith and Bocock (1999) emphasise that the interest of FE to deliver HE was a feature of FE before the widening participation agenda was so high profile. They indicate that the 1987 White Paper on higher education showed the potential for growth in the vocational route from further to higher education. This could be seen through courses such as the BTEC Higher. The Kennedy Report (1997) was supportive of FE in developing FE work only and FE colleges keeping entirely to this as their mission. The report, in fact, warned of 'mission drift' as a concern. In contrast the Dearing Report (1997) supported the growth of HE in FE. Recently, the advent of Foundation Degrees has made the interface between FE and HE very important. The government latched onto this as a way of increasing and widening participation in HE.

The House of Commons Select Committee on Education and Employment (2001) were supportive and encouraging of partnerships between FE colleges and HEIs. They saw this as a way of helping to improve retention and also achievement, arguing that FE colleges have a great deal of experience to contribute to these areas. The Select Committee recommended that the Regional Development Agencies (RDAs) and Learning and Skills Councils (LSCs) should seek to:

> Develop strategic partnerships between further education colleges and regional higher education institutions, in order to provide routes for mature students, and for students who have previously not completed a course of higher education to be able to progress towards entry or re-entry to higher education (House of Commons, 2001b, para 81).

From the above it can be seen that there is the imperative for FE to be come more involved in delivering HE. In order to do this FE colleges will need to consider several areas for development including the professional development needs of the staff currently employed, as well as other risk factors.

The Interface between the Higher Education Funding Council for England (HEFCE) and the Learning and Skills Council (LSC)

HEFCE is the main funding body for HE including HE in FE. The LSC has responsibility for all work delivered in FE colleges and similar settings. Because of the imperative for increased participation through the use of FE, it is essential that HEFCE and the LSC work closely together to ensure that there is no conflict of interests. In 2000 HEFCE produced guidelines for indirectly funded partnerships producing codes of practice for franchise and consortia arrangements. These are both types of practices entered into by HEIs and FECs. The guidelines were put together in order to provide codes of practice that:

> set out guidance on the principles that should be reflected in the consortia agreements that underpin indirectly funded projects, together with introductory commentaries on their application (HEFCE, 2001, p. 1).

HEFCE maintained a firm control on all such arrangements requiring any new consortia to have HEFCE approval before they could be fully established. This has recently been given to the development at a University in the North of England for the Consortium for Post-Compulsory Education and Training (CPCET). This is a consortium of 30 plus institutions with over 2,000 students and is the largest, by far, of any of HEFCE's consortia. In addition, HEFCE state that the arrangements must 'result in high quality teaching and learning for students' (p. 3). Provided that this is the case then HEFCE allow the partners some freedom to determine the actual nature of the arrangements for themselves. However, there have to be clear lines of accountability and they must be financially viable for HEFCE approval, both of which institutions would want to see as part of their agreements.

HEFCE point out that with a franchise arrangement, the responsibility for the students is with the institution that receives HEFCE funding. With an HEFCE-recognised consortium, it is with the institutions delivering the provision. In order to support FECs in their delivery of HE, HEFCE introduced a special HE in FE Development Fund in 1999–2000 and 2001–2002. In order to have access to the funding, FECs had to complete a strategy statement for HEFCE within given parameters. The development fund was specifically for learning and teaching but was also to support the widening participation agenda. This programme of support by HEFCE for HE being delivered in FE acknowledges the variety of provision in terms of scale and significance. HEFCE also state that:

> expectations of accountability and quality in HE have been rising, there is a responsibility to ensure that the students experience in FECs is similar to that in HEIs (HEFCE, 2000, p. 3).

HEFCE also state that they expect colleges to periodically review their HE provision and to have a clear strategy for development. They also acknowledge that FECs could have developed their provision in HE for a number of reasons such as:

- To develop a local or regional mission.
- To develop specialist area of provision.
- To broaden the range of opportunities for students and staff.
- To expand the sources and volume of their funding. (HEFCE, 2000, p. 4)

It can be seen that HEFCE seriously consider the crucial role that FECs can have in increasing HE but that they are also prepared to support FECs in this initiative through additional funding. Although this is the case, HEFCE are keen to ensure that the funding is spent appropriately stating that the development fund could only be used to enhance the HE student experience. Various examples were given to help FECs progress their strategies for developing HE including releasing staff from teaching in order that they can spend time on curriculum, teaching approaches, assessment methods and quality assurance procedures. All of these activities were considered appropriate as were others that related to 'the enhancement of quality and standards of teaching and learning on HE programmes' (HEFCE, 2000, p. 8).

The two agencies, HEFCE and LSC, have recognised that they need to work together to support HEIs and FECs in increasing participation in HE. In doing so they have identified some areas that require particular attention such as the mission of the institution. They have identified aspects of good practice such as release of staff time for development work. All of this was set up as a way of ensuring that FECs were able to respond to increases in HE programmes.

Developing FE to Deliver HE

As part of the agenda to change from an elite to a mass HE system through establishing a variety of provision a development fund for supporting HE in FE was set up by HEFCE as stated above. This was a way for the government to make clear its agenda through specific targeted resources. FE colleges were required to submit their plans for development which were analysed by the then Further Education Development Agency (FEDA). The funding was based on identified priorities in particular 'to enhance the HE student learning experience' (HEFCE, 2000, p. 9). As mentioned it was clear that it could also be used for supporting staff to become experts in teaching and learning in HE through releasing them to spend time on 'developing the curriculum, teaching approaches, assessment methods, quality assurance procedures or any other activity relating to the enhancement of the quality and standards of teaching and learning on HE programmes' (ibid). This gave a great incentive for further education institutions to consider their approach to HE but also to receive funding in order to deliver their priorities in this area. The staffing support was wide reaching and allowed a major investment to be made in supporting staff who were or intended to teach on HE programmes. Further evidence of this is given by HEFCE's approach to staff development when it states that a purpose of the fund is for 'supporting staff development which will have a direct impact on the HE student learning experience...training to improve the reliability of assessment and its consistency of design, marking and moderation and the quality and consistency of feedback to students' (ibid, p. 10). Here HEFCE is encouraging FE colleges to consider a vast range of possible support mechanisms for staff. The funding could also be used for capital expenditure. Any FE college that was considering extending their HE provision was well advised to make a request for development funds from this source.

When FEDA (2001) analysed the requests for funding there were particular patterns emerging. From a regional perspective three factors were identified as being significant in the way FE colleges consider HE. These were remote areas where there is little HE provision, where there has been existing and often long standing FE/HE networks and any sub-regional economic changes. There were several emerging themes identified including the implication of a critical mass, the need for an HE ethos, curriculum and staff development as well as quality assurance. From these themes there were development priorities identified which were:

- HE growth
- HE ethos and environment
- Staff development
- Curriculum development
- Systems infrastructure (HEFCE, 2001, p. 4)

The FEDA report saw the need for staff development in much the same way as HEFCE (2000) did but they acknowledged that HEIs could make a significant contribution to the planning and delivery of staff development in local colleges, although it was stated that there could be some two-way exchanges that could be useful thanks to the curriculum and pedagogy that was evident in further education. They saw the development of the Foundation Degree as a useful new programme for bringing FE and HE closer together both in the development and delivery of the programmes. Other areas of staff development identified for FE staff were improvements in 'staff information, communication and learning technology skills, and subject knowledge updating' (HEFCE, 2001, p. 12).

The joint initiative by HEFCE and the LSC was a significant feature in establishing a way of supporting the government's imperative for increased participation in HE supported by FE colleges. The initiative identified the need for funding to support the development which is important to the FE sector who see themselves as poorly funded in relation to other sectors in education. The fact that there was support for staffing was also important as it is through the staff that the process will be successful. Also acknowledged was the variety of ways in which staff could be supported in their development. This was one way in which a government imperative was supported financially and identified future areas for development.

Conclusion

The national policy context relating to HE and FE is complex, particularly when considering the blurred edges between the two sectors. The history of the relationship between FE and HE has shown how the sectors can work together in delivering governmental agendas such as increased participation rates for higher education. In fact it is difficult to envisage how the recent imperative for extensive growth in HE can be achieved without the involvement of FE. In turn, FE will need to work closely with HE. As indicated by the literature this will have a significant impact on staff within both sectors.

The present position regarding the growth and expansion of HE programmes in order to increase participation has seen a significant shift in funding. HEFCE has assumed responsibility for all postgraduate, first degree, higher diploma and higher certificate courses in colleges of further education. Parry and Thompson (2001) state that the government has planned for 'over half the expansion in sub-degree places to be delivered through the colleges.' (p. 3) This has resulted in colleges being firmly encouraged to think how they can respond to this drive. They are expected to deliver the same quality and standards as HEIs; this can be a real challenge for some further education colleges. One response has been the growth of collaborative arrangements and the development of consortia. These consortia can be clusters of colleges and HEIs in the same area, although there are examples of a wider geographical base for some consortia.

There is the governmental agenda for increased participation in HE and, in particular, from under-represented groups along with the need for FE to be considerably involved in the process. In order to do this there will be implications for those teaching or encouraged to teach HE in FE. However, the involvement of FE in HE is a risk and both HE and FE institutions need to consider these risks carefully from their own perspective before considering initial involvement, or in some cases, increased involvement.

References

Ainscough, V. (1997), 'Reflection in action: Increasing teacher awareness of the learning needs of specific socio-cultural groups', *System*, vol. 25(4), pp. 571–579.

Barnett, R. (1997), *Higher Education: A Critical Business*, Buckingham, Open University Press.

Becher, T. (1989), *Academic Tribes and Territories: Intellectual Enquiry and the Cultures of Disciplines*, Buckingham, Open University Press.

Blatt, I., Hartman, W. and Voss, A. (1999), 'The use of the Internet in university teacher training', *The Internet and Higher Education*, vol. 1(4), pp. 305–315.

Capra, F. (1996), *The Web of Life*, New York, Doubleday.

Dearing Report (1997), *Higher Education in the Learning Society: Report of the National Committee of Inquiry into Higher Education*, London, HMSO.

Field, J. (2002), *Links Between Further and Higher Education – A Contextual Report*, Research Report to HEFCE, London, HMSO.

Gergen, K. (1994), *Towards Transformation in Social Knowledge*, London, Sage.

Gregory, W. (1996), 'Discordant pluralism: A new strategy for critical systems thinking', *Systems Practice*, vol. 9(6), pp. 605–625.

HEFCE (2000), *Higher Education in Further Education: Publication no.00/54*, Bristol, Higher Education Funding Council for England.

HEFCE (2001), *Supporting Higher Education in Further Education Colleges: Publication no.01/07*, Bristol, Higher Education Funding Council for England.

House of Commons (2001), *Sixth Report of the Select Committee on Education and Employment – Higher Education: Student Retention*, London, House of Commons.

Institute for Learning and Teaching in Higher Education (2002), *Annual Report*, York, ILTHE.

Jarvis, P. (2000), 'The Changing University: Meeting a need and needing to change.' *Higher Education Quarterly*, vol. 54(1), pp. 43–67.

Kennedy, H. (1997), *Learning Works: Widening Participation in Further Education*, Coventry, Further Education Funding Council.

Parry, G. (1999), 'Education research and policy making in higher education: The case of Dearing', *Journal of Education Policy*, vol. 14(3), pp. 225–241.

Parry, G. and Thompson, A. (2001), *Higher Education in FE Colleges*, London, Learning and Skills Development Agency.

Parry, G. and Thompson, A. (2002), *Closer by Degrees: The Past, Present and Future of Higher Education in Further Education Colleges*, London: Learning and Skills Development Agency.

Postman, N. (1992), Technopoly, New York, Knopf.

Pring, R. (1999), 'Universities and teacher education', *Higher Education Quarterly*, vol. 53(4), pp. 290–311.

Robertson, D. (1999), 'The Dearing inquiry as process – delegated thinking and the limits of expert advice', *Higher Education Quarterly*, vol. 53(2), pp. 116–140.

Schon, D.A. (1987), *Educating the Reflecting Practitioner: How Professionals Think in Action*, San Francisco, Jossey Bass.

Smith, D. and Bocock, J.C. (1999), 'Participation and Progression in Mass Higher Education: policy and the further-higher education interface', *Journal of Education Policy*, vol. 14(3), pp. 283–299.

Weil, S. (1999), 'Re-creating universities for "Beyond the Stable State": from "Dearingesque"systematic control to post-Dearing systemic learning and inquiry', *System Research and Behaviourial Science*, vol. 16, pp. 171–190.

Chapter 11

Work-Based Learning and its Associated Risk

Gwendolen Bradshaw

Introduction

Health care has recently, been the focus of the news media for good reason. Systems failures and individuals have hit the headlines and exposed the need for an enhanced and more robust approach to the management of risks associated with patient care (Baker, 2001 and Kennedy et al., 2000). It has been acknowledged that even some of the more accepted practices such as mass screening are controversial and not without their risks (Gotzche and Olsen, 2000).

This chapter will provide the background and current approaches to clinical risk management in the NHS and its relevance for those educators in Higher Education who are responsible, together with their NHS stakeholders, for the education of health care practitioners. The ever increasing complex nature of health care provision within the NHS means that there is an element of risk involved. Indeed it would be true to say that on occasions there is a very high risk of adverse events occurring (DOH, 2001). Adverse events being defined as,

> an event or omission arising during clinical care and causing physical or psychological injury to a patient (DOH, 2000a: xii).

Many of these events are not inevitable. Based on a retrospective analysis of patient records Vincent et al. (2001) argue that about half are preventable. The challenge is to learn from these for a number of reasons including the potentially devastating consequences for patients and their families and the anguish experienced by health care staff involved in adverse events (DOH, 2000a; DOH, 2001a; Harpwood, 2001). A staggering 25,000 patients die each year in the NHS, 5,000 of whom die from hospital acquired infections (Comptroller and Auditor General, 2000 and Bristol Royal Infirmary Inquiry, 2001). In addition there are also huge financial implications, for example there is an estimated cost of nearly £1 billion to the NHS as a result of hospital acquired infections and £400 million a year being paid to settle clinical negligence claims (DOH, 2000a). These events and their consequences have undermined the confidence the general public have in the NHS which is another reason to assess and manage risk with a view to achieving better quality care and outcomes for patients. This challenge is not confined to the NHS alone but to health care providers worldwide and to those involved in the education and training of health care staff (Harpwood, 2001). Educators in Higher Education need to be aware that the hospital ward for example, a key area for student learning and their application of theory to practice, can be a dangerous place (Neale et al., 2001). This must be a factor that is considered when engaging in curriculum development (Alaszewski et al., 1998a). Educators are charged with the responsibility to produce health care practitioners who are clinically competent and 'fit for purpose' (UKCC, 1999). The New NHS, Modern, Dependable (DOH, 1997) marks a step change and sets out the Government's aims to ensure that highly trained, competent practitioners are in place to provide care. Initial or basic educational programmes are intended to produce practitioners in whom the public can have confidence of having the pre-requisite knowledge and skills to be admitted to a professional register, gain a licence to practice and do so safely. For example there is a statutory framework that defines the competencies that are required by those practitioners registering on the Nursing & Midwifery Council's professional register (Alaszewski,1998a). All relevant programmes in Higher Education must address these competencies and have appropriate assessment strategies in place. To this end the Department of Health commissioned the Quality Assurance Agency for Higher Education to undertake a Major Review throughout 2004–2006 of all Department of Health funded programmes to ensure that the above is the case. Any programmes within Higher Education Institutions found wanting will be required to put an action plan in place to address the identified deficiencies.

In the context of today's health service delivery with much shorter lengths of stay in hospital, earlier discharges and a public who are becoming increasingly discerning and willing to hold practitioners to account for their actions, the challenge to do this has never been greater (Walshe, 2001; Robinson, 2003). At both the micro level, when individual practitioners can be urged to take on new responsibilities and the macro Government policy level and the introduction of national initiatives, health care practitioners are constantly faced with new technologies and interventions and ever changing roles for which there is an on going need for education to prevent the risk of harm to patients (DOH, 1999). Not only is there a need to think about managing the new risks posed by taking on new roles but it is also important to reflect on the risks associated with the more taken for granted roles that practitioners have (Robinson, 2003).

Background to Risk Management in the NHS

It is worth noting at this point that the term 'risk management' only began to become commonplace in the NHS in the early 1990s with the introduction of a risk management guidance manual for all Chief Executives of NHS Trust Hospitals that was produced by the NHS Executive in 1993 (DOH, 1993). The NHS Executive strongly advised that the guidance be heeded. Prior to this there was no formal arrangement for risk management although many hospitals had components of risk management within their policies and procedures (Walshe, 2001). The following year many Trusts had begun to implement the guidance and had initiated risk assessments (Walshe, 2001).

Since then the whole approach to risk management has undergone a transformation. Rather than being something that was optional and only taken on board by interested clinicians and managers it is now a statutory, core function within NHS Trusts (Vincent and Walshe, 2001).

Adverse Events

Interestingly it was not until very recently that Government health policy made mention of 'harm' or 'adverse events'. Milligan and Robinson (2003) suggest that this may be because of a reluctance to face up to the enormity of the challenge which includes a major educational component or, that there was a degree of ignorance on behalf of the Government regarding the sheer scale of the problem at national level. It has been estimated that approximately 850,000 incidents or errors occur in the NHS annually (Harpwood, 2001). The need to learn from adverse events was introduced in the document entitled 'An Organisation with a Memory' (DOH 2000a). The document was informed by the report of an expert group, chaired by the Chief Medical Officer and convened to consider how the NHS could learn from adverse events. This was followed the next year by the publication of the Government's plan to reduce harm by more clearly identifying adverse events and learning from them. It was entitled Building a Safer NHS for patients (DOH, 2001a). There are a number of ways in which educators in Higher Education can facilitate this learning within pre-registration programmes including the production of reflective practitioners who are committed to lifelong learning.

The inclusion of the Health Service Ombudsman's annual report and various Government enquiries, which are published on a regular basis, in the delivery of the curriculum can provide a rich source of learning about adverse events as a means to the future management of risk. These enquiries include, to name but a few, 'The Confidential Enquiry into Stillbirth and Deaths in Infancy'; 'The Confidential Enquiry into Maternal Deaths' and 'The National Confidential Enquiry into Perioperative Deaths'. As these enquiries provide details of avoidable substandard care together with recommendations for professionals and directions for the future they represent an evidence-based resource for educationalists (Wilson, 2002).

Clinical Governance in the NHS and its Implication for Education

The publication of the White Paper entitled 'A First Class Service: Quality in the new NHS (DOH, 1998), the Document entitled Clinical Governance – Quality in the New NHS (NHSE, 1999) and The NHS Plan – A Plan for Investment, A Plan for Reform (DOH, 2000b) all paved the way for what is now a statutory duty for all NHS Trusts to meet the requirements of clinical governance. Clinical Governance is mainly concerned with procedures and processes including clinical risk management and clinical risk reduction programmes for ensuring the delivery of high quality, evidence-based clinical care in a consistent manner (Milligan and Robinson, 2003). Clinical Governance is viewed as inclusive thus making quality everybody's responsibility and requiring a new style of working which must be reflected in educational programmes (Lilley, 1999; UKCC, 2001). It has been described as:

> an umbrella term for everything that helps to maintain and improve high standards of patient care (Dimond, 2002: 88).

The need for a culture change was recognised with a shift from 'blame' to openness and transparency and a willingness to learn from adverse events and near misses (DOH, 2000 and DOH, 2001). Cultural changes do not simply occur overnight and staff were assured that they would be protected by whistleblowing legislation if they found themselves in repressive organisations (Wilson and Tingle, 1999 and DOH, 2001). This new approach has implications for educators, as the need for additional training for staff may be the outcome of an inquiry into an individual adverse event. In addition pre-registration programmes of study must reflect this new culture. Students must be supported appropriately if they report unsound practices and be protected from victimisation (Dimond, 2002). Close integration of practice and clinical teaching is essential with educators and practitioners working in partnership with both parties taking appropriate responsibility for the student experience (ENB and DOH, 2001).

The Government was keen to introduce an infrastructure that could be owned and implemented locally whilst also being mindful of the need to avoid local variations in standards of care. To this end the Government introduced evidence-based National Service Frameworks (NSF) and created the National Institute for Clinical Excellence (NICE).

NSFs form part of the external reference points which educationalists are required to map against their curricula. This ensures that programmes of education are aligned to service developments. Any guidance produced by the NICE is also expected to be incorporated into programmes of education both at pre- and post-registration level. This ensures that students and practitioners engaging in continuing professional development are being introduced to clinically effective, evidence-based practice of a nationally expected standard.

Further standardisation of the delivery of programmes of education of an acceptable standard saw the introduction of clinical benchmarking. There are now benchmark statements for most professional groups preparing to gain access to professional registers and potentially work in the NHS and again it is the expectation that these will be mapped against relevant programmes of study.

Attitudes and Values as They Relate to Risk Management and Education

Managing risk in the NHS requires practitioners to be able to discuss situations with patients and elicit individual patients' preferences and values (Mohanna and Chambers, 2001). This requires practitioners to be aware of their own attitudes and values.

The assessment of attitudes and values is notoriously difficult to achieve, but it is recognised that these professional attributes are very important (Bedford et al., 1993; Eraut, 1993; Hager et al., 1994). This challenge to assessment practices has sometimes been avoided with the emphasis being placed on knowledge and skills. Limiting the assessment of practice in this way has the potential to deny students the opportunity to learn from their experience and develop the requisite professional attitudes and values (Bedford et al., 1993; Boud et al., 1993; Bradshaw, 1997). Not only does the student need to develop a professional attitude towards those in his/her care but also the appropriate attitudes for critical thinking which is key to the new culture that the NHS is nurturing. These include intellectual humility and the courage to expose poor practices and to contemplate change based on sound evidence, integrity, perseverance and empathy (Miller et al., 1998; Taylor, 2000). Hager et al. (1994) conclude that the most reliable way of assessing attitudes and values is in the context of practice over a sustained period of time. Multiple sources of evidence can be used for the purposes of assessment including the production of portfolios and evidence from prior achievements in addition to the direct observation of the mentor and lecturer. Making the assessment of attitudes and values more explicit within the curriculum can also inculcate in students the need for a strong commitment to the code of professional conduct and explicit accountability for their performance (Chambers and Booth, 2001). Students can be encouraged through the use of reflection, to get closer to the patients' perspectives and to relate to them in more meaningful ways for example, by examining how values and culture influence interactions and care delivery (Usher, 1993; Moon, 1999; Sadala, 1999).

Reflective Practice as an Approach to Risk Management

Extensive research has demonstrated the positive contribution that reflection can make to learning including in particular, learning about risk (Argyris and

Schon, 1974; Alaszweski 1998; Johns, 2000; Robinson, 2003; Wilkinson and Mc Dowell, 2003). Reflection therefore, is seen as an important characteristic of a higher education. However Alaszewski et al. (1998b) found sparse evidence of its use in teaching about risk.

Whilst it is not the intention here to explore theories in relation to reflection in any great detail, a brief conceptual analysis is worthwhile concerning the part it has to play in the reduction of risk associated with clinical practice and patient care. It is generally agreed that the ability to reflect *on* and *in* practice leads to effective learning from practice (Rosie, 2000; NMC, 2002a). Indeed it could be argued that without reflection, learning potential can be missed, with lessons not being learned from adverse events or near misses (Neary, 2000; Wilson, 2002).

Although not all are enamoured with the use of reflection as a means of learning, students are becoming more familiar with reflection as the development of reflective capabilities features in most pre-registration courses. Health care students are being encouraged to learn from their day to day experiences through the use of reflection (Edwards and Knight, 1995; Johns, 2000; ENB and DOH, 2001; NMC, 2002a). This enables students to identify not only what they know but also to gain a better understanding of how they learn (Thorpe, 2000). By embedding reflection within the curriculum as a means of learning, the pre-registration programme can be tailored to the individual student experience as well as meeting the requirements of the professional. body (Dewar and Walker, 1999). It has been argued that the process of reflection on practice,

> validates personal experience as the foundation for learning (Dewar and Walker, 1999: 1465).

When reflection is linked inextricably to practice, the notion of taking a more responsible approach to the management of risk by learning from adverse events and near misses, can lead to the application of that learning by the multidisciplinary team in new future circumstances (Dewing, 1990; Rust, 2002). As with all clinical learning, reflection on practice cannot be taken for granted. In the case of pre-registration students, just because they understand the concept it does not necessarily mean that they can automatically engage in what is a complex endeavour (Brockbank and McGill, 1998). Educationalists must ensure that the process is managed because there is the danger that it is capable of inducing a destructive cycle of self-criticism leading to self-doubt (Atkins and Murphy, 1993; Quinn, 1998; Stefani, 1998; NMC, 2002a). Even when presented in a constructive way as part of the overall approach to clinical governance, students and practitioners can still find the process threatening as they critically re-assess their knowledge, values and feelings and are exposed to uncertainty and doubt. It has been argued therefore, that adequate student support should be available as the focus on clinical learning becomes translated into a sustained change in practice (Kemmis 1985; Hanson, 1996).

Reflection can be emancipating. Occupational socialisation into the health care professions which does not often encourage critique, custom and practice and taken-for-granted assumptions that act as constraints to learning can be revealed and challenged through its use and potential risk of harm can be identified through this process (Taylor, 2000; Wilson, 2002; Milligan and Robinson, 2003). It is important therefore, to encourage students actively to,

> develop the capacity to keep an eye on themselves, and to engage in critical dialogue with themselves in all they think and do (Barnett, 1992: 198).

The use of reflection within the curriculum is intended to develop practitioners who are not only more self aware but whose practice is informed by a number of different perspectives not least of which, is that of the patient (Sadala, 1999). Once an effective practice, which minimises or eliminates risk is identified it can be adopted and disseminated more widely through the use of the National Patient Safety Agency (DOH, 2001a). The National Patient Safety Agency is a key body set up within the national clinical governance framework with a remit that includes the learning from errors. Ultimately it can be argued that students' independence is enhanced through the use of reflection. Programme aims and objectives need to have explicit reference to risk and through the use of reflection students can be encouraged to become more self-aware, develop their critical analysis skills and increase their understanding of risk assessment and risk management by adopting a deeper approach to learning (Alaszewski et al., 1998b).

Student Safety as an Issue and a Responsibility

Clinical education is an integral component of any pre-registration programme providing students with opportunities to prepare themselves for the real world of professional practice. But it can be seen that the reality is that clinical settings, whilst essential for work-based learning, are or have the potential to be hazardous places where students can be harmed or cause harm to others. To prevent students for example incurring a back injury education and training is commonplace for students in relation to moving and handling. However a comparatively new area of concern and study is the increase in violence in care settings. Unfortunately the deaths of several practitioners in the course of their duties have occurred recently. Any programme of study therefore must address this risk and equip students with strategies to deal with actual or potentially violent situations (Littlechild, 2003). It is important to adopt a broad definition of violence within the curriculum that embraces not just physical violence but situations or instances that have an emotionally damaging effect. Littlechild (2003) promotes the RAP/Review model as a method of approaching this issue systematically. This includes recognition, awareness, planning and review activities. He also recommends a comprehensive approach by considering violence at three levels including personal, team and at organisational level.

Students can be coached in safe environments through the use of simulation and be introduced to local policies and Department of Health guidelines (Dimond, 2002). An emphasis should be placed on the practice of violence avoidance.

It is important that lecturers maintain records of all such curricula activity. There have been cases of lecturers being involved in litigation in respect of,

what they have taught, how it was taught and when (Dimond, 2002: 372).

Record keeping and maintaining ones own competence as a lecturer are obviously central to best practice.

The issue of vicarious liability is another example of the need to be mindful of arrangements in place to support students whilst engaging in work-based learning. Students tend to be supernumerary and therefore not considered to be an employee whilst on clinical placement. In the event of an adverse event involving either a patient, equipment or a student it is important that arrangements in relation to liability are addressed and clearly agreed between Higher Education Institutions and stakeholders who provide clinical placements for students. This can often be achieved in negotiation with the relevant NHS Workforce Development Confederation that commissions health care programmes.

Multiprofessional Education and the Concept of Risk

The need for coherent team work is essential when managing risk in care settings given that errors often occur due to different professional groups working in isolation rather than as part of a coordinated team providing seamless patient care (Moss and Paice, 2001; Wilson, 2002). Historically health care professionals were socialised into their respective professional group and did not enjoy the benefits of a multiprofessional education (Cable, 2002). This resulted in competitive, tribal and hierarchical practices with discreet divisions and boundaries which are obviously not conducive to team working (Moss and Paice, 2001). In the past health care workers did not have a full understanding of colleagues roles and did not have an appreciation of the stresses faced by different professionals. Indeed formal training in team working and team dynamics did not feature in pre-registration programmes. Given the very human nature of health care, team work is not seen as optional but essential (Wilkinson and McDowall, 2003). Students not only need to be able to function as a team member but they need to have the capacity to collaborate with peers and other professionals in learning. It has been suggested that the goals of multi-professional education are to develop appropriate attitudes and motivations for working with other professions and the competencies to practice collaboratively (Cable, 2002: 7).

The situation is changing and educationalists have risen to the challenge. There are now examples of very effective multi-professional education being delivered in Higher Education (Chambers and Booth, 2001; Moss and Paice, 2001; Glen, 2002). Morgan (2000) also points to the benefits of not only multi-professional but multi agency education which enables teams to learn to work in a more integrated way with mutually agreed goals and a shared understanding of how to achieve them. This has the potential of helping to address the issue of scapegoating and blaming within the health service by professionals valuing each other's contribution due to an enhanced understanding of what that contribution is.

Alternative approaches to programme delivery have also been introduced by educationalists. Opportunities for teams to learn in their work settings have been identified. Chambers and Booth (2001) argue that to bring about a cultural change teams need to experience interaction with one another as part of the learning process. Cable (2002) introduces a cautionary note by suggesting that any move towards multi-professional education must be evidence based with the ultimate beneficiary being the patient. Many of the policy documents concerning multi-professional education do not refer to its implementation resulting in some quite haphazard and localised initiatives (Glen, 2002). What is crucial however is that educationalists and employers do not create an additional theory practice gap for students with shared learning experiences not being translated into inter-professional working practices which have the potential to enhance the quality of patient care and ultimately reduce risk.

The Quality Assurance Agency for Higher Education has an explicit brief as part of major review to explore the extent to which Higher Education Institutions are responding to the need for the delivery of effective multi-professional education. This will be considered by review teams in the context of the overarching health professions framework and the Quality Assurance Agency code for placement learning (QAAHE, 2003).

Problem Based Learning (PBL) is another example of a strategy that has been successfully utilised to bring multi-professional groups together to learn. PBL is of particular value where programmes of study have a practice element as this element can be integrated and contextualised within the curriculum. Research suggests that PBL enables students to adopt an holistic approach to patient care whilst at the same time acquire the skills needed for team working (Wilkie and Burns, 2003). Both of these attributes are central to clinical governance and the necessity to be able to manage risk.

Both past and present experiences of working as a team member can have a positive as well as a negative influence on adult learners and affect their levels of confidence (Neary, 2000). Developing a curriculum that has an explicit strategy to ensure that work-based experiences lead to learning is important because no assumptions can be made that learning will take place spontaneously (Benner, 1984; Bewley, 1995; NMC, 2002a). Given the complex nature of clinical practice and the types of experiences that students will be involved in or exposed to, there are varying opportunities for learning in the psychomotor, cognitive and affective domains. Practical experience of being a multidisciplinary team member can become, through an interpretative or reflexive process, a form of personal knowledge for students (Usher, 1993). It has been argued that throughout the journey to becoming a professional, students pass through four stages from dependence to counterdependence to independence and eventually to interdependence and team working (Boud, 1988). During this journey it is important that students are given the appropriate level of support and constructive feedback about their performance. In terms of clinical education, facilitating this journey can be a challenge particularly when promoting student independence. There is sometimes a fine line between the development of student autonomy and the educator's responsibility and professional accountability in the event of an adverse event. Whilst students can learn to manage risk by observing role models there comes a point at which they have to develop their own skills. This requires skilled clinical educators based on their experience of supporting students to let go and take a risk but do so in a managed way (Cavanagh, 2002).

The Preparation of Lifelong Learners

Lifelong learning became embedded in national educational policy over a decade ago. Both educationalists and employers saw the skills associated with lifelong learning as necessary for a rapidly changing and potentially unpredictable working environment in the health sector (Training Agency, 1989; UKCC, 2001).

It is now the expectation that all those involved in health care have the skills associated with lifelong learning (DOH, 2001b). A salient goal of Higher Education is that health care students adopt the attitude that lifelong learning is necessary and that they need to acquire the requisite skills (Dearing, 1997; Fryer, 1997; NMC, 2002a). Knowles (1975) highlighted the essence of lifelong learning as being the move from learning how to be taught to learning how to learn. This cultural change and the shifting emphasis from teaching to learning has resulted in more student control and autonomy.

Lifelong learning skills can equip practitioners to realise their potential and also help them to shape, improve and modernise service delivery by playing an effective role in clinical governance (DOH, 2001a; Chambers and Booth, 2001). Students thus develop the ability to take a critical and reflective approach to their own performance and that of others, which aligns with the multi professional approach to risk management in today's NHS (Milligan, 1998). The constant change being experienced by NHS employees with the associated risks involved requires ongoing learning and therefore lifelong learning must be embraced truly as *a pedagogical ethic* (Knapper and Cropley, 2000: 14).

As circumstances and situations can vary so much, students need to be prepared to call on a variety of learning strategies to effectively respond to these experiences and learn from them (Knapper and Cropley, 2000). The acquisition of lifelong learning skills and an enquiring approach to practice have become curriculum outcomes (ENB, 1995; DOH, 2001b). There is a need however, to make students more risk aware and to emphasise risk assessment and risk management as explicit learning outcomes. Lifelong learners adopt a mind set that means that they set out with the deliberate intention of learning. This needs to be organised skilfully if it is to occur in the pre-registration curriculum. A structured approach is required where learning needs identified from near misses and adverse events are met.

The regulatory and the statutory bodies responsible for overseeing the quality of professional programmes have been emphatic about the need for lifelong learning skills being an integral part of any programme. The English National Board and the UKCC have in the past emphasised the centrality of this requirement as a learning outcome and the NMC continue to do so (UKCC, 1999; Phillips et al., 2000; NMC, 2002a).

Patient Involvement in Risk Management and the Curriculum

Patients and carers have a much more prominent role to play in all forms of health care and associated risk management and any curriculum concerned with health care must acknowledge this and be patient centred (DOH, 2001b; DOH, 2002). Students should be aware of the need for patients to have clear roles to play in the promotion and achievement of safety goals (Richardson, 2003). Involving patients and their carers in their health care is not new but actively involving them in risk management in this way is a relatively new concept requiring new ways of working for health care practitioners. It could be argued that a structured approach to risk can result in a more ethical environment in which to practice with mistakes or near misses being explored within the context of a no blame culture (Frith, 1999). Risk assessment in the context of health care can be argued to be as much an art as a science and students require enhanced communication and interpersonal skills and need to value the contribution that patients can make to the management of risk and the reduction of adverse events in an age where there is an increased awareness amongst the general public that health care can actually be harmful (Ryan, 2003; Milligan and Robinson, 2003). It could be argued that they need the skills to engage with the patient at five levels. Firstly to finding ways of explaining risks, secondly to consult with the patient and elicit their preferences and indeed their values, thirdly to support the patient in the decision-making process which may include an element of health education for example, fourthly to actually decide together and finally to act together in partnership (Blundell, 1999; Chambers and Booth, 2001). It is important to capture the patient's perspective and central to this is the notion of informed consent and all of the associated legal and ethical dilemmas. Negative assumptions about individual patient's capacity to make a contribution need to be challenged. Morgan (2000) advocates a very proactive approach with many patients being encouraged to actively participate in the assessment and management of their own risks. Students need skills to work in an environment where patients in their care may well be sceptical of health care practitioners given some of the very negative high profile media coverage mentioned earlier.

The Educational Process and Decision-Making in Relation to Risk

An effective approach to risk management depends very much upon sound decision-making. Dawson defines decision-making as,

> the thoughts and actions associated with a sequence of choices as well as the choices themselves (Dawson, 1992: 195).

It could be argued therefore that risk and decision-making are indeed two aspects of the same process.

All practitioners are held accountable for the decisions they make and in the context of contemporary care the emphasis on an evidence base in decision-making is fundamental. Practitioners are required to incorporate the best evidence into all they do (Gray, 1997). Any decision made can be scrutinised at any time. Within the framework of clinical governance with its national standards, policies and procedures there remains the need for practitioners to exercise their professional judgement based on their expertise and specialised knowledge. Therefore professional judgement and decision-making are important issues for educationalists (Alaszewski et al., 1998b). For practitioners decision-making can be fraught with difficulties and uncertainty, yet a study of social workers, learning disability nurses and district nurses found that there was,

> little evidence that practitioners had been trained in formal decision-making processes and that they used structured decision-making processes (Alaszewski and Alaszewski, 1998b: 123).

Given the associated complexity, uncertainty and the element of ambiguity that the decision-making process may pose to practitioners it is vital that the curriculum makes decision-making skills explicit as a learning outcome. The whole notion of competence should include competence in risk assessment and risk management Very early on in their education students can find themselves involved in very complex decision-making processes, some of which can have major consequences for the patient and indeed the practitioners involved. A structured approach to the teaching of decision-making within the curriculum can help to alleviate some of the anxieties and stresses experienced by practitioners in the work place (Alaszeski et al., 1998a). Given the multi-professional team approach to the delivery of care there is a need for practitioners to be able on occasions to negotiate and perhaps act as an advocate for patients in the decision-making process. Simulation and role-play based on real clinical decisions can be very useful strategies within the curriculum for providing the student with an opportunity to engage in decision-making in a safe environment. However Murphy and Atkins (1994) argue that attention should be given to ensure that students' experiences in the care setting are managed in such a way so that students can learn to manage risk but do so in a controlled way. Alaszewski et al. (1998a) suggest that one way of achieving this is through the use of appropriate role models. Although in the final analysis there comes a point when students have to learn to act with autonomy.

Conclusion

This chapter has considered the context for the management of risk within modern health services. It has identified its significance within the framework of clinical governance and has proceeded to analyse the inclusion of risk management as a formal entity within the curriculum that prepares health service practitioners. As part of this process essential attributes have been considered such as the development of the appropriate attitudes and values, reflective practice, student safety as a responsibility and multi-professional education in the management of risk. Furthermore, the centrality of lifelong learning as a pedagogical ethic, which is necessary to successful risk management along with the greater involvement of patients in the identification of risk and in the curriculum have been explored. The chapter has concluded that decision-making is a crucial element in risk reduction and while this should wherever possible be evidence based there is inevitable scope for the practitioner to employ intuitive evidence that comes from sound professional experience because it has to be accepted that there are many instances where validated evidence does not exist. Hence the need to nurture decision-making as a crucial part of the curriculum for health care professionals.

References

Alaszewski, A., Alaszewski, H., Manthorpe, J. and Ayer, S. (1998a), *Assessing and Managing Risk in Nursing Education and Practice: Supporting Vulnerable People in the Community*, English National Board, London.

Alaszewski, A., Alaszewski, H. and Harrison (1998b), 'Professionals, accountability and risk', in Alaszewski, A., Harrison, L. and Manthorpe, J. (eds), *Risk, Health and Welfare: Policies, strategies and practice*, Open University Press, Buckingham, pp. 89–103.

Argyris, C. and Schon, D. (1974), *Theory in practice: Increasing Professional Effectiveness*, Jossey-Bass, San Francisco.

Atkins, S. and Murphy, L. (1993), 'Reflection: a review of the literature', *Journal of Advanced Nursing*, vol. 18, pp. 1188–1192.

Baker, R. (2001), *Harold Shipman's Clinical Practice 1974–1998*. Department of Health, London.

Barnett, R. (1992), *Improving Higher Education*, SRHE/Open University Press, Buckingham.

Bedford, H., Phillips, T., Robinson, J. and Schostak, J. (1993), *Assessing competencies in nursing and midwifery education*, English National Board, London.

Benner, P. (1984), *From Novice to Expert: Excellence and Power in Clinical Nursing Practice*, Addison-Wesley Publishing Company, California.

Bewley, C. (1995), 'Clinical teaching in midwifery – an exploration of meanings', *Nurse Education Today*, vol. 15, pp. 129–135.

Blundell, C. (1999), 'Competence in healthcare', in Wilson, J. and Tingle, J. (eds), *Clinical Risk Modification: A Route to Clinical Governance*? Butterworth Heinmann, Oxford, pp. 141–171.

Boud, D. (1988), 'Moving towards autonomy', in Boud, D. (ed), *Developing student autonomy in learning*, Kogan Page, London.

Boud, D., Cohen, R. and Walker, D. (1993), *Using Experience for Learning*, The Society for Research into Higher Education and Open University Press, Buckingham.

Bradshaw, A. (1997), 'Defining "competency" in nursing (Part i): a policy review', *Journal of Clinical Nursing*, vol. 6, pp. 347–354.

Bristol Royal Infirmary Inquiry (2001), *Learning from Bristol. The report of the public inquiry into children's heart surgery at the Bristol Royal Infirmary, 1984–1995*. Department of Health, London.

Brockbank, A. and McGill, I. (1998), *Facilitating Reflective Learning in Higher Education*, The Society for Research into Higher Education and The Open University Press, Buckingahm.

Cable, S. (2002), 'The context – why the current interest?', in Glen, S. and Leiba, T. (eds), *Multi-professional Learning For Nurse*, Palgrave, Basingstoke.

Cavanagh, M. (2002), 'Being a mentor', in Canham, J. and Bennett, J. (eds), *Mentorship in community Nursing: Challenges & Opportunities*, Blackwell Science, London, pp. 180–187.

Chambers, R. and Booth, E. (2001), *Clinical Effectiveness and Clinical Governance Made Easy*, 2nd. edn., Radcliffe Medical Press, Oxford.

Comptroller and Auditor General (2000), *The Management and Control of Hospital Acquired Infection in Acute NHS Trusts in England*, Department of Health, London.

Dawson, S. (1992), *Analysing Organisations*, 2nd. edn, Macmillan Press, London.

Dearing, R. (1997), *Report of the National Inquiry into Higher Education*, HMSO, London.

Department of Health (1993), *Risk Management in the NHS*, HMSO, London.

Department of Health (1997), *The New NHS, Modern, Dependable*, HMSO, London.

Department of Health (1998), *A First Class Service: Quality in the new NHS*, Department of Health, London.

Department of Health (1999), *Making a Difference; Strengthening the nursing, midwifery and health visitor contribution to health and healthcare*, Department of Health, London.

Department of Health (2000a), *An Organisation with a Memory*. Report of an expert group on learning from adverse events in the NHS chaired by the Chief Medical Officer, The Stationary Office, London.

Department of Health (2000b), *The NHS Plan- A Plan for Investment, A Plan for Reform*, HMSO, London.

Department of Health (2001a), *Building a Safer NHS for patients*: Implementing 'An Organisation with a Memory', The Stationary Office, London.

Department of Health (2001b), *Working Together, Learning Together*, The Stationary Office, London.

Department of Health (2002), *Involving Patients and the Public in Health Care*, The Stationary Office, London.

Dewar, B.J. & Walker, E. (1999), 'Experiential learning: issues for supervision', *Journal of Advanced Nursing*, vol. 30(6), pp. 1459–1467.

Dewing, J. (1990), *Reflective Practice*, Senior Nurse, vol. 10(10), pp. 26–28.

Dimond, B. (2002), *Legal Aspects of Nursing*, 3rd edn, Longman, London.

Dineen, M. and Walshe, K. (1999), *Clinical Negligence litigation and the NHS*, Project Report 7, Health Services Management Centre, The University of Birmingham.

Edwards, A. and Knight, P (1995), 'The assessment of competence in higher education', in Edwards, A. and Knight, P. (eds), *Assessing Competence in Higher Education*, Kogan Page, London.

English National Board (1995), *Creating LifeLong Learners: partnerships for Care*, English National Board, London.

English National Board and Department of Health (2001), *Developments in multiprofessional education. Placements in Focus. Guidance for education in practice for health care professionals*, ENB and DOH, London.

Eraut, M. (1993), *Assessing Competence in the Professions*, Methods Strategy Unit, Educational Department, Sheffield.

Frith, L. (1999), 'Clinical risk modification and ethics', in Wilson, J. and Tingle, J. (eds) (1999), *Clinical Risk Modification: A Route to Clinical Governance?*, Butterworth Heinmann, Oxford, pp. 172–186.

Fryer, R.H. (1997), *Learning for the Twenty-first Century: First Report of the National Advisory Group For Continuing and Lifelong Learning*, DfEE, Sheffield.

Glen, S. (2002), 'Inter professional education: the way forward', in Glen, S. and Leiba, T. (eds), *Multi-professional Learning For Nurses*, Palgrave, Basingstoke.

Gotzche, P.C. and Olsen, O. (2000), 'Is screening for breast concer with mammography justifiable?', *The Lancet*, vol. 355, pp. 129–133.

Gray, J.A.M. (1997), *Evidence-based Healthcare*. Churchill Livingstone, Edinburgh.

Hager, P., Gonczi, A. and Athanasou, J. (1994), 'General issues about assessment of competence', in *Assessment and Evaluation in Higher Education*, vol. 19(1), pp. 3–16.

Hanson, A. (1996), 'The search for a separate theory of adult learning. Does anyone really need andragogy?', in Edwards, R., Hanson, A. and Raggatt, P. (eds), *Adult*

Learners, Education & Training: boundaries of adult learning, Routledge in association with The Open University, London.

Harpwood, V. (2001), *Negligence in Healthcare. Clinical Claims and Risk*, Informa UK Limited, London.

Johns, C. (2000), *Becoming a Reflective Practitioner*, Blackwell Science, London.

Kemmis, S. (1985), 'Action research and the politics of reflection', in Boud, D., Keogh, R. and Walker, D. (eds), *Reflection: Turning Experience into Learning*, Kogan Page, London.

Kennedy, I., Howard, R., Jarman, B. and McLean, M. (2000), *The Inquiry into the Management of Care of Children receiving Complex Heart Surgery at the Bristol Royal Infirmary. Interim Report-Removal and Retention of human Material.* The Bristol Royal Infirmary, Bristol.

Knapper, C.K. and Cropley, A.J. (2000), *LifeLong Learning in Higher Education*, 3rd edn., Kogan Page, London.

Knowles, M. (1975), *Self-Directed Learning. A Guide for Learners and Teachers*, Follett Publishing Company, Chicago.

Lilley, R. (1999), *Making Sense of Clinical Governance*, Radcliffe Medical Press, Oxford.

Littlechild, B. (2003), 'The risk of violence and aggression to social work and social care staff', in Kemshall, H. and Prichard, J. (eds), 5th edn., *Good Practice in Risk Assessment and Risk Management 1*, Jessica Kingsley Publications, London, pp. 159–175.

Miller, A.H., Bradford, W.I. and Cox, K. (1998), *Student Assessment in Higher Education*. A Handbook for Assessing Performance, Kogan Page, London.

Milligan, F. (1998), 'Defining and assessing competence: the distraction of outcomes and the importance of educational processes', *Nurse Education Today*, vol. 18(4), pp. 273–280.

Milligan, F. and Robinson, K (2003), 'Introduction, aims and mapping health care', in Milligan, F. and Robinson, K. (eds), *Limiting Harm in Health care. A Nursing Perspective*, Blackwell Publishing, Oxford, pp. 1–16.

Mohanna, K. and Chambers, R. (2001), *Risk Matters in Healthcare: communicating, explaining and managing risk*, Radcliffe Medicine Press, Oxford.

Moon, J. (1999), *Reflection in Learning & Professional Development. Theory & Practice*, Kogan Page Ltd, London.

Morgan, S. (2000), *Clinical Risk Management. A Clinical Tool and Practitioner Manual*, The Sainsbury Centre for Mental Health, London.

Moss, F. and Paice, E. (2001), 'Training and supervision', in Vincent, C. (ed), *Clinical Risk Management: Enhancing patient safety*, 2nd ed, BMJ Books, London, pp. 341–354.

Murphy, K. and Atkins, S. (1994), 'Reflection within a practice – led curriculum', in Palmer, A., Burns, S. and Bulman, C. (eds), *Reflective Practice in Nursing*, Blackwell Scientific, London.

Neal, G., Woloshynowych, M. and Vincent, C. (2001), 'Exploring the causes of adverse events in NHS hospital practice', *Journal of the Royal Society of Medicine*, vol. 94, pp. 322–330.

Neary, M. (2000), *Teaching, Assessing and Evaluation for Clinical Competence: A practical Guide For Practitioners And Teachers*, Stanley Thornes (Publishers) Ltd., Cheltenham.

NHS Executive (1999), *Clinical Governance: Quality in the new NHS*, Department of Health, London.

Nursing & Midwifery Council (2002a), *Requirements for Pre-registration Midwifery Programmes*, Nursing & Midwifery Council, London.

Nursing & Midwifery Council (2002b), *Code of Professional Conduct*, Nursing & Midwifery Council, London.

Phillips, S., Schostak, J. and Tyler, J. (2000), *Practice and Assessment: An evaluation of the assessment of practice at diploma, degree and post graduate level in pre-and post-registration nursing and midwifery education*, English National Board, London.

Quinn, F. (1998), *Continuing Professional Development in Nursing: A Guide for practitioners and educators*, Stanley Thornes, Cheltenham.

Robinson, K. (2003), 'Being a professional – a defence against causing harm?', in Milligan, F. and Robinson, K. (eds), *Limiting Harm in Health care. A Nursing Perspective*, Blackwell Publishing, Oxford, pp. 42–60.

Rosie, A. (2000), 'Deep Learning', *Active learning in Higher Education*, vol. 1(1), pp. 45–59.

Rust, C. (2002), 'The impact of assessment on student learning', *Active Learning in Higher Education*, vol. 3(2), pp. 145–158.

Ryan, T. (2003), 'Risk, residential services and people with mental health needs', in Kemshall, H. and Prichard, J. (eds), *Good Practice in Risk Assessment and Risk Management 2*, 4th. edn, Jessica Kingsley Publications, London, pp. 159–173.

Sadala, M.L.A. (1999), ' Taking care as a relationship: a phenomenological view', *Journal of Advanced Nursing*, vol. 30(4), pp. 808–817.

Stefani, L. (1998), 'Assessment in partnership with learners', *Assessment and Education in Higher Education*, vol. 23(4), pp. 339–350.

Taylor, B.J. (2000), *Reflective Practice: A Guide for Nurses and Midwives*, Open University Press, Buckingham.

Thorpe, M. (2000), 'Encouraging students to reflect as part of the assignment process', *Active Learning in Higher Education*, vol. 1(1), pp. 79–92.

Training Agency (1989), *Enterprise in Higher Education, Guidance for Applicants*, Employment Department Group, Sheffield.

United Kingdom Central Council (1999), *Fitness for Practice. The UKCC Commission for Nursing and Midwifery Education*, United Kingdom Central Council, London.

United Kingdom Central Council (2001), *Professional self-regulation and clinical governance*, UKCC, London.

Usher, R. (1993), 'Experiential learning or learning from experience: does it make a difference', in Boud, D., Cohen, R. and Walker, D. (eds), *Using Experience for Learning*, The Society for Research into Higher Education and Open University Press, Buckingham.

Vincent, C., Neale, G. and Woloshynowych, M. (2001), 'Adverse events in British hospitals: preliminary retrospective record review', *British Medical Journal*, vol. 322, pp. 517–519.

Vincent, C. and Walshe, K. (2001), 'Clinical risk management and the analysis of clinical incidents' in Clememts, R. (ed), *Risk Management and Litigation in Obstetricks and Gynaecology*, Royal Society of Medicine Press Ltd, London, pp. 79–93.

Walshe, K. (2001), 'The development of clinical management', in Vincent, C. (ed), *Clinical Risk Management: Enhancing patient safety*, 2nd ed, BMJ Books, London, pp. 45–60.

Wilkie, K. and Burns, I. (2003), *Problem-Based Learning*, Palgrave, Basingstoke.

Wilkinson, J. and McDowall, J. (2003), 'Harm reduction in context – the scope of nursing practice', in Milligan, F. and Robinson, K. (eds), *Limiting Harm in Health care. A Nursing Perspective*, Blackwell Publishing, Oxford, pp. 61–78.

Wilson, J. and Tingle, J. (1999), 'Conclusions and the way forward', in Wilson, J. and Tingle, J. (eds), *Clinical Risk Modification: A Route to Clinical Governance?*, Butterworth Heinmann, Oxford, pp. 187–195.

Wilson, J. (2002), 'Principles of clinical governance', in Wilson, J. and Symon, A. (eds), *Clinical Risk Management in Midwifery*, Books For Midwives, Oxford, pp. 1–14.

Chapter 12

Educating for Risk: How Social Work Degree Students Prepare to Practise as Social Workers

Ros Day

Introduction

Social workers deal with risk in relation to a large number of different groups of service users. Risk to children who are in danger from adults who are also their carers is probably the most high profile in the sense that cases which go disastrously wrong make headlines in the media and sometimes result in public inquiries. However, risk is also an issue for social workers who are working with mental health service users. The public policy agenda seems to emphasise the risk to the public posed by mental health service users. This may therefore mean that the risks to the service users themselves of medication or of abuse or discrimination are downplayed. Social workers working with older people may have to assess the risks or benefits of remaining in their own home or moving into supported accommodation. Thus risk and the assessment of risk are an integral part of many types of social work.

In this chapter I will discuss risk, using examples from social work relating to child welfare. I will then consider how social work students are prepared through their training to deal with risk, reflecting in particular on the courses and students I work with. Lastly, I will draw the two aspects of this discussion together to make some tentative conclusions about how social work students are and might be, prepared to meet risk in their working lives as social workers.

Risk in Promoting Children's Welfare

'I recognise that those who take on the work of protecting children at risk of deliberate harm, face a tough and challenging task.' (Laming, 2003: 3)

'There is currently no mechanism for routinely identifying those children who are at risk of harm or getting into trouble.' (Denham, 2002)

'Without ignoring the importance of effective child protection, improving quality of life rather than minimising risk may provide a better sense of purpose for everyone concerned about child welfare.' (Bentley, cited in the Guardian, 24.9.2003)

'The murder of seven-year-old Toni-Ann Byfield, shot dead with her convicted crack-dealer father in north London last week, has raised concerns about how well social workers assess the risks posed to children who are under their protection.' (The Guardian, 24.9.2003)

The above quotes illustrate the confusing picture that might face a would-be social work student considering entering the social work profession in the twenty first century. Lord Laming's quote suggests that the trainee social worker is entering a challenging and difficult arena where some children are deliberately harmed by the people who are supposed to be caring for them. The first Minister for Children and Young People, John Denham MP seems to be proposing that the job of dealing with children at risk of deliberate harm might be improved by establishing better systems, procedures and mechanisms. So the intending social work student might wonder if their proposed career may involve them in implementing new and developing systems and proce-dures for dealing with risks to children. The third quote considered here may lead the social work trainee to wonder about the emphasis in the first two quotes and think about how far their role as a social worker will be about improving children's welfare through improving the quality of their lives and might ponder how this could best be achieved. Lastly, the aspiring social work student will be all too aware that when children are harmed but are known to social services their work may well be criticised; as has been the case after the murder of Toni-Ann Byfield. Social work assessments of risk of harm to children are therefore both an integral part of social work, but also, if some disaster occurs and a child dies, of the public's scrutiny of social workers and their daily work.

Each new public inquiry into the non-accidental death or injury of a child known to social services has led to further scrutiny of the work done by social workers, in particular, to protect vulnerable children. Since the death of Maria Colwell in 1973 until the Laming Report in 2003 into the murder of Victoria Climbie; a series of public inquiries have problematised the ways that social workers have acted, or failed to act, when a child has been killed but is 'known' to social services. Social workers have been criticised for doing too much or too quickly or on insufficient evidence in some cases: as in Cleveland in 1986–7or Orkney in 1991 where children were removed from their homes in cases of suspected sexual abuse. In these cases the rights of parents were seen as being flaunted and the professionals were viewed as some sort of family storm troopers. Alternatively, social workers have been parodied in the press for their naivety in believing parents will look after their children and for failing to act quickly enough to remove children from family settings that they later died in. This CE 'damned if you do and damned if you don't' culture of blaming social workers for children's deaths, has been discussed and analysed by social work academics and other cultural analysts in recent years.

One of the key words that appears in the scrutiny of social work 'failures', as these child deaths are often presented, is the word 'risk'. Douglas (1992), in her outstanding series of essays analysing 'risk and blame', suggests the development of a 'blame culture' in modern societies such as the United States of America and the U.K.. She points out that since the 1970s 'risk' has become, 'an academic growth area' (1992: 10) a period which has also seen the development and professionalisation of risk analysis, based on notions of rational individual choice. Her political analysis of risk which sees it as located within the morality of each culture and therefore implicitly political, is very different to the 'scientific', objective and individualistic approach of the risk analysts. Douglas insists that 'risk' must be seen in its social context not as a matter of individual choice which extracts the individual decision-maker from their social context. She sees the dominance of the term 'risk' as a new cultural phase in which every death has to be, *'chargeable to someone's account ...'* (1992: 15), where death cannot be accepted as part of life, but must be blamed on someone, preferably with the possibility of financial compensation for the dead person's relatives. Douglas establishes that in modern societies 'risk' has come to be seen in only negative terms. In the past the term 'danger' might have been used, but 'risk' has a more technical and scientific nuance, which fits a modern industrialised culture better.

Douglas's analysis can be applied to the situation of the contemporary social worker. In the context of the deaths of children known to social services, the dangers they face are primarily from their carers. However, it is the front-line social workers who are blamed for failing to correctly assess that the child was 'at risk' from her carer. Therefore the culture of blame focuses on the perceived failings of social workers rather than the dangers that some children face from their carers within family settings. This emphasis on risk and blame therefore means that technical fixes, new and better procedures and better trained social workers are seen as the solution, rather than a critical analysis of the dangers to children of family life in modern societies. I would argue that this is profoundly political and represents a discourse which does not problematise family relations but instead focuses blame on organisations and workers. This organisational and procedural emphasis fits very well with the emphasis of John Denham MP in his 2002 speech and in some of the recommendations of both the Laming Report (2003) and the Green Paper 'Every Child Matters' which followed its publication. Our would-be social worker might be feeling somewhat daunted in their choice of career having considered some of this debate.

Unpicking the Meaning of the Term 'Risk'

In a chapter entitled 'Managing Risk and Decision-Making', aimed at the first generation of under-graduate social work students on the new B.A.s in Social

Work that began in September 2003, O'Sullivan (2002: 269–276) notes that concern about risk amongst social work practitioners has led to an increase in proceduralism and defensive practice. Thus social workers may try to carefully follow procedure and cover their backs, resulting in unnecessary caution to the detriment of children's interests and their own job satisfaction. He is sceptical about the uncritical use of risk assessment checklists which oversimplify the complexity of factors that will have to be considered when making an assessment of risk in each particular situation. He states that risks should only be seen as part of any assessment and have to be looked at alongside needs and resources (see also Milner and O'Byrne 1998: 25). Alternatively, he proposes the use of strengths and hazards analysis as developed by Brearley (1982) and Kemshall and Pritchard (1996). In this type of analysis the term risk is replaced by both the positive term 'strengths' and the negative term 'hazards' thus making the assessment a better rounded balance of positives and negatives associated with any change or decision to maintain the status quo. He is at pains to point out that he is not proposing 'excessive' risk-taking but feels that the assessment he suggests will lead to informed risk-taking. He also emphasises the importance of recognising that any future oriented changes are always complex and uncertain and not straightforward or unproblematic.

In the earlier book by Brearley (1982) he explores a variety of concepts often related to risk from his analysis of the use of the term risk in the Insurance industry and in technical and scientific fields. These concepts are: probability; uncertainty; hazard; danger; risk taking. Brearley proposes that social workers are mainly concerned with managing hazards (1982: 27–28): that is with trying to minimise loss and negative outcomes for the service users they work with. He suggests that hazards and dangers can be separated out: 'hazards' referring to existing factors (actions, events, deficiencies etc.) that introduce or increase the possibility of an undesirable outcome; whilst 'dangers' refers to a feared outcome of a hazard (a loss outcome) (1982: 83). For any one situation where risk is being assessed a list can be made of the hazards and dangers for each person involved: a child, a mother, a father, a grandmother, a social worker for instance. This can be set against a list of 'strengths' or positive factors which decrease the likelihood of dangerous outcomes. These lists can be further refined by consideration of predisposing and situational hazards (1982: 84) and can also be prioritised by considering the gravity of the danger, its importance or its imminence. The comparative lists of hazards/ dangers and strengths can be made for the current situation and for each potential course of action. Brearley recognises that this process is both time consuming and not necessarily straightforward: for instance one factor: 'being in hospital', may be both a strength and a hazard in certain circumstances. However he feels that such a framework allows the social worker and service users to be involved in careful reflection before actions are taken.

'The risk analysis framework will not remove the fact of a variability in possible outcomes. Nor can it remove uncertainty and the inevitable element of subjectivity in social work.' (Brearley, 1982: 91)

He emphasises that social work by its nature is uncertain and such careful analysis is therefore only a tool to enable social workers to continue working in risky situations where they might otherwise become paralysed by anxiety about the uncertain outcomes of their work (1982: 134–5).

Case Study

Many Social Work programmes in universities began a new Bachelor of Arts degree in September 2003. The move towards making social work a degree only profession reflects changes that have occurred in other public sector welfare professions, such as teaching and nursing. It could be argued that this change will improve the status of social work as a profession. The three year degree gives students a longer time to learn relevant theory and research as well as to experience a wider range of practice placements.

The new social work degrees are governed by the National Occupational Standards for social work under the auspices of the General Social Care Council. Included in the 'operational process skills' as one of the 'competences' is the ability to 'manage risk'. 'Key Role 4' encompasses both 'unit 12' 'Assess and manage risks to individuals, families, carers, groups and communities' and 'unit 13' 'Assess, minimise and manage risk to self and colleagues'. Therefore assessment and management of risk to a wide range of individuals and groups is seen as an integral part of the social work role (see www.topss.org.uk for further details of these National Occupational Standards).

In order to explore how one particular course is preparing its students for managing risk, I interviewed the course director. She saw the main context for students to learn about risk in teaching students about assessments in general. A number of first level modules allow students to be introduced to the concept of risk, from a variety of perspectives. The first module in which students will explore the concept of risk is an introductory module in Social Work Theory and Legal Perspectives. This module is taught in the second term of the first year, and thus students will be able to start to think about risk fairly early on in their course. The module is taught by an experienced social work academic alongside a practicing lawyer. This facilitates students in learning about both the theory and concepts associated with risk and the ways that risk is encountered in legal and practice settings. During this term the students are out of the university for four days a week doing their first practice placement. This therefore allows students to see how the theory they are learning is operationalised in practice. The connections between theory, research and practice are actively explored with the students throughout the second and third terms of their first year.

The course director saw the approach to learning about risk as necessarily multi-layered as students will develop their understanding of risk through later second and third year modules and in two later practice placements. Later modules allow students to consider risk in more depth within particular areas of social work, such as mental health and working with people with disabilities. Final year specialist modules about working with adults, or with children and families, also incorporate critical understanding of risk. In their second and third placements students will encounter how risk is operationalised in a variety of practice settings and will be encouraged to build on their initial learning about risk. Varied understandings of risk are also encountered in third level modules dealing with multi-disciplinary working and with communication in social work. The course director felt that students' understanding of the complex realities of social work practice enables better understanding and allows the students to apply what they have learned. Agencies who provide students with placements were questioned by the Placement Coordinator about which of the Key Roles outlined for social workers should be included in their first placements. Interestingly they all suggested that Key Role 4 dealing with risk was best left until the students' second and third placements. This arguably illustrates the complexity that social work agencies attribute to working with risk.

The course director suggested that students vary in their confidence about dealing with risk. She pointed out that many students don't initially realise that risk is one aspect of most assessments because the word is not specifically used, or perhaps is not clearly defined. Students sometimes wanted identified sessions on risk but the course director felt that it was better integrated into a number of modules across the whole programme and throughout the three years as this allows a deeper and better informed understanding of the complexity and variety of risk that students will encounter as social workers. She reflected that high profile cases in the media about social work 'failures' make students acutely aware of their individual responsibilities as social workers and of the necessity of accountability. In some cases, students are anxious about their ability to respond to risk. The course director expressed concern that defensive practices in social work may stop social workers from being as imaginative, inventive and creative as they might otherwise be. She observed that students who experienced placements in organisations where they felt supported from within the organisation through constructive supervision and positive management were able to grow in confidence as they felt both supported and trusted. However, students who experienced management that was intrusive and constantly felt under surveillance tended to be conservative and unable to take risks.

I also questioned second year Diploma in Social Work students at one university about their understanding of risk. I asked them to explain what they understood by the term 'risk'. The majority gave a predominantly negative definition: mentioning harm, negative outcomes or injury. However some saw risk as being about 'balancing probability with possibility': identifying possible harm and possible benefits. Secondly I asked them how far they felt their social work course had prepared them to deal with risk. All students felt that they had been well introduced to a number of aspects of understanding throughout the whole course. Some students specifically mentioned the difficulty of dealing with risk as a student on placement in the light of changing procedures for assessing risk. Some mentioned anxieties about the risks they would face as social workers if they took the wrong actions: for instance that they would lose credibility, may experience mental health problems, face disciplinary action or litigation. Opinion varied on the need for a specialist module about risk as part of the course, and a minority thought this would be helpful. Other students were more concerned with keeping up-to-date with changing models of risk assessment when they started practicing as social workers after they qualified.

Lastly, I interviewed recently qualified practicing social workers who are currently working in social work area teams. One social worker, working with children and families stated that risk is integral in all aspects of her work. She is involved in the assessment of risk for the service users she works with, for instance the risks to a child of the social worker doing further emotional damage to an already damaged child. A social worker must also weigh up the risks to herself as a professional in working with children and their families. These risks include risks of physical attack by service users and the emotional risks involved in some of her work in distressing circumstances. These difficult aspects of the work are hard to prepare for. She suggests that whilst courses can prepare new social workers to be aware of risk in a general sense, it is easier to learn about the realities of risk as it is experienced in the particular area of social work that you specialise in after completing your initial professional training. Thus, she views the understanding of risk as best located firmly in practice settings. She felt that training specific to the actual specialism and job role should be ongoing as part of a social worker's professional development. Another worker, specialising in work with adult mental health service users, pointed out that risk assessment which really involved a service user in understanding and reflecting upon their current situation and possible changes they might make could be empowering and help the service user recover a better quality of life. Unfortunately she did not feel that all workers were equally committed to taking the time and making the necessary effort to enable this to happen, meaning that risk assessment was sometimes imposed upon service users rather than involving them as integral to the process.

Conclusion

In this chapter I have discussed the confusing and somewhat contradictory picture facing would be social work students when they consider risk in relation to social work. Reflecting on Douglas's analysis of our culture as one that emphasises, individualises and technicises risk, our social work student may, rightly, expect to be faced with an array of apparently technical risk assessment and management checklists. However, reading the work of Brearley and O' Sullivan the student may feel that they could be more actively involved in assessing risk by breaking it down into hazards, dangers and strengths and then analysing any situation in the light of this analysis. This gives the social worker more professional autonomy and creativity and therefore may be, I would argue, more satisfying. However, this ideal may not be achievable in practice if the new worker finds themselves in a busy office with a complex and demanding caseload. For this to work well there needs to be sufficient investment in time and training for new social workers, and this therefore raises issues of central government funding of social services.

The would be social worker may also feel that they would be blamed if anything went wrong in cases they were working on. Certainly, Douglas establishes the existence of a 'blame culture' within societies with an emphasis on risk. Cases like that of Toni-Ann Byfield do lead to scrutiny of social work action or inaction, in the media and by politicians. There is a difference between being held accountable and being blamed, with the latter being much less justifiable and clearly worrying the existing students I interviewed. A social work culture that is defensive may be the reality that many new social workers find in their offices and may not be the best circumstances in which to practice.

Lastly, the social worker may feel anxious about their choice of career, recognising that they will be working with the complexities and messiness of people's lives. The authors I have considered and the National Occupational Standards for Social Work make clear that uncertainty and risk are integral to social work. However, by giving students and social work staff the confidence and frameworks to work with risk they may find this challenging task ultimately satisfying.

References

The Guardian (24/9/2003), *When the Wild World's Roots are in the Home.*

Brearley, C. Paul (1982), *Risk and Social Work*, Routledge and Kegan Paul, London.

Denham, J. (2002), 'Address to the local government association seminar on supporting children and their families', Local Government Association, London.

DfES (2003), *Every Child Matters*, Cm 0672, The Stationery Office, London.

Douglas, M. (1992), *Risk and Blame: Essays in Cultural Theory*, Routledge, London.

Dowie, J. (1999), 'Communication for better decisions: not about "risk"', *Health Risk and Society*, vol. 1(1), pp. 41–53.

General Social Care Council (GSCC), *Code of practice for social care workers*, GSCC, London.

Kemshall, H. and Pritchard, J. (eds) (1996), *Good Practice in Risk Assessment and Risk Management*, Jessica Kingsley, London.

Laming, H. (2003), *The Victoria Climbie inquiry report*, Cm 5730, The Stationery Office, London.

Milner, J. and O'Byrne, P. (1998), *Assessment in Social Work*, Basingstoke Macmillan.

O'Sullivan, T. (2002), 'Managing risk and aecision making', in Adams, R. et al., *Critical Practice in Social Work*, Basingstoke Palgrave.

Parton, N. (2001), 'Risk and professional judgement', in Cull, M-A. and Roche, J. (eds), *The Law and Social Work*, Basingstoke Palgrave.

Chapter 13

Knowledge Capture, Knowledge Rendering and Knowledge Use in a Metropolitan Fire Service

Trevor Austin

Introduction

Inquiries into knowledge capture and use have hitherto focused primarily on commercial organisations who seek to gain competitive advantage through individual and organisational development (Blackler, 1995). Such inquiries have yielded interesting typologies (Blackler, 1995) and revealed significant contrasts between formal descriptions of work and the ways in which work is actually carried out (Brown and Duguid, 1991).

A large metropolitan fire service offers a different milieu in terms of work practices, hierarchical structures and the relationships between knowledge, learning and action. Here, a range of significant risks rather than commercial imperatives are at work. In this context knowledge is 'rendered', that is, significantly reduced and simplified, to make it accessible during acute situations. This rendered form of knowledge, henceforth referred to as a Standard Operating Procedure (SOP), emerges as an organisationally significant 'thing'. But how does it connect with the action? Is it an harmonious and dualistic one as Wenger (1998) suggests, or is it a more uneasy and potentially counter-productive one where practice and procedure become disconnected so that personal and group views conflict with the organisational ones?

In exploring these relationships SOPs also emerge as important for training and learning since there are important connections between how knowledge is captured, rendered and then conveyed as organisational views of tasks and their resolution. There is a training and learning paradox here since SOPs are 'stiff' forms of knowledge that are often inadequate in highly dynamic situations. Using such procedures with rich, local practices rendered out, may actually increase risk rather than reduce it. Hence, the case study brigade, in depending on routinised forms of knowledge, may need to consider different processes of shared understandings and therefore different forms of learning and training.

The chapter is structured around answering these questions and exploring the relationships that exist between knowledge, learning and action. The initial section considers some of these relationships. The organisational view of risk and the ways in which it is reduced are then considered. The case study brigade's own definition of risk as 'a measure of the likelihood that the harm from a particular hazard will occur, taking into account the possible severity of the harm' (see Home Office, 1998) is used throughout. The closing section reports on the status and impacts of SOPs as reported by a sample of fire service trainers and operational staff, and re-considers their role in risk reduction. Finally, the implications of these findings are considered with reference to the implications for training and organisational learning more generally.

Risk, Learning and Knowledge

The focus upon rendered knowledge arises from a broader awareness of fire service activity. In particular, the approach to and delivery of, training activity and the ways in which learning from incidents is held and used. The SOPs currently have a central role in this since they embody organisational views of tasks, which in turn inform broader training patterns. Like the SOPs, which I will discuss later, training is conceived and delivered in standardised forms and is highly behaviourist in character. By this I mean that knowledge is presented in its finished form so that learning is centred on standardised drills. Learning is thus highly observable, at least in practical scenarios. Much training is also focused on equipment and key tasks both within initial training and the operational training that follows it. It is also particularly amenable to observation and competence-based systems of functional analysis and accreditation (Jones and Moore, 1993). The brigade concerned has recently introduced a National Vocational Qualification (level 3) in Fire Operations for initial and probationary training and is actively looking at ways to extend the competency model into other functional areas. Indeed, the Fire Service nationally is introducing a competency model to underpin all of it's training and professional development.

There is of course a potential tension between packaged and specified levels of performance and the highly dynamic situations in which fire crews frequently find themselves. How can such training, centred as it is on the 'unit' level and the work of the individual, prepare fire fighters for 'real world' activity which is undertaken almost exclusively in groups and which requires the integration of several skills? The brigade's general approach to training and its growing attachment to competency formed the initial focus of this study since the relationships between learning (training), knowledge and action are generally portrayed as central to organisational development (Garvin, 2000).

It is to the knowledge component of that relationship that I now turn. Knowledge is held to be a central feature of post-industrial societies and much work has been done by Blackler (1995), among others, into the ways in which that knowledge is held. In one hundred observations of training sessions, knowledge was invariably presented as highly stable in ways that parallel the tension between knowledge and action in the argument set out above. Furthermore the question needs to be addressed, how do the knowledge forms of the brigade as apparently fixed, procedural forms of knowledge, sustain and inform those operating in highly dynamic and potentially dangerous situations? Researchers such as Brown and Duguid (1991, p. 1) have noted how 'formal descriptions of work and of learning are abstracted from actual practice'. This suggests that the links between knowledge and action, mediated through or around organisational views of tasks, could be revealing, with additional implications for training and other knowledge forms.

Further questions emerge from these ideas. One of the most intriguing, though difficult to answer, is the extent to which highly procedural knowledge, the 'embedded' form described by Blackler (1995), could actually heighten rather than reduce risk. The logic inherent in this of course is that procedure somehow conditions and predisposes those who practise to certain responses and that such conditioning can be dangerous in novel or unexpected situations. In this milieu the role played by SOPs thus becomes compelling since there is a potential 'double-bind'. Thus, following procedures can, a priori, condition the right responses yet may not fit local variations. Contrariwise, deviating from the procedures in order to respond to local conditions carries the potential for blame if things go wrong. Such comments are highly speculative but raise important questions as to the decision-making of incident commanders as they reconcile risks to their team, to members of the public and to valuable property. They also reflect the politics of organisations and work since controlling practice is seen as controlling risk. This requires a clear view of what needs to be reified and what can be left to participation (Wenger, 1998) and the ways in which participation itself can be shaped by good training and learning.

While the initial sections of this chapter will describe the methodology and report findings from interviews and documentary sources, the concluding sections will synthesise theory, policy and evidence from the sources described above.

Risk Management in the Fire Service

There are two elements to risk assessment across the United Kingdom (UK) Fire Services. The first of these is Operational Risk Assessment and the second is Dynamic Risk Assessment. Both systems are driven by incidents but the first set is directly concerned with the situations that confront fire-fighters while the second is a generic process of responding to risk regardless of the incident. Confusingly, the Operational Risk Assessment is broken down into some thirty-two 'Generic Model Risk Assessments'. These are categorised into five sections and have been produced to help brigades in their response to regulatory requirements. These five sections are:

- Responding to emergencies
- Carrying out rescues
- Fighting fires
- Incidents involving transport
- Generic hazards

Each Generic Risk Assessment has three sections. First, there is a description of the scope of the activity covered, the significant hazards and risks, the key control measures and technical references. Secondly, there are bullet-point lists of considerations (many of which find their way into the SOP's) and, finally, a summative table of the risk assessment. In 'lay' terms these identify the nature of risk in particular situations, for example at car fires or people trapped in collapsed buildings. These are detailed and comprehensive descriptions and represent accumulated experience from thousands of incidents. Senior officers periodically review these, though 'use' is confined to incident commanders. Those who lead the fire crews at incidents undertake assessment of risk.

Standard Operating Procedures are also informed by Dynamic Risk Assessment (Home Office, 1998) which enshrines the moral, economic and legal aspects of health and safety. That is recognising and controlling risk. Brigades have a responsibility, in common with other employers, to protect employees under Sections 2 and 3 of the Health and Safety at Work Act (1974). They must also seek to protect the public and the environment when attending incidents. Additionally in the case of the public, the Court of Appeal decided in 1997 that a fire authority could be held accountable in respect of property loss resulting from negligent fire fighting by its fire officers. This decision followed a case where a fire officer attending an incident shut a sprinkler system down leading to the spread of a fire and the subsequent destruction of a building (Hartshorne et al., 2000).

Dynamic Risk Assessment is defined as 'the continuous assessment and control of risk in the rapidly changing circumstances of an operational incident' (Home Office, 1998, p. 10). This system has a number of key features but two are worthy of note. First, as stated above, the overall responsibility for the application of the system lies with the incident commander. At a small incident this may be the most senior fire-fighter present; at a very large incident it could be the Chief Fire Officer for the brigade. The second feature is that incidents and the responses to them are divided into three stages: The initial stage, development stage and closing stage.

The initial stage is the most crucial phase in that it involves the early evaluation of the incident, the risks that are present and how these might be reduced. Decisions made at this stage are frequently irreversible and are made at high speed. Once the initial risk assessment has been done (a mental process) the incident commander must then select and apply safe systems of work. This is the point at which procedural knowledge is invoked, including of course, the SOP. Commanders are then required to assess the chosen system of work against the risks involved. They are required to pose and answer the question 'are the risks proportional to the benefits?'

The development stage requires an incident commander to constantly monitor a situation, reviewing the effectiveness of existing control measures. Particular vigilance is required to ensure that new hazards are identified and controlled. Incident commanders must also ensure that the operational activities themselves don't produce risks to people or the environment or that fire crews do not become fatigued.

The closing stage ensures that the process of dynamic risk assessment continues until all personnel and machinery has left the incident. Information for the post-incident review is gathered at this stage. Incident commanders de-brief crews before they leave the incident.

It will be clear from the above that there is immense pressure on incident commanders to assess risk appropriately and to be reflexive in their thinking and operation as the incident unfolds. SOP's constitute, as we shall see, a broad guide to action but much is left to the training, experience and support given to the individual concerned. If the incident itself is highly novel then past experience, whether organisational or individual, may be a limited guide to action.

In drawing attention to a generic risk assessment, the aim is to highlight how procedural knowledge both shapes and falls out of wider processes. The generic practices described here were referred to in an earlier section as operational risk assessments which despite the term 'generic' are specific responses to types of situations encountered by operational fire-fighters. The three sections dealing with these practices have also been set out. They are important in that they validate the brigade's current practices and shape other forms of knowledge such as Standard Operating Procedures. They also illustrate a definitive, organisational view of tasks and, when rendered, contribute directly to SOPs.

The Generic Risk Assessment for incidents involving rescues from trenches or pits for example, begins by cross-referencing the material to relevant legislation and other Generic Risk Assessments. Incident Commanders 'learn' or rehearse these assessments during desktop exercises but also revisit them in post-incident evaluations. In the trench collapse example significant risks and hazards are identified along with the key control measures. For example a significant hazard is the weight of soil (1.25 tonnes per cubic metre) and a key control measure might include the use of ladders and air bags for shoring. The attention of incident commanders is drawn to six technical references. The lists of control measures and other considerations are very detailed and could never be used operationally. Hence, this knowledge is distilled or rendered into a Standard Operating Procedure, a short summary of key points from the Generic Risk Assessment and the Dynamic Management of Risk and full operating procedures. In rendering these sources considerable information is lost and is, it is assumed, held elsewhere, such as in practice. Fire crews refer to this as 'experience' and, as we shall see, it is the dominant knowledge form. The extent to which knowledge is 'rendered' to make it accessible and useful at an incident can be gauged by comparing a generic risk assessment with the full and standardised operating procedures that follow it. The SOPs, the distillation of highly complex and technical information, are laminated and carried by fire crews to operational incidents. I will describe their subsequent use later.

The Relationships between Knowledge and Work Practices

The potential relationships between an organisational view of tasks and the way in which work is actually carried out have already been alluded to whilst considering the work of Brown and Duguid (1991). Citing the work of Orr (1987, 1990) they illustrate how an organisation's view of work can overlook and even oppose what and whom it takes to get a job done. They further assert that 'it is the actual practices, however, that determine the success or failure or organisations' (Brown and Duguid, 1991, p. 2). These observations are of direct relevance in this study since, as we shall see, SOPs are rarely invoked at incidents but function as 'knowledge of last resort'. At the heart of this of course is the organisational assumption that complexity can be successfully mapped onto simple canonical steps. In the case of private companies of course such use of 'rendered' knowledge is underpinned by a reduction in initial and on-the-job staff training and labour costs. In the case study fire service it is about reducing organisational risk, both in terms of injuries and of litigation. Giddens (1976, 1979, 1986), on the other hand, focuses on the idea of routinisation itself – the habitual, taken-for-granted activities of day to day working. Here, knowledge is locked into practice and wholly implicit. Giddens (1976, 1979, 1986) rightly recognises the importance of making such implicit knowledge accessible using the term 'knowledgeability' to capture the highly 'learned' nature of day to day work. Procedural knowledge in the Fire Service could be seen then as an attempt to frame and express accumulated experience in ways that link it to 'embrained' or conceptual knowledge. However, making knowledge visible does not inevitably lead to its use. Giddens remarks that:

> Knowledge of procedure, or mastery of the techniques of doing social activity, is by definition methodological. That is to say, such knowledge does not specify all the situations which an actor might meet with, nor could it do so; rather, it provides for the generalised capacity to respond to and influence an indeterminate range of social circumstances (Giddens, 1989, p. 22).

This infers that distilled or rendered versions of knowledge can be re-combined to construct transferable responses to real world problems. No novel situation is beyond resolution by knowledge of procedure and the mastery of specific techniques. If I understand Giddens correctly, it raises an interesting question regarding the way in which mastery and procedure become combined to resolve novel situations. My own inquiry suggests that mastery itself either absorbs or discards procedure and does not rest easily alongside it. The relationship between the procedure and knowledge locked into practice appears to be an inherently unstable one.

Blackler's (1991) work also raises fundamental questions about where knowledge is held, and whilst his typology is highly permeable, it helps to identify knowledge forms and how knowledge shifts within organisations. Whilst Blackler's work is also interesting for conceptualising aspects of work practices it is entirely grounded in commercial settings. Nevertheless, it becomes clear that, on the surface at least, the Fire Service is what Blackler (1991) would term a 'knowledge-routinised' organisation. That is, where knowledge is embedded in technologies, rules and procedures. Yet the work of a fire service is dynamic, it does not operate a production line and has to respond to novel situations and unforeseen tasks. Hence, it can be said to embody features of other organisations in Blackler's (1991) typology. Two overlapping terms used by Blackler (1991) resonate here in conveying the unique nature of fire service work. These are 'expert' and 'expertise'. A fire service has few experts in the terms intended by Blackler (1991); there are no black-boxed skills, expertise is commonly held and held in common. There are hierarchical and historical reasons for this. One is that there is a single point of entry into the Fire Service, a common point or origin regardless of subsequent career trajectory. The second is that fire fighters become the source of much new knowledge and inform the procedures themselves. They are at the heart of the action and experience first hand the ways in which changing design, technology and social settings throw up the unexpected. It is a management responsibility to 'render' this knowledge into new procedures and to encourage their use among those who initiated the new knowledge. Another reason is that senior fire officers still attend live incidents, albeit infrequently. Thus, the functional separation of those who undertake core activities and those who supervise them is more diffuse than might be expected in what others (see Hartshorne et al., 2000) have termed 'quasi-militaristic' organisations.

The work of Wenger (1998) in distinguishing between the explicit and the tacit, what is represented and what is assumed, extends, confirms and disrupts a priori views about procedure and work in a fire service. Of course much of it, including Wenger's work, focuses on the ways in which individuals become a part of communities of practice, how co-operation as incidental activity helps to resolve real-world problems unrecognised by codified procedures. In a fire service, communities of practice and procedures are integrated and formalised even if the processes of induction, initial training and early accreditation are somewhat individualised. Like Brown and Duguid's (1991) technicians, Wenger's (1998) claims processors find short cuts as well as forms of interdependence to define and shape their communities of practice. Fire fighters reproduce identical processes but in a more formal context and where practice is honoured and theory is disdained. The role of the SOP in connecting the action with knowledge is thus an uneasy as well as an unstable one.

I have already noted drawing on the work of Brown and Duguid (1991) how formal descriptions of work and of learning are abstracted from actual practice. This circularity probably accounts for the way in which they are disconnected. They represent practice itself. However SOPs are not only informed by practice; a wide range of outside sources also shapes them. All change is externally initiated, the brigade does not 'imagine' odd or unexpected events. SOPs are informed for example by new manufacturing standards (e.g. air bags in cars), central government (e.g. the potential use of dirty bombs) and the Health and Safety Executive. Some discretion is exercised by the brigade in the timing and implementation of changes but most external change is incorporated following the guidelines recommended by the issuing authority. There is no discretion in the case of Improvement Notices. The Health and Safety Executive issue these following the deaths of fire crews. These are infrequently issued, the last one following the deaths of two fire fighters at a poultry factory in Hereford in 1994. Health and Safety issues and such notices have an immediate and significant affect across all brigades. As Hartshorne et al. note:

> The HSWA is working to directly affect the activities of brigades served with notices, but is also having an influence on other brigades, and indeed a more significant influence than the influence of negligence liability (Hartshorne et al., 2000, p. 517).

The Methodology

Any attempt to describe and analyse the capture, rendering and subsequent use of a procedure, even an apparently straightforward item such as a SOP, will require a multi-method approach. The nature of the information needed and the setting from which it would be drawn, required eliciting views and reactions from practitioners as well as using documentary sources and direct observation. An exploratory approach framed both the data gathering and the subsequent analysis. In gaining insights into the ways that Standard Operating Procedures are initiated, revised, disseminated and used, I undertook seven semi-structured interviews with senior and junior fire service staff across different functional areas of the case study brigade. Surveying and 'gutting' documents provided considerable background to the formal processes and procedures, as well as the organisational view of the ways in which tasks, both situationally and in terms of generic processes, should be carried out. Direct observation of training sessions was undertaken initially to fulfil the requirements of a university training course but the range, location and number of those observations provided clear insights into the nature of training and learning for both novices and operational fire fighters.

These methods contribute to what is largely a descriptive approach with some reflexive accounts. Extended quotations from the interviewees are used to evoke a clear sense of practitioner views of SOPs. This approach reveals the connections between the actions and the procedures. In linking research questions to research strategy Robson suggests that 'what' questions 'lend themselves to a flexible design strategy which is likely to be a multi-method case study' (2002, p. 36). Of course, documentary sources and interviews are second-hand. They rely on organisational and individual memory, interpretations of events as well as feelings and attitudes. Hence there was an intent to observe 'real' events which can be seen as a clean source of date. It has inherent validity.

The process of analysis can be likened to 'grounded theorising' where qualitative data is generated by the perspectives of various groups involved in a setting, the documentation of the problems that they face in their lives, and the description of the strategies that they have developed to deal with problems. As Sapsford and Jupp point out though, 'this provides a general framework for the analysis, but the substance must come from the data' (1995, p. 13).

The responses to the questions were analysed in a practical and straight-forward way. The responses were read and re-read and notes were made alongside comments which seemed to confirm or challenge the findings of the authors cited above. This involves of course, selecting some parts of the data and ignoring others. In some areas individual terms are highlighted while in others extended quotations are used where it appears to voice something said by others or something that was revealing or profound. No systematic content analysis was undertaken. Rather, the responses were left to speak for themselves with themes or terms emerging from the 'thick description' (see Geertz, 1988).

In adopting this approach a number of themes did emerge that seemed to disrupt as well as confirm the relationships between knowledge forms and work practices espoused by Giddens and others. These themes centre on the ways in which procedural knowledge and work practices are 'incorporated' one into the other; where procedural knowledge is used as a last resort or where the relationships between the explicit and the tacit are 'uneasy' or 'unstable'.

Research Background

The work of the metropolitan brigade used for this research is similar to other emergency services in large urban areas and reflects social and economic problems as well as the traditional activities of domestic fires and road traffic accidents. It is one of 52 public fire authorities in England and Wales whose duties to provide fire and other cover are set out in the Fire Services Act (1947). The case study brigade covers an area of 800 square miles and serves two million people. During the financial year 2000–2001 it handled 90,720 emergency calls and responded to 51,749 incidents. Of these, 2,896 were malicious calls and 2,583 were fires in domestic premises. Attendance at fires still dominates the brigade's work (11,673 fires involving people and property and 15,726 small fires such as burning rubbish) although the proportion of special service calls is growing. These include road accidents and chemical spillage. There is no legal obligation to attend these latter incidents. There were additionally 8,516 cases of arson and 17,314 false alarms with good intent. In the same year 16 people were killed by fire and 44 fire-fighters were injured. To meet this workload the brigade has 1,698 full-time fire-fighters, 162 retained (part-time) personnel and 234 non-uniformed staff. There are 50 fire stations which can deploy 66 front-line appliances. The workload and pattern of work vary according to geographical location. The busiest stations are in large urban areas where 5,000 incidents may be attended in a year. Stations close to motorways are also very busy. The quietest stations may attend less than 500 incidents each year and will not be permanently manned. The brigade has been commended for reducing deaths from fire from 40 per year in 1992 to 16 in 1993. Greater effort is being placed on fire prevention but the resources of the brigade, including its training effort and knowledge base, are largely directed to attending incidents.

Establishing the relationships between the SOPs and action involved exploring the perspectives held by the seven interviewees regarding definitions, experience and the issues they associated with using the SOPs. Although two of the respondents were in a training role, all had substantial operational experience (at least 15 years). Three of the interviewees were part of a centralised operations function and were responsible for the rendering of information into SOP format. The remaining respondents were deployed as operational fire fighters, one of whom was a station commander.

The Status and Impact of Standard Operating Procedures

The interviewees began to elaborate on the role of SOPs when they were asked to define and describe them. All underscored the dominance of practice over procedure, how participation had displaced the reified. Some responses settled on a 'common-sense' view of SOPs with phrases like an 'idiot's guide to fire-fighting' being used by one respondent. Others stressed more neutral terms such as a 'checklist' and a 'condensed guide from policy' which clearly link back to organisational views of practice and indirect attempts to control it. Only one interviewee defined them as 'safe working practice for use at an incident' – their formal and correct role. In a similar vein, other responses alluded to the ways in which they might connect with the action stating that they are a 'guide to action' or a 'confirmatory tool'. One trainer described them as a 'utopian ideal' implying the kind of disconnected role for SOPs that many were to assert later in their interviews. All of the respondents made some connection with risk assessment insofar as SOPs could help incident commanders to avoid silly or avoidable mistakes though this in no way guaranteed their use at an incident. Another interviewee asserted that they might reduce the number of short cuts or corner cutting that had been going on in the past. The formalisation and standardisation of responses to incidents thus begins to emerge. Most of the interviewees stressed that 'they make you safety aware'. This in turn implies something that is one step removed from the action.

The particular connections that exist between the organisation's view of a task and how these might contrast with actual practice began to emerge. Four interviewees (those who were operational at the time of the research) said they were hardly used – that they had become disconnected from practice or incorporated into it. All interviewees suggested that they were probably only used in certain circumstances because most work at incidents was 'done automatically'. It was suggested that the rendered information in the SOPs was so distilled that it had lost its purpose. References were made to their use in new and novel situations whilst it was noted how in busy stations such situations rarely arose. When prompted most interviewees conceded that novices to a station or to the brigade might use them but they stressed that such individuals are always put on the busiest fire tender in order to acquire knowledge quickly. Procedural knowledge was rarely invoked at incidents and never in training. Knowledge, it was suggested, was not held in procedures but in the fire crews themselves. Here, participation rather than reification is given 'objective' status. The remarks of a station commander illustrate and clarify the kind of use to which incident commanders might put an SOP. His comments include related issues and I quote them at length as a way of integrating wider concerns and views.

> SOPs lay down normal thought processes. They reflect the list culture of the fire service and the routine mentality that goes with it. An incident doesn't follow a list. It is the unknown we need. We routinely ignore most SOPs. 80–90 per cent of work at an incident is done automatically. The only question I need to ask at an incident is whether it is safe. Can I commit personnel? If I'm unsure about something I ring mobilising (the communication centre). They are usually written the wrong way around. The information you need is at the very end. We need non-standard operating procedures. Just having the wind blowing a different way can alter the whole way you respond to an incident. They don't affect the outcome of an incident. I'd be quite concerned if one of my watch commanders was using one at an incident.

Such comments underscore how procedural knowledge is used as a last resort and how it is disconnected from practice. What Wenger (1998) refers to as 'reificative stiffness' – the way in which the rigidities of policies have to be bent to stop them becoming counter-productive – begin to emerge here. Incidents are dealt with using the tacit knowledge of the crews to resolve the tension between the rational (their response) and the habitual (the 'stiff' procedure). Another fire officer, currently in a training role, suggested that SOPs were not yet settled, even though they had been around since 1996. He also noted that incident commanders were reluctant to deviate from them even though:

> a lot of things aren't standard. People stick to what's in them even though they're not actively used at incidents.

The relationship between the SOPs and practice is thus seen as an uneasy one since interviewees gave differing views on the impact of SOPs. Those who used them saw them differently to those who rendered them. Some viewed them as a guide with considerable scope for discretion, while others felt that as part of the risk assessment process they should operate more as a checklist.

The uneasy and problematic relationship between procedural knowledge and work practices is further illustrated and extended by a number of other responses made by the interviewees. Several of them regarded SOPs as 'too basic' to be useful; arguing that they enshrined common-sense thinking which could be ignored as it is already known. Yet, the interviewees freely acknowledged that they could be caught out in novel or unexpected situations. In disconnecting the procedures from the action, obscure or forgotten information is that which needs to be invoked. Of course, a large fire service is not a homogenous organisation in terms of the demands placed upon it. Whilst the relationship between procedures and practice in a busy fire station can readily be characterised as 'uneasy', 'unstable', 'disconnected' or 'last resort', the situation in other parts of the organisation may be rather different. Here the novel and unexpected are commonplace. The disconnection between procedure and practice also takes on new forms as new or inexperienced crews build their shared practices. Additionally, I referred earlier to the virtual absence of specialists or experts in the fire service but several interviewees described how this situation is currently changing very rapidly as hazardous materials and technical rescue officers are deployed to an increasing number of incidents. Hence, the way in which knowledge is held is changing but not in ways that necessarily invoke SOPs.

Risk, Knowledge and Standard Operating Procedures

This inquiry has sought to explore some of the relationships between particular knowledge forms and how these are used to control the work practices of fire officers and fire fighters. Their observations on these connections suggest that these relationships are as problematic as those described elsewhere (see Brown and Duguid 1991 and Wenger, 1998). However, this is not an oppositional relationship, which hinders or compromises working practices, but a more subtly unstable, uneasy and disconnected one. This arises both from the nature of fire service work (dangerous, dynamic and resolved in short time scales) and the organisational responses to and views of those tasks. These attempts to provide codified behaviours that seek to convey flexible (though essentially static) responses to highly dynamic situations are inherently problematic in their relationship to risk. As significant contributors to these procedures, fire fighters have absorbed them into their practice leaving incident commanders to invoke them in obscure ways (knowledge as last resort) to resolve the unexpected and the novel. This constitutes a 'paradox' of risk since procedural knowledge forms may not provide the necessary local and shared understandings that fire crews appear to need. Blackler (1995) for example, draws a sharp distinction between the embedded knowledge of routinised organisations which focus on familiar problems and encultured knowledge where the focus is on novel problems. The fire service may need to re-define the nature of the problems it faces and therefore the way in which it defines risk itself.

The ways in which the relationships are mediated through training processes are also interesting and potentially significant. There is a paradox here too that runs in parallel with knowledge and risk. In focussing on a 'standard' kind of learning where the knowledge or skill is deemed stable and well defined and where there is a competent trainer who knows what is to be learned, risk is heightened because crews are learning something that isn't stable or well understood in advance.

Conclusion

It is clear from work practices of fire crews that the live action is held to be central and the procedural disdained, though this relationship shifts up and across the organisation. Work practices and procedure also converge in ways that are not reproduced elsewhere (Lave and Wenger, 1990). However, as abstractions of past and accumulated practice, enlightened by expert views, SOPs appear not to function in the ways that they were intended. As knowledge rendered from a range of sources they over-simplify and denigrate tasks and in attempting to distil knowledge and practice, become disconnected from it. Yet, actual practice inevitably involves tricky interpolations between procedure and situated demands as incident commanders seek to reduce financial and human risks. However, these are not improvised strategies but 'tacit knowledge', collective and cumulative, brought to bear in 'known' but infinitely novel situations. This approach and these relationships do not always protect the organisation either from injuries to workers or litigation from those who have not been well served.

References

Blackler, F. (1995), 'Knowledge, knowledge work and organisations: an overview and interpretation', *Organisation Studies*, vol. 16(6), pp. 102–126.

Brown, J.S. and Duguid, P. (1991), 'Organisation learning and communities of practice: toward a unified view of working, learning and innovation', *Organization Science*, vol. 2, pp. 40–57.

Garvin, D. (2000), *Learning in Action – A Guide to putting the Learning Organisation to Work*, Harvard Business School, Boston.

Geertz, C. (1988), 'Works and lives: The anthropologist as author', Polity, Cambridge.

Giddens, A. (1976), *New Rules of Sociological Method*, Hutchinson, London.

Giddens, A. (1979), *Central Problems of Social Theory*, Macmillan, London.

Giddens, A. (1986), *The Constitution of Society*, Polity Press, Cambridge.

Hartshorne, J., Smith, N. and Everton, R. (2000), *Caparo under Fire: A study into the effects upon the Fire Service of Liability in Negligence*, Blackwell, Oxford.

Jones, L. and Moore, R. (1993), *Education, Competence and the Control of Expertise*, Carfax, Abingdon.

Lowe, J. and Wenger, E. (1990), *Situated Learning: Legitimate Peripheral Participation*, Institute for Research On Learning, IRL Report 90-0013 Palo Alto, CA.

Orr, J. (1990), *Talking about machines: An Ethnography of a Modern Job*, Unpublished Ph.D thesis, Cornell University.

Robson, C. (2002), *Real World Research*, Blackwell, Oxford.

Sapsford, R. and Jupp, V. (eds), (1995), *Data Collection and Analysis*, Sage, London.

Wenger, E. (1998), *Communities of Practice: Learning Meaning and Identity*, Cambridge, Cambridge.

Chapter 14

Negotiating Risks in Career Development

Charles P. Chen

Introduction

This chapter attempts to address and elaborate on the notion of risk in the context of vocational and career psychology. Notwithstanding an increasing interest in the topic of risk in a range of disciplines in the social sciences and humanities (for example, Caplan, 2000; Lupton, 1999a, 1999b), the notion of risk is less frequently and explicitly discussed in the vocational psychology and career development literature. Thus, knowledge enhancement in theory and practice in the careers studies is called upon to draw more attention to the risk phenomenon – a dynamic and complex variable that has more significant impact on individuals' vocational wellbeing than ever before in our current world of work and beyond. Following this intent, the chapter sets out to show the relevance of integrating the risk concept into the consideration of individuals' worklife and career development experiences. In understanding the risk construct from academic and lay perspectives, the chapter intends to consider and illustrate more optimal ways of risk management in one's life-career development practice. It argues that for effective risk-coping behaviour, individuals need to learn to locate and embed the risk construct within a more holistic, resilient, and constructive thinking frame. More specifically, the chapter discusses the role and function of risks in the broad context of vocational and career psychology, outlining the rationale and necessity to understand and deal with the risk construct in one's worklife reality. Based on that, the chapter proceeds to propose some considerations that will help individuals negotiate and cope with risks in their vocational life experiences, yielding helpful implications for career development practice and intervention.

Comprehending Risks in the Worklife and Career Context

To comprehend the risk phenomenon in the context of individuals' worklife and career development, this section will first present a rationale of recognizing vocational risks. It will then examine some main sources of vocational risks.

Finally, it will take a look at how the notion of risk is delineated and perceived in vocational psychology. Combined, these three aspects attempt to provide some conceptual foundation for negotiating and managing risks in people's life-career journey.

Recognition of Vocational Risks: A Rationale

The notion of risk has captured increasing attention in several areas within the general domain of social sciences and humanities for the last two decades (Bauman, 1993; Beck, 1992; Caplan, 2000; Douglas & Wildavsky, 1982; Giddens, 1994; Lupton, 1999a, 1999b; Wynne, 1996). Scholars and researchers have looked at the risk phenomenon in a variety of human contexts that include social, societal, political, cultural, economic, technological, and other environmental dimensions. Social scientists, especially sociologists, social anthropologists and philosophers in sociology have made considerable effort in explaining the role of risk in our postmodern and postindustrial society. These explanations appear to provide much needed intellectual insights in understanding the movement and function of a complex macro-ecological system in our world today – the continuing changing context of post modernity. The knowledge yielded at this philosophical level is indeed stimulating. Parallel to the scholarly debate it has generated about the critical social and societal issues a risk society has to deal with systematically in the postmodern era, it points to the necessity of comprehending and dealing with the risk construct as a common phenomenon in lay people's daily life experiences. This is because it is at this more practical and micro-level that the lay public becomes aware of the risk impact on their everyday life experience, seeking ways to deal with the risk emergence. Risk-taking and risk-coping, therefore, become not only the topic of epistemological debates among the experts, but also meaningful discourses in lay people's life narratives (Wynne, 1996).

Individuals' worklife or vocational aspects of life experience are a pivotal component of one's total life structure (Chen, 2001; Peterson & Gonzalez, 2005; Super 1990). Similar to other aspects of one's social and personal life experiences, one's worklife involves various risks. They range from minor risk variables such as taking on a boring piece of work assignment, to more serious risk factors such as choosing a wrong occupation that is conflicting with one's sense of value and/or personal interest. The worklife-related risk has its apparent impact on a person's vocational wellbeing, and consequently affects other aspects of one's total life as well, given that vocational wellbeing is part of a person's general wellbeing (Amundson, 2003a; Crites, 1981; Cochran, 1990; Young & Collin, 1992). This interconnectedness of one's life experience and vocational experience necessitates the need to focus on studying, understanding, and more importantly, seeking ways in managing risks in people's worklife and career development.

Drawing attention to the risk phenomenon in the vocational context is, therefore, a worthwhile effort that aims to eventually enhance one's total life quality. Of note, the dynamic and fast-changing nature of the current world of work generates many more risk factors than ever before (Caplan & Teese, 1997; Cappelli, 1999; Cartwright & Cooper, 1997). This reality calls upon scholars, researchers, and practitioners in vocational and career psychology to collaborate more closely in searching for creative ideas and effective mechanisms that can help people cope with risks in a risky world of work. Likewise, workers who are actively engaged in their vocational aspects of lives and prospective workers who endeavour to enter the world of work may benefit from gaining increased risk awareness as well. This awareness can make them more advantaged in a self-helping process, that is, the more knowledgeable they are about the risk phenomenon, the better they are prepared to encounter the risk circumstance, and the more capable they become in dealing with the risk factor.

Source Analysis of Vocational Risks

There are a variety of risks in people's worklife and career development experience, and these risks are caused by an array of very diverse, dynamic, and sometimes complicated reasons. While some of the risks may be generated by natural causes, the majority of the risks are largely the results of human interaction. Although this section of the discussion is intended to take a very brief glance at some of the risk phenomena related to people's worklife and career development experience, it is important to note that these phenomena can never be separated from other aspects of people's life experience. This is because, as mentioned earlier, vocational life is always an integral part of one's total life experience. Thus, it is impossible to funnel vocational risks out of other risks in one's general life experience. Neither is it possible to make vocational risks as isolated variables that only have impact on people's worklife and career development experience. In this sense, vocational and career risks are always perceived and handled within the broad life-career context.

Social and Societal Risks

Worklife is a form of social action and activity, and thus it is first and foremost affected by risks yielded from the general social and societal environment. As the original sources for nearly all kinds of risk factors, the social and societal environment here reflects a very broad and inclusive human ecological system rather than a narrowly defined social domain (Patton & McMahon, 1999). Termed 'macro-sociological-ecology (MSE)', this vast and comprehensive system attempts to serve as a large umbrella that covers an array of branches that form the macro and micro social functioning of both the general society and the individuals who make a living in the society. The general social and societal environment as presented by the MSE system covers a range of major facets that are social, cultural, political, economic, and technological in nature.

It is these facets of the MSE system that provide the breeding basis to generate risk dynamics affecting people's vocational aspects of life.

The social and cultural conditions can always play a vital role in constituting risk factors (Caplan, 2000; Lupton, 1999a, 1999b). A deep-rooted social and/or cultural value may affect one's career choice in a profound way. Gender stereotyping, for instance, is a very typical example in this regard. Historically occupations were very often divided along the gender lines. With the emergence of feminist and other human rights movements, the past several decades have witnessed some substantial effort of the general public in breaking the gender barriers in the world of work. Notwithstanding such effort, gender stereotyping still remains a problem in people's worklife and career development experiences (Herr, Cramer, & Niles, 2004; Zunker, 2002). While this is a common problem in many working environments, some occupations, especially those which have traditionally been dominated by one gender, tend to pose more risks for the other gender to enter and/or to progress more smoothly. It has been argued that female professionals such as lawyers may sometimes have to take the risk of postponing their career advancement or even leaving their professional career for the sake of maintaining a more healthy family life (Krakauer & Chen, 2003). Also, the so-called 'glass-ceiling' effect in some organizations in the corporate world poses an invisible yet very concrete risk for female middle-level managers to advance to a higher level management position.

Likewise, while men choosing to enter traditionally female-dominated occupations has become a more common phenomenon, it is not unusual that a male nurse might take the risk of being perceived as either 'too feminine' by some people, or 'not possessing enough nurturing capacity' by others. Values and social perceptions as such is just one kind of basis for risks affecting individuals' vocational life. There are numerous other variables in the social and cultural domain that may become the sources of risks. Aspects such as social class, social interaction and relationships, communication norms, and other elements and dynamics that operate and maintain the functioning of the social and societal structure, can generate direct or indirect risk factors to people's worklife and career development (Hotchkiss & Borow, 1996; Johnson & Mortimer, 2002). These social and cultural risk factors may not often arise as dramatic and devastating as some other risk phenomena caused by economic turmoil or environmental disasters, the impact of the social and cultural risks cannot be overlooked. This is because these risks tend to affect individuals' worklife and vocational wellbeing in a more subtle, routinely, and long-lasting way.

The other two major risk dimensions in the MSE system are political atmosphere and economic circumstance. Almost any slight change or shift in economy brings direct risky possibilities to people's worklife (Sharf, 2002). For example, the increased value of a nation's currency may strengthen the status of the currency in the international monetary market. Unfortunately, this very same strong currency may cause the rise of the production cost, and as a result, reduce the competitiveness of the country's export business. As the business is declining, there will be a need to reduce labour costs in the export production sector. Thus, the possible layoff will become a very real high risk that overshadows the job security of workers in this particular sector. A situation as such can very often affect the overall economy in a negative way by reducing consumer confidence and sending pessimistic signals to the entire labour market of the country, creating risks of hiring freeze, layoffs, job loss, and other forms of involuntary unemployment such as forced early retirement.

Various kinds of changing dynamics in the world of work are economically driven, and they reflect shifts in economy (Bridges, 1994; Hall, 1996; Rifkin, 1995). Under the name of increasing productivity, the workplace transformations such as restructuring, downsizing, outsourcing, and merger, just to mention a few, bring real risks to not only those workers who have to leave their present worklives, but also those who may at the moment continue to stay with their jobs. While the immediate job loss may not be a high risk for this latter group of workers, they can face risks of a heavier workload, a disrupted working environment with lower morale, and consequently enduring a higher level of work-related distress. As illustrated, the vital connection between the economic situation and the labour market trends has determined the pivotal role of the economic dimension in forming, developing, and reforming risk dynamics in people's vocational life.

The political situation can certainly pose risks to people's worklife in a direct manner. For example, the government's decision to avoid providing subsidy or terminate financial support to a sector of the industry may result in a possible shutdown of the industry. This may generate the real risk of job loss for workers in this very industry. The introduction of a new regulation or change of an existing policy can also generate challenges for business practice in certain occupations and industries, making worklife in these contexts more risky than ever before. In the meantime, political environment often yields risks in an indirect manner, that is, it affects other risk dimensions in the MSE system, which in turn, poses direct risks to people's worklife and career development experience. For example, a turbulent and unstable political environment is likely to negatively affect the economy toward a downturn. As a result, a gloomy economic trend will strain and burden the labour market, causing a range of work-related risks previously mentioned.

One pivotal source of risks to people's worklife today is the fast-advancing technological revolution in the 21st century and beyond. The profound advancement in natural and applied science research in the post-industrial era has changed the way of human living in a drastic and profound manner. New technological changes marked by biochemical and genetic engineering, especially by the sweeping power of information sciences and computer technology, have totally transformed not only the way the world functions, but also the way lay people live their daily routines. The unprecedented and revolutionary transformations in technology have no doubt brought great benefits to our worklife. For example, it is difficult for many of us to imagine that we would be functioning normally in our workplace today without having access to the Internet and computer.

In the meantime, just like many other human triumphs upon the world, the continuing development in new technology poses risks to people in the world of work. Automation in the workplace requires a much smaller, but more highly educated and skilful workforce, and as a result, signaling the risks of job loss for many current workers. The rapid development of new information technology (IT) also accelerates the disappearance of some sectors of the industry deemed as outdated and inefficient, increasing the risks of unemployment for many workers. Even the 'bubble economy' has become a severe side effect of the overly-heated IT industry in the last decade. Its ramification has been painfully felt by the entire Western industrial world for the last 3 or 4 years. Tens of thousands of very experienced and skilful workers in the IT related sectors encountered the risks of losing their jobs. Meanwhile, the new university graduates with a computer science related major of studies have realized that they are facing the real risk of not finding employment in the high tech sector that was supposed to provide them with much promise for future career prosperity.

Natural and Environmental Risks

Any changes in natural and environmental conditions can affect aspects of human living, including the vocational aspects of people's lives. It should be noted that the term 'environmental' can encompass a very broad range of meanings such as sociocultural, political, and economic milieu. Yet, the notion of environmental condition here focuses solely on the natural environment such as weather, climate, geography, and other facets associated with the nature of things in human life. These natural events and conditions can sometimes become influential sources of risks that have considerable impact on individuals' worklife and career development experiences. Extinction and disappearance of natural resources may create the real risk of driving people out of work. A very typical example in this respect was the moratorium order imposed by the Canadian government in its Atlantic Provinces a decade ago due to the endangered disappearing of some major fishery stocks in the Atlantic Ocean along the Canadian coast line. When the risk of moratorium of the fishing industry in these Canadian coastal regions became real, the workers who had a family tradition of working in this industry for generations were devastated and traumatized. They felt the loss of their vocational identity while experiencing their livelihood to be stripped off their hands.

Similar situations also occurred when other forms of natural resources such as mining and forestry were drained. Workers were facing the risk of job loss, as their resource-based vocational life had to be scaled down substantially or come to a complete halt. There are many other circumstances that can demonstrate how various environmental conditions imposing risks in people's vocational wellbeing, can alter their way of making vocational choices. For example, natural disasters such as severe drought and animal disease create serious risks that may threaten the worklife of workers in the farming industry. For many, the risk of financial loss becomes the reality, depriving them of their annual income that was supposed to be the return of their hard work and other cost investment to maintain the farming operation. For some, their operation may be totally ruined, and they just have to be forced out of the farming business due to the reality that the financial loss has become too enormous to bear.

Summary of Risk Interactions

Of note, the natural and environmental sources of risks are very often intertwined with other social and societal risks in the MSE system. Political atmosphere, economic circumstance, and technological development can all interplay with the natural and environmental conditions, generating and altering the risk dynamics that will affect people's worklife and career development experiences. For example, ill-planned and unsustainable economic and technological growth are often exploiting the natural environment in an excessive manner. The end result of such development is destructive and harmful in maintaining a harmonious balance between human and nature, yielding more new risks to all aspects of human living, especially vocational aspects of lives. There has been scientific evidence that the risk phenomena such as the disappearance of natural resources and natural disasters affected by climate change, are all closely connected to the way that nature is treated by humankind.

Likewise, social, political, and economic factors can interact in a complex manner in generating risks. As such, trade disputes between nations that are very often driven by domestic politics (or so-called 'national interest'), can yield devastating economic risks for certain sectors of the economy. An example in this regard is the heavily-hit workers in the forestry industry in Canada due to the continuous softwood lumber export-and-import dispute between Canada and the United States. Another similar example that shows the combination of how the natural and economic variables intertwine in generating risks is the recent Mad-cow Disease crisis that has already resulted in several billion dollars of financial loss of the beef industry in Canada. Because of the finding of one case of Mad-cow disease, the United States (Canada's major destination for its beef export business) has to impose a suspension of the Canadian beef import. The main reason for the United States to maintain this ban is that it wants to make sure that its beef export business to other countries, especially to its Asian market, will not be negatively affected.

As has been illustrated, many natural and environmental risks that people have to encounter in their vocational lives and career development are ultimately social and societal. To understand this nature-nurture interrelationship is essential to develop a comprehensive and integrated worldview in discerning how risks originate, evolve, and shift in human living in general, and in people's vocational aspects of lives in particular. With an increased comprehension in this respect, more effective ways can be found to deal with the risks emerging from people's worklife and career development contexts, whether such risks stem from social and societal or natural and environmental sources, or a combination of both.

Risk Conceptualized in Vocational Psychology

Notwithstanding the less usage of the term 'risk' in a direct and explicit manner, the risk phenomenon is not an unfamiliar aspect in vocational and career psychology. It is actually often considered a vital component in the vocational psychology literature, especially in some main theoretical models in career development and career counselling. Yet, most of the time, the risk concept is not directly identified as it sounds, but rather, is addressed in an indirect manner. The notion of risk is very often implied when theoretical assumptions concerning the role and function of risks are proposed. This section of the current discussion aims to explore and elaborate on the risk phenomenon implied and/or indicated in some major theoretical models in vocational and career psychology, providing some conceptual foundation for risk-taking and risk-coping considerations in career development practice.

A central principle in the person-environment correspondence theory (Dawis, 2002), also known as work adjustment theory (Dawis & Lafqust, 1984), is to find a good fit or more harmonious match between the workers' needs and the requirements of the workplace. Work adjustment is very often needed to make the two sides, that is, the personal needs and work requirements, more adaptable to each other, because a perfect fit between the two sides seldom happens.

This adjustment process, however, does not always yield a satisfactory result. While the individuals try to adjust to the demands of the working environment, they may take the risk whether they try to accommodate the work demands by altering their personal needs or make a decision to leave the working environment for good. In the former situation, they may take the risk of caving in to work environment or work requirements that are in conflict with their interest, values, and other personal needs. In the latter case, the risk factor they face is that the next new work environment they intend to enter may not be as ideal as that which they had originally expected. The new workplace may also have similar problems, or other new problems that they have never anticipated and experienced in the current work environment. As a result, a new process of work adjustment may be needed.

The central implication here suggests that work adjustment can be a useful means to reduce risks in one's worklife, yet, the risk factor itself as a common and influential dynamic will not vanish from individuals' worklife. It points to a simple truth that the existence of risks is definite while the disappearance or avoidance of risks in the vocational context is merely a relative phenomenon based on human-environment interaction. As new risks, expected or unexpected, continuously emerge in people's vocational lives, individuals have to make constant adjustments in dealing with various risk dynamics. As such, risks are encountered and dealt with when individuals continue their life journey, in which worklife and career development is an essential part. Vocational and career risks will never stop surfacing, but rather, people try to understand and resolve these risks in a more satisfactory manner and with an ongoing effort.

A risk-coping behaviour seems to be reflected by the principle of compromise as defined by Gottfredson (2002). In her theory of circumscription, compromise and self-creation, Gottfredson (2002) reasons that key psychosocial variables such as intelligence, gender, and social prestige can play a vital role in influencing individuals' vocational behaviour. As individuals become more aware of the intellectual capacity, gender identity, and social class involved in their career decision-making, they start to perceive the possibilities and non-possibilities while choosing their most accessible career options. To reduce the risks of entering into a vocational field that is deemed not attainable, individuals make compromises in their career choice. Options with high risks, that is, those options that are considered not pertinent to one's sex roles, social class, or intellectual caliber, are ruled out. On the contrary, alternatives with low risks to achieve, that is, those options that are thought to be more realistic and obtainable, are often selected as the viable career choices. As such, the process of compromise occurs as individuals narrow down their career options, during which high-risk options are being replaced by low-risk options.

Some newly emerging theories in vocational and career psychology, represented largely by the social constructivist school of thinking, have incorporated the risk factor into the career development process by recognizing the complex social and environmental contexts in which individuals' worklife takes place and functions. The notion of context is given considerable attention in theoretical approaches such as social cognitive career theory (SCCT) (Lent, Brown, & Hackett, 2002) and the contextualist explanation of career (Young, Valach, & Collin, 2002). The construct of context is a broad concept that covers a variety of dynamic and complex situational variables affecting the individual's vocational aspect of life. Within these contextual dimensions, there are often unfavorable variables that can bring difficulties and hurdles to individuals' vocational wellbeing. Presumably, the more contextual barriers and hindrance one has to encounter, the more risks one has to take in achieving an optimal career outcome.

Some of these contextual risks appear to parallel negative circumstances engendered by the factor of 'environmental conditions and events', one of the essential features of Krumboltz's social learning theory of career decision-making (Mitchell & Krumboltz, 1996). The tenet of environmental conditions in Krumboltz's theory points to a broad domain rather than a narrowly focused dimension. A diversity of variables such as political, social, cultural, economic, technological, and demographic conditions in the macro-sociological-ecology (MSE) system as previously discussed can become the triggers for risks to people's worklife and career choice. Likewise, adversity in the natural environment can also generate risky conditions affecting people's vocational aspects of life. These natural and environmental conditions interplay with other social and societal factors, forming a complex and dynamic ecology in the individual's worklife.

This integral ecological system has been elaborated in a comprehensive manner by systems theory framework (STF) to career development (Patton & McMahon, 1999). According to Patton and McMahon (1999), individuals' career choice and decisions are not merely a matter of personal preference, but rather, an individual propensity that is shaped and re-shaped by the variety of factors in the MSE system within which the person makes his/her vocational choice. Sometimes, the nature of the influencing factors seems to present themselves in an explicit way. That is, such factors are evident to a person that they would either facilitate or hinder his/her career preference under the circumstance. At times, however, these pros and cons are closely intertwined within a career decision-making context, making it impossible to produce a clear-cut simple solution to a career problem. Weighing the pros and cons within the MSE system in this kind of situation is about, in fact, assessing the risks involved in searching for a more pertinent solution to the career problem. Hopefully, this search will lead to a better comprehension of the nature of the risks involved, and more importantly, the possible impact of the risk factors on a particular worklife and career development choice. A better understanding as such forms a valid base, upon which individuals generate relevant coping mechanisms in controlling and minimizing the possible negative impact rendered by the risk factors. Consequently, a more desirable career decision, albeit not totally risk-free, may be reached and implemented.

Perhaps the most recent theoretical model that points more directly to the role of risk is the planned happenstance theory proposed by Mitchell, Levin, and Krumboltz (1999). The central premise of this conceptual framework is that individuals have to capitalize on the events that emerge in their lives. Planned happenstance is the human intentional action to utilize these life events in an optimal manner. It focuses on the critical need to help a person adopt an open and constructive attitude in dealing with the chance variable that occurs in one's career exploration and decision-making process. To master the chance factor in careering, the person has to normalize planned happenstance in life-career experiences, to transform curiosity into opportunities for learning and exploration, to produce desirable chance events, and to overcome blocks to action. Obviously, risk management is an unavoidable task when the person tries to minimize negative chances and maximize optimal chances in choosing a career option.

Negotiating and Managing Career Risks

As presented, a review of the rationale, the categories and sources, and the psychological explanations of the risk phenomenon in people's worklife and career context appear to be helpful. It has not only confirmed the existence, but also demonstrated the role and function of the risk factor in people's vocational aspects of life. To recognize and make sense of the risk factor in this context is certainly critical to provide us with a sound educational foundation for an increased awareness of the risk phenomenon. Based on this foundation, I wish to highlight the importance of conceptualizing the risk component in vocational and career psychology practice in this section. The awareness enhancement on the theoretical level is necessary for knowledge advancement. In the meantime, it is equally, if not more important, that the theoretical knowledge can become the directive and stimulating threshold for guidance toward better ways of living. This principle of linking theory to practice may hold particular relevance to incorporating the risk phenomenon – one of the most common phenomena of human living – in individuals' vocational aspects of life.

With this goal in mind, this section attempts to propose some general considerations in dealing with the risk component in the vocational context. For convenience in illustration, the forthcoming discussion will be generally framed in a helping situation in which a career counsellor and a client work together to tackle the risk factor in career planning and exploration. Yet, these considerations for intervention are by no means to be restricted only in this context. They are intended to offer some practice-oriented guidelines and ideas to a wider range of relevant audience in the broad domain of vocational and career psychology. This audience may include career development practitioners such as educators in careers and vocational education, vocational psychologists and consultants, human resource development personnel, life-career skills trainers and coaches, vocational guidance workers, employment and job-placement counsellors, professional development specialists, and other helping professionals who work in a variety of career development intervention contexts (Niles & Harris-Bowlsbey, 2002). Of note, these considerations in dealing with vocational and career risks may also be adopted as self-helping guidelines while individuals endeavour to cope with risks more effectively in their own worklife experience and career development practice.

Increasing Risk Awareness

Although vocational and career risks may take very different forms, and their impact on individuals' worklife experience may also vary because of dynamic and complex contextual reasons, the existence of risks is definite. In other words, whether recognized or not, the risk factor will be an unavoidable variable that accompanies one's vocational life experience. As a prerequisite to negotiate and manage possible risks, it is necessary for individuals to possess a sense of risk in their worklife and career development contexts. Career counselling should make this helping task a priority in the intervention process. The counsellor can help the client become more conscious about the risk construct as a general phenomenon in one's vocational planning and career decision-making. Based on that, risk factors that might be relevant to a particular personal situation can be explored and dealt with. The client needs to become cognizant of the simple reality that any engagement in the world of work will never be risk-free. This means that in one's vocational journey, encountering risks is a continuous and never-ending experience, while eluding risks is only a relative and tentative phenomenon. The risk factor needs to be incorporated into the whole picture while exploring career options and making a career plan.

The counsellor can constantly remind the client about the possible risks involved in the planning process. As the person who is directly engaged in the exploration process, the client can often become too involved in one or more aspects of the career problem, while overlooking other variables that may also be part of the problem. As a result, possible risk factors may not be given enough attention, or even be recognized by the client. The counsellor's role as an intentional spectator will be pivotal in the helping process. That is, the counsellor is in an easier position to see the existing and emerging risks that might be missed or ignored. Moreover, such risk factors are brought to the table, being shared openly with the client. As risks, whether minor or substantial, are very often entangled with each step of a career decision, the client is much better off to be constantly alerted to the risk component through the entire decision-making process. In doing so, the counsellor helps the client have more exposure to the risk phenomenon, making the client feel more comfortable to always include the risk factor in considering a career option.

It should be noted that in order to enhance the client's sense of risk in career exploration, the counsellor should be sensitive to the risk factor, and be capable of observing and envisioning the risk factors in the context of the client's career planning and exploration. Without this sensitivity, it would be difficult for the counsellor to become proactive in facilitating the client to draw attention to the risk construct in considering and forming career alternatives. The counsellor should also feel comfortable to bring the risk component into the helping process. From the part of the counsellor, seeing the risk factor and its possible ramifications is necessary, yet not sufficient. The counsellor's knowing of risk only becomes relevant to the helping process and its ultimate outcome if the risk phenomenon is communicated to, and to be well received by the client. This requires that the counsellor remain mindful and intentional in sharing with the client the need to pay attention to the existing and possible risks whenever necessary. This is indeed to do a pertinent and indispensable service to the vocational wellbeing of the client. The counsellor must not feel reluctant and hesitant to be unequivocal about the risky reality in nearly all kinds of career choice and decision-making situations. In the meantime, the way of communicating this reality to the client should be, and can be, framed in a skillful manner. The central goal here is to find more facilitative ways that will help the client increase a sense of risk in dealing with career issues.

Several points may be of particular relevance in this regard. First, a good counsellor-client work alliance is a must. Without this healthy rapport or trustworthy working relationship, it would be extremely difficult for the counsellor to convey a credible message to the client. In experiencing the rapport firsthand, the client feels that a focus on the risk component is a well-intentioned service for his/her vocational wellbeing. Second, the explanation of risk factors should remain situational and flexible. For example, some clients may need more time and space to increase their risk awareness through some in-depth self-exploration, while others may prefer that the counsellor could be more directive, highlighting the risk factors in a more focused and explicit manner. Third, the risk factor should always be framed in a problem-solving context. Tabling the risk factors on the client's career map is important. Yet, it is even more important that the central focus is on finding the appropriate strategies to manage the possible risk factors. A desirable helping situation is to let the client feel truly that by paying attention to the risk phenomenon, he/she is working with the counsellor to tackle a necessary aspect, just as any other relevant worklife and career-related aspects, in searching for a more optimal solution to a career problem (Cochran, 1994).

Strengthening Risk-Taking Stamina

Parallel to an increased sense of the risk phenomenon in worklife reality, one needs to have a right state of mind in coping with the risk factor, similar to what Chen (1997) defined as challenge preparation. In other words, it is equally, if not more, important that a person should possess the psychological stamina to encounter the risk dynamic in real worklife and career experiences. A main task of career counselling, therefore, is to help the client build and reinforce this psychological strength. Taking a risk often involves some degree of uncertainty. It implies that there is a possibility for a less desirable or even negative outcome when implementing a career decision. The client who is directly engaged in the career decision-making situation needs to grow a sense of comfort toward the uncertain and less desirable reality. Such a sense of comfort requires not only the awareness and understanding of the risk phenomenon, but also the psychological endurance to live with a risky experience. It is this psychological strength that forms the essential mindset to endure the expected and unexpected 'blow' resulted from risky circumstances. Without this capacity to coexist with the risky aspects in one's worklife experience, the client may find it extremely difficult to cope with risks effectively.

An advisable step in the helping process is to normalize the existence of the risk phenomenon in one's worklife and career experience. The counsellor can facilitate the client to adopt a more constructive attitude in facing the risk component in a career planning and exploration situation. The client comes to realize that risks of different nature and different degree are very often part of the dynamics involved in the career planning process. The risk influence is not going to disappear because of human intention to avoid or ignore its existence. Thus, a sense of fear and denial must be replaced by an attitude of normality and acceptance. Just like other variables often deeply entangled with one's life experience, the risk phenomenon can be seen as a common aspect that accompanies one's vocational life experiences.

In acknowledging the risk factor as a normal companion in his/her career exploration, the client is encouraged to approach the risk phenomenon with a welcoming disposition. The client realizes the necessity of including rather than excluding the risk component while forming a career direction. Given that risks involved in a career option will affect the outcome of this very career option in one way or another, a more proactive stance to live with the risk phenomenon allows the person to exercise more control in managing these risks. Rather than feeling vulnerable or even fearful about the possible risks, a person with more psychological stamina is able to focus on how to deal with the risk reality. By devoting more time and energy to risk-understanding and risk-coping action, limited resources can be used more effectively and efficiently in solving real career problems. The counsellor can help the client build and reinforce a sense of strength in this regard.

First, the client needs to have the time and space openly sharing his/her views and feelings about the possible risks involved in a career decision-making situation. This opportunity of sharing is very helpful as it provides some clue with respect to the client's attitude toward the risk phenomenon. A clearer understanding of where the client stands helps the counsellor adopt more relevant helping strategies to meet the specific needs of each client. Meanwhile, an in-depth exploration as such also helps the client become more conscious about the reasons behind his/her own reluctance or resistance to accept the risk component in choosing a career option or dealing with a challenge in worklife.

Second, the counsellor needs to facilitate the client to normalize feeling of anxiety and other negative emotions associated with the sense of uncertainty caused by the risk reality. As the client is encouraged to take a closer look at his/her daily life experiences, he/she becomes aware that taking risks is not a rare incident, but a lay experience that one encounters frequently. The client comes to realize that he/she has been actually involved in risk-taking and risk-coping behaviour in various personal and social life situations either consciously or unconsciously. Thus, feeling anxious or fearful about the risk impact is unnecessary. Encountering risks is not an unfamiliar life phenomenon for an individual. Rather, it is part of the norms entangled in many aspects of one's life, including one's vocational life. Risks may not always be handled in a desirable way due to various reasons, especially those factors that are beyond the person's control. Yet, life experience proceeds with the constant emergence of the risk phenomenon. In seeing the emerging risks as a normal aspect, the client increases a sense of comfort and confidence while being engaged in risk-taking and risk-coping situations. This sense of normality provides the client with more psychological strength and a positive attitude to live with the risk reality in career planning and decision-making contexts.

Third, there is a need to constantly check the level of psychological strength the client has in dealing with possible risks while solving a career problem. The client is reminded of the critical importance in maintaining this level of stamina while managing the risk component in his/her vocational life experiences. With a trustworthy counsellor-client work alliance in place, the counsellor can challenge the client to elaborate on the concrete preparation he/she has should the risk component yield an anticipated or unanticipated negative outcome. Being aware of the risk existence and having the psychological readiness to live with the risk phenomenon is very important. It is equally important that the psychological stamina will always stay in place so that the person feels more comfortable and confident in dealing with constantly emerging uncertainty generated by risks in one's worklife. With a constant reminder and analysis of the possible 'worst case scenario', the client may increase his/her tolerance of uncertainty while becoming more prepared to find ways of dealing with possible negative outcomes derived from a risk-taking experience.

Maintaining an Open Stance

The importance of maintaining an open stance is a very familiar recurring theme in the career psychology literature for the last decade. Academics and practitioners alike have recognized the significant role and function of individuals' openness and flexibility in coping with worklife and career issues (Amundson, 1995; Chen, 2002; Cochran, 1997; Gelatt, 1989, 1991; Krumboltz, 2003; Mitchell & Krumboltz, 1996; Peavy, 1993; Schlossberg, & Robinson, 1996). This open attitude is pivotal because it provides individuals with the necessary mindset for facing changes – an essential human quality of being psychologically adaptable to a fast-changing world of work. Career counselling intervention can help the client foster and reinforce a sense of openness in career choice and in the decision-making process. The central goal here is to help the client understand that while an open attitude is an advisable state of mind in dealing with virtually any kind of career exploration and development issues, it is especially worthy of attention in risk-taking situations that involve high levels of uncertainty.

This calls upon the individual in career exploration to stay flexible when facing the risk reality. The counsellor helps the client understand that risk-taking naturally involves a certain level of uncertainty in one's career experience. An optimal way of dealing with these uncertain aspects in career planing and problem solving is to have more options available. The more options one has, the better coping methods may be selected for solving a career problem. To generate a range of options requires that the person is open to new and creative ideas, and is flexible to use these ideas while encountering the risk reality in the world of work. The main rationale for remaining flexible is to let the client adopt a broader vision that may provide new ways for comprehending a career problem, and new alternatives to cope with the problem in a more constructive manner. A range of options will lead to more possibilities in looking at the risk factor from different angles. This helps the client use different perspectives in examining the risk factor. Although the risk component remains the same, it might be analyzed and framed differently, shedding new light on the coping strategies that are worthy of consideration.

The client comes to realize that in order to negotiate with risks in worklife and career experiences, he/she needs to maintain an open mind. It is this open mindedness that will help one adopt a tentative attitude in risk-taking and risk-coping behaviour. It is much more effective if risk assessment is conducted in a situational and contextual manner. For example, to categorize the level of each risk factor is advisable in generating more effective coping mechanisms. Different kinds of psychological and tangible preparations are needed for high risk and low risk variables in a career decision-making situation. With an open mind, the client finds that very often the criterion for measuring the magnitude and impact of a risk component is not static. This is to say that there is no rigid boundary that divides a high risk and low risk component. This assessment depends very much on how the individual will look at the nature of the risk and its potential impact on his/her particular career and worklife development experience. The scope and magnitude of the risk influence, i.e., either high or low, is only relative in nature. That is, there is no absolute and clear-cut line between a high risk and a low risk. Also, these two levels of risk aspects can be transferable to each other if they are examined by the same person who is willing to adopt different perspectives, make some adjustment in his/her worklife preference, and/or prioritize his/her career goals in different ways. To facilitate a sense of open-mindedness, therefore, is of pivotal importance in setting up a basis within which the client can make open negotiation with emerging risk factors. Dynamic, situational, and most of all, more creative strategies can be found and utilized in taking on vocational and career risks.

Enhancing Risk-Coping Competency

A key aspect in becoming more effective in coping with the risk reality lies with a person's capacity in risk management. In other words, the person needs to be competent when he/she is called up to deal with an emerging risk in a career development situation. Negotiating with risks is not an aimless attempt, but rather, it is a well-thought-through reasoning process based on the information one possesses at the moment the risk arises. The essential requirement here is that the person needs the necessary skills in coping with the risk component. Perhaps the first and foremost important condition to form these skills is that one has to be knowledgeable and cognizant in knowing how to encounter the risk phenomenon. To do so, the person must have the intellectual insight to understand the nature of an emerging risk, to examine and anticipate possibilities associated with the risk, and to execute effective coping strategies.

Although it is impossible to anticipate the exact outcome of a career risk one has to take, a focus on insight development provides the client with more intellectual preparation to envision the possible trend of a career problem. This will hopefully lead to an increased sensitivity to change, an interest in different alternatives, and moreover, an accumulation of new information in assessing pros and cons in one's career choice and decision-making. A main task of career counselling, thus, is to help the client develop and accumulate forward-looking insight. The more insight the client gains, the more knowledgeable he/she will become in tackling an emerging career risk. Career counselling can certainly encourage and challenge the client to broaden the existing knowledge scope through constant acquiring of new visions and ideas. In the meantime, it is also pertinent to facilitate the client to reflect on, and utilize his/her knowledge of risk predicating and risk coping from past worklife and career experiences. Notwithstanding the reality that not all human estimation of the risk factors can be accurate, insight development and accumulation will provide a more rational foundation for generating effective coping mechanisms.

Guided by the insight, the client should consider how to translate ideas into action (Amundson, 2003b; Chen, 2002; Cochran, 1997; Young & Valach, 2002). Insight has no real meaningfulness until it is implemented via human action. A range of applicable coping skills must accompany the implementation of insight. Several points may be of particular relevance in this regard. First, promoting lifelong and transformative learning is of essential importance. This kind of learning is intentional, purposeful, and developmental. It aims to incorporate constant changes into one's life-span, including one's vocational aspects of life. The person learns to cope with all kinds of life experiences, including risk coping in a career development context. Like other learned skills in life, risk-coping skills are essentially rooted in one's learned experiences. As the client starts to pay more attention to his/her past learning experiences, he/she may be quite surprised by the amount of resource in the personal repertoire. The career counselling process helps the client become more aware of these skill resources, making use of them, and transferring them into the present circumstance of examining and managing career and worklife risks.

Second, the client needs to realize the importance of becoming an intentional learner who endeavours to assess the risk factors and deal with them in a situational way (Law, 1996; Patton & McMahon, 1999). This is to say that the learned coping skills are not used to deal with career risks dogmatically, but rather, in a contextual manner (Young, Valach, & Collin, 2002). It is particularly worth noting that each client may be better off if he/she follows an individual learning plan in skill development and enhancement. It is this individual learning process that will respect and emphasize the special learning needs of each individual, making the learning experience a much more contextual and relevant process that will be meaningful to the person.

Third, with the open stance and psychological stamina, the client must have some concrete preparation before taking on the risk component. A couple of back-up plans should be in place in case the first coping attempt does not manage the risk factor in a desirable manner. The more such preparation is in place, the more possibility for an optimal outcome in a risk management situation. Although there can be no guarantee that such preparation will work each time, the client is better off with the preparation than without preparation. A more advisable approach is to have several scenarios and options planned when encountering a career risk, especially a risk that is complex and multifaceted (Schlossberg & Robinson, 1996). Being in the role of both a helper and an observer, the counsellor can play the role of a learning facilitator who encourages the client to be proactive in preparation. Meanwhile, the counsellor should not hesitate to play the role of an educator and consultant who gives direct guidance if necessary, and provides the client with concrete advice in forming viable options for managing the risk component in the client's worklife and career development experiences.

Conclusion

Risks are part of the norms individuals have to encounter in their worklife and career development experiences. This reality has become an increasingly frequent phenomenon of the world of work in our post-modern and post-industrial society. Risk-taking and risk-coping is not an alternative, but a must while individuals are engaged in their vocational aspects of life. As such, workers and prospective workers need to have the necessary psychological and tangible preparation in dealing with the constantly emerging vocational and career risks. To become effective agents who are capable of managing the risk reality, individuals should possess a high level of awareness and sensitivity, increase the mental stamina, possess the right attitude, and enhance the actual coping competency. Although these aforementioned professional helping and self-helping considerations do not intend to be inclusive of all the major coping mechanisms, they seem to provide some viable alternate strategies for the risk-taking and risk-coping action in the vocational and career development context.

A vital point worthy of reiterating is that vocational risk coexists and interacts with other risks in one's personal and social life dimensions. Risks in the vocational dimension can not be separated from risks in other personal and social life domains. Thus, coping strategies that will work effectively have to take a comprehensive and integrated approach in addressing the dynamic and complex nature of a vocational and career risk. That is, very often people can only make more sense of a career risk if this very risk is understood and dealt with in a broad and general life-career context. In this sense, taking and coping with vocational risks is part of an integral endeavor to promote and improve a person's general life quality. The mastery of risk-coping experience will certainly improve one's vocational wellbeing. An illuminated worklife wellbeing provides more energy, resource, and vitality for the welfare of other personal and social life aspects, which in turn, makes the person more competent in taking on and coping with risks emerging from his/her vocational life. This reflects a more positive and constructive cycle for risk negotiation. The key mission of career intervention aims to establish and enhance this more optimal and healthy cycle, helping individuals achieve more career and vocational success in a risky world of work.

References

Amundson, N.E. (1995), 'An interactive model of career decision-making', *Journal of Employment Counseling*, vol. 32, pp. 11–21.

Amundson, N.E. (2003a), *The physics of living*, Ergon Communications, Richmond, BC, Canada.

Amundson, N.E. (2003b), *Active engagement: Enhancing the career counselling process (2nd ed)*, Ergon Communications, Richmond, BC, Canada.

Bauman, Z. (1993), *Postmodern Ethics*, Blackwell, Oxford.

Beck, U. (1992), *Risk Society: Towards a New Modernity*, Sage, London.

Bridges, W. (1994), *JobShift*, Addison-Wesley, New York.

Caplan, G. and Teese, M. (1997), *Survivors: How to keep your best people on board after downsizing*, Davies-Block Publishing, Palo Alto, CA.

Caplan, P. (2000), 'Introduction: Risk revisited', in P. Caplan (ed), *Risk Revisited* (1–28), Pluto Press, London.

Cappelli, P. (1999), *The new deal at work: Managing the market-driven workforce*, Harvard Business School Press, Boston.

Cartwright, S. and Cooper, C.L. (1997), *Managing mergers, acquisitions and strategic alliances*, Butterworth-Heinemann, Jordan Hill, Oxford, England.

Chen, C.P. (1997), 'Challenge-preparation: The "3E" approach in career counselling', *Journal of Vocational Education and Training*, vol. 49(4), pp. 563–571.

Chen, C.P. (2001), 'Career counselling as life career integration', *Journal of Vocational Education and Training*, vol. 53(4), pp. 523–542.

Chen, C.P. (2002), 'Integrating action theory and human agency in career development', *Canadian Journal of Counselling*, vol. 36(2), pp. 121–135.

Cochran, L. (1990), *The sense of vocation: A study of career and life development*, State University of New York Press, Albany, NY.

Cochran, L. (1994), 'What is a career problem'? *The Career Development Quarterly*, vol. 42, pp. 204–215.

Cochran, L. (1997), *Career counseling: A narrative approach*, Sage Publications, Thousand Oaks, CA.

Crites, J.O. (1981), *Career counseling: Models, methods, and materials*, McGraw-Hill, New York.

Dawis, R.V. (2002), 'Person-environment-correspondence theory', in D. Brown (ed), *Career choice and development* (4th ed), Jossey-Bass, San Francisco, pp. 427–464.

Dawis, R.V. and Lofquist, L.H. (1984), *A psychological theory of work adjustment*, University of Minnesota Press, Minneapolis.

Douglas, M. and Wildavsky, A. (1982), *Risk and culture: An essay on the selection of technological and environmental dangers*, University of California Press, Berkley, California.

Gelatt, H.B. (1989), 'Positive uncertainty: A new decision-making framework for counseling', *Journal of Counseling Psychology*, vol. 36(2), pp. 252–256.

Gelatt, H.B. (1991), *Creative decision-making*, Crisp Publications, Los Altos, CA.

Giddens, A. (1994), 'Living in a post-traditional society', in U. Beck, A. Giddens and S. Lash (eds), *Reflexive modernization, politics, tradition and aesthetics in the modern social order*, Polity Press, Cambridge, pp. 56–109.

Gottfredson, L.S. (2002), 'Gottfredson's theory of circumscription, compromise, and self-creation', in D. Brown (ed), *Career choice and development* (4th ed), Jossey-Bass, San Francisco, pp. 85–148.

Hall, D.T. (ed) (1996), *The career is dead – long live the career: A relational approach to careers*, Jossey-Bass, San Francisco.

Herr, E.L., Cramer, S.H. and Niles, S.G. (2004), *Career guidance and counseling through the life span: Systematic approaches (6th ed)*, Pearson Education, Toronto.

Hotchkiss, L. and Borow, H. (1996), 'Sociological perspective on work and career development', in D. Brown and L. Brooks (eds), *Career choice and development* (3rd ed), Jossey-Bass, San Francisco pp. 281–334.

Johnson, M.K. and Mortimer, J.T. (2002), 'Career choice and development from a sociological perspective', in D. Brown (ed), *Career choice and development* (4th ed), Jossey-Bass, San Francisco, pp. 37–81.

Krakauer, L. and Chen, C.P. (2003), 'Gender barriers in the legal profession: Implications for career development of female law students', *Journal of Employment Counseling*, vol. 40(2), pp. 65–79.

Krumboltz, J.D. (2003, August), 'How happenstance implements positive psychology', *Paper presented in the 111th Annual Convention of the American Psychological Association*, Toronto, Ontario, Canada.

Law, B. (1996), 'A career-learning theory', in A.G. Watts, B. Law, J. Killeen, J.M. Kidd and Ruth Hawthorn (eds), *Rethinking careers education and guidance: Theory, policy and practice*, Routledge, New York, pp. 46–71.

Lent, R.W., Brown, S.D. and Hackett, G. (2002), 'Social cognitive career theory', in D. Brown (ed), *Career choice and development* (4th ed), Jossey-Bass, San Francisco, pp. 255–311.

Lupton, D. (1999a), *Risk*, Routledge, London.

Lupton, D. (1999b), *Risk and sociocultural theory: New directions and perspectives*, Cambridge University Press, Cambridge.

Mitchell, K.E., Levin, A.S. and Krumboltz, J.D. (1999), 'Planned Happenstance: Constructing Unexpected Career Opportunities', *Journal of Counseling and Development*, vol. 77, pp. 115–124.

Mitchell, L.K. and Krumboltz, J.D. (1996), 'Krumboltz's learning theory of career choice and counseling', in D. Brown and L. Brooks (eds), *Career choice and development* (3rd ed.), Jossey-Bass, San Francisco, pp. 233–280.

Niles, S.G. and Harris-Bowlsbey, J. (2002), *Career development interventions in the 21st century*, Pearson Education, Upper Saddle river, New Jersey.

Peavy, R.V. (1993), 'Envisioning the future: Worklife and counselling', *Canadian Journal of Counselling*, vol. 27, pp. 123–139.

Peterson, N. and Gonzalez, R.C. (2000), *The role of work in people's lives: Applied career counseling and vocational psychology*, Wadsworth/Thomson Learning, Belmont, CA.

Rifkin, J. (1995), *The end of work: The decline of the global labor force and the dawn of the post-market era*, G.P. Putnam, New York.

Schlossberg, N.K. and Robinson, S.P. (1996), *Going to plan B*, Simon & Schuster, New York.

Sharf, R.S. (2002), *Applying career development theory to counseling (3rd ed)*, Brooks/Cole, Pacific Grove, C.A.

Super, D.E. (1990), 'A life-span, life space approach career development', in D. Brown and L. Brooks (eds), *Career choice and development: Applying contemporary theories to practice* (2nd ed), Jossey-Bass, San Francisco, pp. 197–261.

Wynne, B. (1996), 'May the sheep safely graze? A reflexive view of the expert-lay-knowledge divide', in S. Lash, B. Szerszinski and B. Wynne (eds), *Risk, environment and modernity: towards a new ecology*, Sage, London, pp. 44–83.

Young, R.A. and Collin, A. (1992), *Interpreting career: Hermeneutical studies of lives in context*, Praeger, Westport, CT.

Young, R.A. and Valach, L. (2000), 'Reconceptualising career theory and research: An action-theoretical perspective', in A. Collin and R.A. Young (eds), *The future of career*, Cambridge University Press, New York, pp. 181–196.

Young, R.A., Valach, L. and Collin, A. (2002), 'A contextualist explanation of career', in D. Brown (ed), *Career choice and development* (4th ed), Jossey-Bass, San Francisco, pp. 206–252.

Zunker, V.G. (2002), *Career counseling: Applied concepts of life planning (6th ed)*, Brooks/Cole, Pacific Grove, CA.

Chapter 15

Diversity, Risk, Excellence and the Public Good in Education

Kay Adamson

Introduction

The evolution of a public debate during 2003, about the nature and purpose of higher education in Britain and how it ought to be funded, which arose after the publication of the Department for Education and Skills strategy document *The Future of Higher Education* (DfES, 2003) offers a useful framework within which to explore the varied relationships that are detectable between the different fields of diversity, risk, excellence and the public good in education. Consequently, this chapter aims to examine the theoretical constructs that have been employed in this debate and how they have been reported. Much of this focus will be on the *Financial Times* which has reported extensively on the debate and where broadly, but not exclusively, there was a general support for the introduction of variable top-up fees as a means of increasing the revenue base of universities. The basic principle is that higher education institutions should be able to set their own fees up to an annual maximum per programme of £3,000. The idea being that different types of programmes both incur different levels of costs and are differentially attractive to students, with the result that fees should reflect this (DfES, 2004, paras. 16, 37). The part played by the *Financial Times* was particularly interesting not only because of the fact that one of its former editors, Richard Lambert, headed up a government report on the future relationship between business and the universities, but also because of its general support for the New Labour project, despite a popular view of it, as the newspaper of the financial world. That the *Financial Times* covered the debates in the way it did suggests that the financing of universities is of more than ordinary interest. Although the debate took place on a national stage, the proposals themselves are directly applicable only to England and Wales, as education is a devolved matter in Scotland and the Scottish Executive has (at least for the moment) ruled out the use of top-up fees to finance higher education in Scotland. That said, the proposals will have an indirect effect on Scottish universities, not least in terms of what higher education is seen to be about. As a result, this chapter has opted to include aspects of the discussion in Scotland where this discussion can illuminate aspects of the broader debate. This chapter begins with a discussion of the meanings of such expressions as public good, diversity and excellence before exploring how these can be interpreted through the prism of risk.

Public Good

It is useful to begin with the issue of what constitutes a public good because it provides an illustration of the manner in which words and ideas are always in evolution so that they can reflect the nature of contemporary political debate. Our starting point is the definition of a public good in the 1972 Penguin *A Dictionary of Economics* (Bannock et al., 1972). It defines a public good as 'those goods which because they cannot be withheld from one individual without withholding them from all, must be supplied communally' (Bannock et al., 1972). The authors also point out that in areas such as housing, hospitals and education, such goods could 'in principle' be supplied privately thus rendering these fields ones that cannot necessarily be considered to be a 'pure' public good. However, the reading of the caveat 'in principle' is one of closure and of an absence of probability within the context of the early 1970s. It is also an understanding of the meaning of 'public good' that is very close to the definition that is found in John Rawls' influential *A Theory of Justice*. In *A Theory of Justice,* Rawls argued that a public good had two characteristic features, namely 'indivisibility and publicness' (Rawls, 1972, p. 266). However, just as important, were the decision-making processes that determined what proportion of 'total social resources' should be devoted to 'public goods'. Given that Rawls's book was published at the same time as the Penguin *Dictionary of Economics,* and that they both used the example of 'national defence' as the means to explain what constituted a 'pure' public good, it is reasonable to conclude that there was a degree of consensus in 1972 on both sides of the Atlantic concerning the broad meaning of 'public goods'. However, both Rawls and Penguin's *Dictionary of Economics* also indicate that there is room for genuine political debate over what ought to be considered to be a public good and therefore what the appropriate provision of such a public good should be. By also admitting that 'in principle' such goods could be supplied privately, they left open a space within which it was possible for the political debates of the 1980s and 1990s in the United Kingdom to take place. These debates which occurred under the Conservative majority governments of first Margaret Thatcher, and secondly, John Major, were influenced by the complex legacy of anti-communist inspired thinking associated with, for example, Frederick Hayek in works such as *The Constitution of Liberty* (1960), which focused on the degree to which government was and ought to be responsible for the social provision of goods. These debates posed enough questions about the reasonableness of education's position as a public good that they not only prepared the ground for the debate that has taken place over the funding of higher education, but they also contributed to the idea that this debate was an eminently reasonable one.

The impact of these debates 'can clearly be seen in the shift of meaning that is found in the 2000 *Collins Dictionary of Economics* (Pass et al., 2000) where public good is described as:

> those goods and services that are provided by the state for the benefit of all or most of the population; and which are normally paid for out of generalized taxation as against individual consumers purchase of it in the market place; consequently, there is not normally a direct link between consumption and payment (Pass et al., 2000).

Although this definition might not immediately seem dissimilar to that found in the 1972 Penguin *Dictionary*, two major shifts have taken place. In the first of these, there is the explicit introduction of the concepts of the consumer and the market. The second shift occurs because the definition itself is no longer located under the heading of 'public goods' but is actually found under the heading 'social goods' or 'merit goods'. The latter itself raises a number of subsidiary issues that are relevant for discussions of diversity and excellence as those almost always involve an appeal to the concept of 'merit', which is in practice a rather difficult concept to define. For the moment, what is significant from the 2000 definition is the consumption/payment issue as it is this that has been central to the arguments that have favoured the charging of top-up fees. Furthermore, if it is assumed that the political debate has already taken place in the sense that pre-emptive decisions had been taken to pay for education by means other than through generalised taxation then higher education could no longer be viewed analytically or normatively as a 'pure' public good. The magnitude of the shift that this represented, accounts for why higher education has been increasingly viewed as no longer a 'pure' public good. Indeed it can be measured by that part of the debate that even questions whether the state should have any interest at all in funding higher education. In a sense, if higher education has indeed ceased to be a 'pure' public good then logically there is no necessary reason why the market should not determine access to it. If access is to be determined by the market, the corollary in terms of equal opportunities ought then to be that no special provision is required because higher education is open to all. It is the equal chance/equal treatment perspective revisited in a new guise. There are two problems with this formulation. The first is that it assumes that there is a level playing field but as Ball (2003) and Reay, Davies, David and Ball (2001, p. 868) have argued, 'despite the ending of the binary divide in 1991, existing material advantages of a small cluster of elite institutions have been maintained'. The second problem is that if education is presumed to be open to all, by virtue of it functioning through the medium of the market, there remains no obvious rationale for why the state should then regulate access. In other words, government regulation is rendered obsolete, access becomes a matter for individual institutions to regulate. However, that the state has not recognised the implications of its own transformation of higher education from a clear public good into one that is part public good and part a function of the

market is indicated by the absence of consent to the Bill's proposals and
the Minister for Higher Education, Alan Johnson's need to defend the role of
government in an interview with the *Financial Times* (10/11/04). Johnson
argued that 'it was the role of government, not university vice-chancellors, to
set a maximum fee according to what it felt was fair and politically acceptable'
(Financial Times, 10/11/04). It might, at first glance, seem reasonable for the
government to seek to retain its ability to regulate the sector by arguing that
fees should be varied according to either the cost of the course itself or
the subsequent market value of the course. By admitting the principle of
variability on market-related grounds, it has made its task of regulation in the
long-term, unsustainable, particularly as the vision that is increasingly
presented is of a university system that will become more and more differentiated. Characteristic of this move towards differentiation is the increasing use
of terms such as 'elite', 'world class', 'research', 'leading', 'non research-
intensive', 'modern', and 'teaching', as a basis for justifying the kinds of
proposals that were the basis of the DfES's *The Future of Higher Education.*

Before leaving this part of the discussion, it is also worth recalling the
argument made by Michael Walzer (1983) in *Spheres of Justice. A Defence of
Pluralism and Equality.* Walzer's argument allows for the incorporation into
the discussion, of another important characteristic of 'public goods', namely
that before one can discuss who are the agents for the distribution of social
goods, it is necessary to have taken account of the processes of the conception
and creation of those goods (Walzer, 1983, p. 6), and how they have been
named and given meaning. Distribution is then 'patterned in accordance with
shared conceptions of what the goods are and what they are for' (Walzer,
1983, p. 7). However, to do so, also requires knowing the nature of the 'social
good' that arises from such an identification (Walzer, 1983, p. 9). The social
good that has been identified in the British debate, is Britain's ability to
compete internationally; whilst the private good is the capacity of individuals
who have had a higher education, to raise their overall life-time earnings.
Finally, Walzer crucially points out that the attached social meanings and
consequently just and unjust distributions, change over time because they have
an historical character. The truth of the historical character of such social
meanings attached to what is considered by the parties to be just and unjust
distribution is central to an understanding of why there has been a debate over
the funding of higher education and why it would come to a head over the
question of whether it was legitimate for the English and Welsh universities via
the agency of the state to charge variable fees to students. In other words, it
was precisely because what was the 'good' in question, how it ought to be
named and the nature of its meaning, had not been agreed by all the parties
that the debate became so increasingly acrimonious during 2003. Such
discussions and consequent agreements are, as Habermas (1990) argued,
central to the democratic political process in contemporary western societies.
However, the degree of dissent that was generated is not only illustrative of
flawed dialogic processes but also of a growth of a sense of insecurity about

the future that develops as the state withdraws from its role as the insurer for social risks. The result, as Castel (2003) argues, is a steady growth of opposition to any changes that the state may propose.

Diversity and Excellence

Although an attempt will be made to separate the ideas of diversity and excellence, it has to be acknowledged that in public discourse, these are more usually linked together. It seems in the first instance more appropriate to treat them in this way before trying to separate them in order to argue that their realities are in many ways, different. One example of just how the two are used inter-connectedly was illustrated by a Financial Times editorial (Financial Times 24/06/03). The purpose of the editorial was to comment upon the United States' Supreme Court's decision to uphold the disputed principle of affirmative action that the University of Michigan's Law School had been operating in its school's admissions' policy. The Supreme Court made two rulings, and the *Financial Times* editorial commented on each of them. The two rulings were:

1. By a 5-4 majority, to uphold the law school's 'practice of using race as a factor in admissions in order to increase the diversity of the student population' by extending 'the definition of a constitutional compelling interest to include the educational benefits that flow from a diverse student body'.

2. By a 6-3 majority, it ruled 'unconstitutional the university's practice of awarding extra points for race in the admissions process. As the university merely checked that an applicant was a member of a minority group before awarding 20 additional points in the admissions process ...' This practice 'was not deemed narrowly tailored to achieve educational diversity'.

The Editorial concluded that by making the principle of using race in admissions constitutional but demanding that it was used intelligently, that is 'alongside many other factors to broaden their student body or their staff' – 'the twin principles of excellence and diversity have been upheld.' Those factors, the intention of which was to broaden either of the pools from which the student body or staff were recruited, ought to aim to take account of 'individual circumstances' and not be general to the groups concerned because the Editorial noted middle-class blacks often receive a better education than blue-collar whites. Clearly both in the US Supreme Court ruling and the Editorial whilst they had emphasised that the immediate beneficiaries were individuals, there had also been a presumption that both diversity and excellence had a value beyond the individual who might receive a benefit from a decision that had been reached on the basis of those criteria. That this presumption is more generally made was nicely illustrated in an article by

Martin Wolf (Financial Times, 28/11/2003) where Wolf concluded that the five
bases of a first-rate university system in today's world are:

Excellence – diversity – freedom – resources – access

As I have already suggested, a precise understanding of the composition of
each of these five bases and whether or not they are necessarily compatible
under a single regime is generally resolved in England and Wales, by the
advocacy of the variable top-up fees solution. Yet, as we continue to unpick
the two concepts of diversity and excellence, the possibility of containing these
within a single regulatory regime seems both analytically and normatively very
difficult. The problem arises from the need to reconcile market driven criteria
with those of social engineering as each produces different kinds of
compromises. The DfES in *The Future of Higher Education* argued that its aim
was to balance 'wealth creation' and the ability of universities 'to compete on
a world stage'. The social justice agenda was to be pursued through the
appointment of a Higher Education Access Regulator whose role would be
to 'develop a framework for Access Agreements for each institution' but
alongside an increase in the availability of two-year foundation degrees.
However, although there appears to be both analytical and normative
problems in aligning these different goals of diversity and excellence, they have
nevertheless been widely subscribed to by higher education itself. For example,
the Convenor of Universities of Scotland and Principal of Robert Gordon
University, Professor Bill Stevely, has argued (*Financial Times*, 27.11.2003)
that Scotland's approach to Higher Education ought to be seen as a hybrid
between the American model of selectivity and concentration, and the
European model of breadth and equity, thus making Scotland, a model of
inclusive excellence.

Even a literal reading of how the Scottish hybrid is arrived at poses some
difficult questions about the perceptions and understanding of the different
ways in which university sectors in different parts of the globe operate. In the
first place, there is no single American model, the sector is highly differentiated
with many different kinds of institutions, some selective and some not.
Secondly, what is the intended meaning of 'concentration'? Geographically,
universities are found in multiples in every state in the USA. If concentration
is used in the business sense where only a few firms compete in certain sectors,
this is hardly true of a sector that includes the large public University of
California, extending over several different campuses, and a small college such
as Wesleyan University, in Middletown, Connecticut. There are self-evidently
different resource levels between different universities. Even a university so
frequently cited as Harvard, only became a significant national player in the
1940s when research funding shifted from the private foundations to the
government and Harvard, which had previously been considered to have been
a college that served the national political elite and the Boston gentry, was
changed into one that competed for the best graduate students (Turner and

Turner, 1990). With regard to 'selectivity', private universities such as Harvard are selective but the large publicly-funded state campuses are not.

Turning now to Professor Steveley's second characterisation of a 'European model of breadth and excellence'. Did he mean breadth of study, of student body or of equal access for all? These questions have to be asked as there are a wider range of higher education institutions in most European Union countries than this vision suggests. In some countries, public and private institutions exist alongside one another, as in Belgium. In France, not only is the private sector a significant player but parts of the system, are highly selective such as entry to the *grandes écoles*, and moreover as Bourdieu has shown in *The State Nobility. Elite Schools in the Field of Power* (1996), it does matter what your family background is, if you desire entry to such schools. Moreover when the entry criteria are diluted, new institutions are founded in order to ensure that the elite continues to retain its overall hold on the 'field of power' that is education. At the same time, the mass public universities while they may accept any student who has the baccalaureate, maintain their selectivity by managing it through an examination system that takes place at the end of the first year by which time the student body is culled. Consequently, although the idea of Scotland as 'a model of inclusive excellence' may make good political sense, if its meaning is dependent upon how the other two exemplars are understood then what it means is far less clear.

Diversity

Having shown that it is common practice to link together ideas of diversity and excellence, what I want to do now is separate these two concepts from each other. In order to proceed, I will begin with a closer examination of the variety of meanings that the heading of 'diversity' has incorporated during the year 2003. As Habermas (1989) has pointed out, how such meanings are understood are both an essential part of the processes of public discourse and also part of the process by which certain sections of the community bring their private interests into the public sphere. In terms of the debate that took place in British higher education during 2003 and the first weeks of 2004, it is possible to identify the following uses of the idea of diversity. That there should be different types of institutions providing higher education; That there should be different types of provision available. That different types of institutions and provision are necessary in order to reflect the presence of different groups in society, some of whom have been excluded by the nature of existing institutions and provision. These different groups have then normally been identified in terms of social class, ethnic origin, gender, and the degree of access that these groups are viewed as having had. This approach can be said to closely mirror Bourdieu's idea of the parts played by what he has called the social and cultural capital that is built up by the *habitus* of different social groups (Bourdieu, 1996). The relevance of Bourdieu's idea of capital and its impact on excluded social groups is further underpinned by the wider view of the Labour government that within the United Kingdom it has proved consistently difficult for some social groups to thrive.

Excellence

On the other hand, diversity and excellence have generally been seen, as the discussion in this chapter has argued, to be essentially two aspects of the same educational ideal, and consequently to be two elements of the same discourse. In the debate that took place in the UK during 2003, although this link was maintained within public discourse, excellence has also been presented in terms of two additional and separate dimensions. Firstly, excellence is essential to achieve international competitiveness. Secondly, all institutions should be able to achieve excellence, but only on the basis that they adjust what it is they do to reflect the characteristics of the social groups for which they are providing.

Outlining the Different Risk Positions

Analysing the nature of the risk positions that have been adopted by government policy-makers in part, depends upon whether diversity and excellence are treated together or separately. However, there would seem to be two principal types of risk or dangers that are seen as being involved. In the first place, there are those civil dangers that might affect the social well-being of contemporary British society. The most obvious of these stems from the government's agenda on social exclusion and the perceived social disorder/ discontent and the consequence thereof that might result from the exclusion of certain well-identified social groups from the public or rather private benefits of education. In this instance, to avoid social disorder, government policy-makers focus on policies that aim to encourage both individual enterprise and fair competition. The sub-text of their position is the belief that with some assistance, individuals being responsible for their own destinies, will be able to win out. However, in spite of the public commitment to excellence for all, the emergence of a legitimated public discourse that aims to 'pick winners', to concentrate resources on those universities (read companies) that are most successful, means excellence has been primarily conceived in terms of issues of competitive advantage. Therefore, although the results are perhaps very different, risk has actually been identified in both situations as a question of insurance. This means that the diversity/excellence evocation of risk falls very much within the parameters of the risk literature in the governmentality field and more especially the framework that was proposed by Ewald (1991).

Indeed, it is the competitive advantage/insurance idea of risk that has emerged from the 'governmentality' approach to risk that I now want to pursue beginning with the exposition in Ewald (1991, pp. 197–210) that risk can be viewed simultaneously as calculable, collective and a capital.

How then do the universities fit within this kind of schema? In the first place, universities are clearly being viewed in terms of their position as a capital resource that is at one and the same time, collectively owned but which delivers an individual benefit. Consequently, it is possible to calculate the value of what the university produces and what individuals gain from their experience there. However, government policy also aims to maintain a global economic position by managing the risks that result from the various points of intersection of inequalities. It is this contradiction between the value of the university to the state as a perceived generator of wealth and the calculated benefit to the individual through their participation that has made the 2003 debate one in which parties to it have been found, much like boxers in the ring, aligned in opposing corners. This debate has been further complicated by the other reading of excellence. This has meant that the position taken in this chapter is a usage of 'risk' in a largely Foucauldian sense, in that it argues that the various debates, however internally contradictory they are, are nevertheless concerned with risk as an issue of 'governmentality'. It is also necessary to view universities, in a manner that is reflective of them as institutions that operate in a relationship with each other as well as the government. This view of universities as institutions is more effectively understood using the framework provided by Douglas and Wildavsky (1982). In other words, a view of risk that takes into account those links between risk selection and culture, and more particularly their discussion of the characteristics of 'borders'. Douglas and Wildavsky (1982) use the idea of 'borders' to explore the ways in which opposition to state policy can operate simultaneously outside the recognised practices of the state but at the same time be increasingly drawn into those same practices. The characteristics of these different organisational positions have been systematised by Lupton (1999a) and Crook (1999) as a matrix that consists of the two axes: group ethos and grid position. According to this model, the two camps are as follows: pro-variable top-up fees are on the low group ethos/low grid position or are 'individualists', whilst the anti-variable top-up fees occupy the corner of high group ethos and low grid position or are 'egalitarians'.

The Douglas and Wildavsky formula helps to account for why there has been different responses not only from individual universities but also from the different bodies that have represented them. The number of such bodies – the Russell Group, the Coalition of Modern Universities (CMU), Meg (Mixed economy group of further education colleges), Council for Industry and Higher Education (CIHE) and Universities UK is reflective of the presence of very different institutional cultures and positions that universities and other institutions that seek to provide higher education in the United Kingdom have. These in turn reflect the historical trajectories of their positioning on the excellence – diversity continuum. Such organisational arrangements are reflections of past historical inequalities which in turn allow the elite who have been the main beneficiaries to rewrite the rules of the game, as and when they perceive their interests to be threatened (Ball, 2003; Bourdieu, 1996). The emergence of the Russell Group, representing self-styled 'elite universities' and categorised on the basis of their dominance in research, has permitted a series of repositionings amongst the universities that will almost certainly have the effect of retaining existing patterns of dominance in higher education. Using the cultural perspective on questions of risk that is associated with Douglas and Wildavsky (1982) makes it possible to appreciate that to understand the complexity of risk in the contemporary social world requires that one takes account of how particular external events can impact on different players in the field. Thus, where it concerns the institutions themselves, the govern-mentality approach is less useful. Instead, it is better understood in terms of ethos and grid position. Taking a culturalist perspective on risk does not, however, explain the specifics of the highly acrimonious character of the politi-cal and public debate that did take place as the different players had to deal with the constantly shifting proposals on 'top-up fees' that emerged during 2003. For that, it is more pertinent to use the framework of the risk and governmentality approach.

The growth of the opposition to the introduction of top-up fees during 2003 should be read as a measure of the ambiguity contained in the proposals. Bauman (1991) wrote of the need in modernity to live with ambivalence. The proposals themselves have been ambivalent in that neither their immediate effects nor their long-term effects on the provision of higher education have been, in practice, self-evident. They have been presented throughout in terms of two arguments which are epistemologically difficult to reconcile. On the one hand, there have been the two public good arguments. They have simultaneously emphasised social justice and the extension of opportunities from the few to the many alongside higher education as a component of national economic policy and the nation's capacity to compete globally in the 'knowledge economy'. This position was taken by the Secretary of State, Charles Clarke on ITV's Jonathan Dimbleby show (18.1.2004). In his opening statement, Charles Clarke argued that the United Kingdom is living in an increasingly competitive world and therefore must make the best use of the skills and talents of its people. However, this position is offset by the individual and utilitarian arguments focused exclusively on the private long-term benefits to the individual and therefore the reasonableness of individually-based payments. The DfES's document *The Future of Higher Education* also interwove these different positions which served to increase the level of confusion felt by the individual who has to make a decision and consequently their sense of insecurity and uncertainty or risk (see also Ball (2003) on the problem of having too much choice).

It is the interplay between these conflicting arguments that allows the extended use of Ewald's (1991) identification of 'insurance' as *abstract technology*. Using such identification, education can then be thought of as one of the methods by which government insures itself against the risk of the national economy failing to grow and prosper. Failure would mean not only that the economy could not generate sufficient jobs, but also that it could not generate them at the right level to ensure that it could compete at a global level. Returning to Ewald's (1991, pp. 201–5) identification of 'risk' as comprised of three aspects, that it should be *calculable, collective,* and *a capital,* and applying these to education, we find that all three of these characteristics are being employed. Higher education is being rendered as *calculable* given that the fundamental basis of the government's argument for justifying 'top-up fees' is that there are long-term individual earning benefits – also backed up by the September 2003 OECD report *Education at a glance.* This showed that 'the financial return from going to university is greater in Britain than anywhere else in the developed world.' (Financial Times, 17/09/03). There is a separate debate about why education should have this kind of payback in the UK but that discussion is outside of the main focus of this chapter, even though it does form part of the utilitarian justification for individuals being responsible for final payment. Ewald's second aspect that the risk concerned has to be *collective* in the sense that the benefit is shared by the whole community is also fulfilled; whilst at the same time there are ongoing processes of selecting and dividing up the risks through the redesign of the institutions involved so that they can increasingly perform different functions, with the result that risks are shared out amongst a wider population. Finally, higher education is also being identified as *a capital* because the view is that the individual achieves additional material advantage from access to it. This is reminiscent of Bourdieu's general discussions of 'capital' as well as his specific discussion of the uses of the different forms of capital in education by the bourgeoisie (Bourdieu, 1996) or, after Ball (2003), the 'middle-classes'. Both Bourdieu and Ball illustrate that even where there is government intent towards democratisation, the means that they use, enable existing elites to simply shift the boundaries. Ewald himself, deals with this particular issue through the medium of his discussion of insurance and 'justice'. Ewald quotes the nineteenth century French social thinker, Proudhon, to argue that even though insurance can be bought by everyone, what insurance actually buys is security. However, security is a state of being that in practice, increases through the social classes even as the premium for its purchase falls. Therefore, the rich continue to be able to buy more for the same amount (Ewald, 1991, p. 206). In education, the Government argues that education is for all, 'top-up fees' plus accompanying redistributive measures such as bursaries will therefore act to ensure that it is not only available to all but that more of those who might not otherwise have been able to obtain its advantages are able to do so. However, even within the terms of their own vision, structures are already being put in place that will mean in practice that those who will benefit most from the changes will be other than those that the changes are allegedly aimed at. The *Future of Higher Education* states that 'the bulk of the expansion will come through new types of qualification tailored to the needs of students and of the economy' and that the means will be the expansion of 'the number of foundation degree places' and through '2+' models. These are programmes that have two initial years of study leading to a qualification, which then has to be topped-up for full value by a further period of study. Studies in the USA of '2+' models have indicated that the effect of these programmes is to concentrate the already disadvantaged within a narrow range of programmes that have limited options for exit (Richardson and Bender, 1987). Reay, Davies, David and Ball (2001) show that students who come from ethnic minority and/or working-class backgrounds have a greater propensity to opt for 'local' institutions because not only do they feel more at home there; but also, their 'A' level grades tend to be lower as a result of their need to work whilst studying. Consequently, as Richardson and Bender (1987) had already shown for the United States, such students are more likely to be found in precisely those institutions that are less prestigious and which will be encouraged to offer the new types of qualification. This means that going to university, is, except for a small minority, unlikely to dramatically alter overall life chances. Taken together with two other policies, namely the extension of the use of the title of university to institutions that do not fulfil the normally understood criteria of a university as a place where both research and teaching take place; and the ongoing classification and hierarchical ordering of existing institutions according to what has been deemed by government to be the global potentiality of the institution then the relationship between education, government and wealth production changes in a number of significant ways, irrespective of the references to a focus on teaching. After all institutional value-added has little to do with what it does and rather more to do with the doors that it is perceived to open.

One important consequence is that it becomes necessary to look rather differently at both the ways in which the idea of market is being used, as well as the arguments that focus on the relationships that might exist between the universities and business. Whilst market has been primarily presented in terms of a presumption of individual market gain/advantage, it is equally possible to take the view that the 'knowledge economy' is in practice a direct and unambiguous reflection of the requirements of the reproduction of capital in the current age. In this form, the beneficiaries are not necessarily the individual but the state, employers and business. *The Future of Higher Education's* emphasis on 'reputable and truly employer-focused higher education qualification' (DfES, 2003, para 5.13) is rather more suggestive of a change in the relationship between capital accumulation and education than simply a debate over alternative sources of funding. However, even though, the agenda has been ostensibly about the search for a wider (or more diverse) range of funding sources, there have been rather mixed messages. On the one side has been situated the UK government and British business all arguing that business is a viable alternative source of funding; whilst on the other there have been a number of interventions from commentators in the United States suggesting that whilst business can provide cash resources, these should not be seen as primary resources for overall budget augmentation rather they are about breaking even on specific projects. If such funding is only about breaking even, it means that in practice, relying on an expectation that business sources of finance will provide a viable long-term alternative source for funding higher education, is over-optimistic.

The final consideration is the public/private distinction in its US/UK dimension. The debate over public and private, the role of external funding and the establishment of endowment funds have all been key elements in the proposals. Indeed chapter 7 of 'The Future of Higher Education' argues that 'the way forward is through endowment' (DfES, 2003, paras 7.16 to 7.19). However, the attractiveness of this proposal belies the difficulties ahead in achieving it. Furthermore, it is also reflective of a very partial interpretation of the US history of endowment funds and their intimate links with the particular character of the origins of many of the US universities, and more especially, a much sharper distinction between what is a private and a public university. In the UK, universities have no recent history of independent formation, only one private university, the University of Buckingham which opened in 1976 with sixty-five students can be said to parallel its US counterparts. However, it has remained relatively small (the student body was under seven hundred students in 2003) and is therefore a marginal player in British higher education. Consequently, drawing the public/private distinction in the UK rests on an ambivalence of meaning. As such, the position taken by the 'elite' universities in the form of the Russell Group that if the Government wants the best in the world it is necessary to give more support to the best universities runs parallel with the understanding that a student attending a 'best' university will be able to expect to command a higher salary on exit. The presumption of rational actor decision-making that underpins this, is also present in government policy-making. However, as the localism question has indicated, actors may be less rational in this single sense than thas been assumed. They perceive the risks entailed in opting out of their social environment. However, if the Russell Group institutions view their market position in those terms then perhaps it is not the role of government to provide support to them. Consequently, there may be a case for letting those institutions who see themselves as well-funded become private. The government then deals with the question of access by concentrating funding on truly public institutions.

Conclusion

The debate over top-up fees has revealed the fragility of the unintentional opening up of the higher education sector by the transformation of the former polytechnics into universities in 1992. However, the subsequent growth in regulatory systems whether of teaching or research, has served to reassert the market advantages of the older institutions. Whether the proposed Director of Fair Access to Education will make a significant difference depends on the intended aim. Meanwhile, the choice of a fee-based system to fund university education should be seen as an essential part of the reassertion of old class domination that was challenged by expansion and democratisation in the new universities. It can be said that order has been reasserted, and it can be expected that there will be a growth in differentiation between the various institutions. Although the Secretary of State, pledged that a review of the level of fees will not take place before 2009–10, with such a review subject to parliamentary approval, already institutions that consider their market value to be sufficient to warrant higher fees have challenged the overall package (Financial Times, 17/18/04); whilst the heads of CMU universities argue that their level of under-funding means that they have no choice but to charge the maximum (Financial Times, 24/25.1.2004) suggests that top-up fees ought to only be seen as an interim solution to a problem that is still to be resolved. One such solution is endowment funds financed by *alumni*. The future is indeed uncertain.

References

Ball, S.J. (2003), *Class Strategies and the Education Market. The middle classes and social advantage*, Routledge Falmer, London and New York.

Bannock, G., Baxter, R.E. and Rees, R. (1972), *The Penguin Dictionary of Economics*, Penguin Books, Harmondsworth.

Bauman, Z. (1991), *Modernity and Ambivalence*, Polity, Cambridge.

Bourdieu, P. (1996), *The State Nobility. Elite Schools in the Field of Power*, Polity, Cambridge.

Castel, R. (2003), *L'insécurité sociale. Qu'est-ce qu'être protégé?*, La République des Idées, Seuil, Paris.

Crook, S. (1999), 'Ordering Risks', in Lupton, D., *Risk and Sociolcultural Theory. New Directions and Perspectives*, Cambridge University Press, Cambridge, pp. 160–185.

Department for Education and Skills (2003), 'The Future for Higher Education', http://www.dfes.gov.uk/highereducation/hestrategy.

Department for Education and Skills (2004), 'Higher Education Bill', http://www. publications.parliament.uk/pa/cm200304/cmbills/035/en/04035x.

Douglas, M. (1992), *Risk and Blame: Essays in Cultural Theory*, Routledge, London.

Douglas, M. and Wildavsky, A. (1982), *Risk and Culture. An Essay on the Selection of Technological and Environmental Dangers*, University of California Press, Berkeley, Los Angeles.

Ewald, F. (1991), 'Insurance and Risk', in G. Burchell, C. Gordon, and P. Miller, *The Foucault Effect. Studies in Governmentality*, Harvester Wheatsheaf, Hemel Hempstead, pp. 197–210.

Financial Times (24/06/03), 'Affirmative Action. The Supreme Court takes a principled stand'.

Financial Times (19/09/03), 'Ministers seize on survey findings to back fees policy'.

Financial Times (27/11/03), 'Motor that needs 5-star fuel'.

Financial Times (28/11/03), 'Set Universities free to compete'.

Financial Times (17/18/04), 'Top-up plans insufficient, say colleges'.

Financial Times (24/01/04), 'Most new universities plan charges near top'.

Habermas, J. (1989), *The Structural Transformation of the Public Sphere. An Enquiry into a Category of Bourgeois Society*, Polity, Cambridge.

Habermas, J. (1990), *Moral Consciousness and Communicative Action*, Polity, Cambridge.

Hayek, F.A. (1960), *The Constitution of Liberty*, University of Chicago Press, Chicago.

Lupton, D. (1999a), *Risk*, Routledge, London.

Lupton, D. (1999b), *Risk and Sociocultural Theory. New Directions and Perspectives*, Cambridge University Press, Cambridge.

Pass, C., Lowes, B. and Davies, L. (2000), *Collins Dictionary. Economics*, HarperCollins, Glasgow.

Rawls, J. (1972), *A Theory of Justice*, Oxford University Press, Oxford.

Reay, D., Davies, J., David, M. and Ball, S.J. (2001), 'Choices of Degree or Degress of Choice? Class, "Race" and the Higher Education Choice Process', *Sociology*, vol. 35(4), pp. 855–874.

Richardson Jr, R.C. and Bender, L.W. (1987), *Fostering Minority Access and Achievement in Higher Education – the role of urban community colleges and universities*, Jossey-Bass publishers, San Francisco and London.

Turner, S.P. and Turner, J.H. (1990), *The Impossible Science. An Institutional Analysis of American Sociology*, Sage, London.

Walzer, M. (1983), *Spheres of Justice. A Defence of Pluralism and Equality*, Basil Blackwell, Oxford.

Chapter 16

Educating About Donor Insemination: Managing Risky Identities in Donor Insemination

Catherine Donovan and Nigel Watson

Introduction

Within public health discourse there is a long tradition for associated agencies to provide patients with information on treatments and on how to avoid or minimize health related risk. In the United Kingdom a concern of this kind can be traced back to the nineteenth century when the public health reformers set about improving housing and environmental conditions in the industrial cities. During the twentieth century however, there was a gradual shift away from general population approaches towards a focus upon individual social behaviours and most recently upon lifestyle. (for a full discussion of these developments see Ashton and Seymour 1988, chapter 2). Given this shift towards individual responsibility and developments in mass communications, advice has most commonly been delivered via a leaflet, a video and now web pages. This form of activity has usually been located as part of general health education.

One outcome of this form of information is the construction of the patient as an active subject who can responsibly make the necessary changes to avoid and/or minimise perceived risk. It implies that the individual is in a position to weigh technical evidence and arrive at a balanced objective assessment. However whilst the concept of risk is closely associated with biomedical discourse through a common emphasis upon calculative and predictive outcomes which are objectified and removed from social value, this is not necessarily true of public perceptions. As Douglas (1990) has pointed out, risk in everyday discourse means danger and risks are perceived as negative. In this respect the conjunction of education and risk makes for the potential construction of socially negative activities and by association, socially negative groups of people.

In this chapter we will examine the information that is made available to potential recipients of donor insemination (DI) and semen donors by the Human Fertilisation and Embryology Authority (HFEA). This was set up under the aegis of the Human Fertilisation and Embryology Act 1991 (HFE Act, 1991) to grant licenses, produce guidelines that interpret the legislative framework for best practice and oversee developments in reproductive and genetic engineering. We intend to discuss the ways in which this information educates potential recipients of DI and donors of sperm by both constructing and reinforcing the normative use of DI; and reproduces normative families and parenthood. In particular we will show how the biomedical discourse through which the information is articulated constructs the use of DI as a legally regulated medical treatment for infertility whilst neutralising its impact as an alternative method for conceiving babies and constructing families.

Donor Insemination has been surrounded by controversy ever since its use in Britain was first made public (Barton, et al., 1946). This assisted conception technique (ACT) involves the insemination of a fertile woman with a stranger's sperm at ovulation. The then Archbishop of Canterbury commissioned a report published in 1948 on the use of insemination that concluded DI should be banned because it undermined the sanctity of marriage being tantamount to adultery and because of the effect on the resulting children of knowing their origins (Haimes, 1998; Snowden and Mitchell, 1981). These objections represent a set of anxieties that has been articulated in relation to DI ever since.

DI threatens many of the fundamental normative assumptions that exist in British society about family, reproduction and parenting. The genetic basis of kinship is challenged since the social/legal father is not the genetic father of the child(ren) yet the mother is; heterosexual sex is not required for conception to occur which opens up the possibilities of its use by 'anybody' who desires children; and the genetic father is deliberately shut out of the kin and family relationships he is responsible for and which result from using DI. More recently the possibilities have been understood by a growing number of women that DI offers the chance for autonomous motherhood (Klein 1984; Hornstein, 1984; Saffron, 1994). DI threatens to give rise to social chaos (Snowden and Mitchell, 1981).

Yet all of these anxieties – articulated by powerful groups in society such as religious groups, pro- (heterosexual, nuclear) family groups and conservative groups – have not led to the use of DI being banned. Rather the trend has been towards regulation and the management of perceived risk. The arguments have been won that DI – along with other ACTs that rely on donated gametes – are on the whole positive techniques that, when medically managed and legally regulated, assist in providing those who want children the opportunity to conceive, bear and give birth to children who are genetically related to at least one member of a couple relationship. A balance has been struck, it would seem, between on the one hand, the use of a technique that requires the use of quite 'abnormal' social relations and organisation and on the other, the reproduction of as near a 'normal' experience of conception, pregnancy, childbirth and motherhood as possible. This balance has been maintained, we would argue, by the successful medicalisation of infertility and the location of the provision of ACTs within the medical sphere. In this context it is interesting to reflect upon the way in which the idea of a social threat becomes entwined around the apparently neutral concept of risk articulated through an associated medical discourse.

The Medicalisation of Donor Insemination

The emphasis on regulation rather than an outright ban has been facilitated by several factors. The recommendations of the Warnock Report (1984) have probably been among the most important. The HFE Act, 1991 was based on the Warnock recommendations and provide the framework within which DI is provided. Two of the most important recommendations were those that confirmed infertility as a legitimate 'malfunction' requiring medical attention and recommended that DI should be offered as a medical treatment under the supervision of licensed medical practitioners. The recommendations provided the basic conditions within which DI could be successfully produced as a 'respectable' medical concern.

First medical practitioners as respected professionals with a monopoly on issues of the body and intimate experiences such as attempting conception are very well placed to act as an honest broker between potential recipients of DI and donors of sperm (Novaes, 1998). Second the embedding of DI as one of an array of ACTs effectively medicalises its application and through an association with predictive scientific practices, allows for the easier embedding of DI within risk discourse. Donovan (1993) found that different clinics adopt different protocols for administering DI each of which are presented as best practice. For example, the range of fertility investigations carried out on the women, at what stage and with what consequences for medical intervention and treatment with drugs; the identification and timing of ovulation; the number of inseminations administered per cycle; the number of cycles constituting a course of treatment and so on.

The medicalisation of the organisation of insemination creates a context within which the technique is constructed as a treatment of infertility rather than an alternative method of achieving conception. Within this context it can easily be forgotten that women successfully organise to self-inseminate and that for any woman to conceive using DI she must be fertile. The biomedical model, constructed through a discourse including labelling recipients as 'patients', DI as 'treatment' and the construction of medical/health 'risks', confirms this definition and gives secondary importance to the social implications and consequences of using DI.

Thirdly, biomedical discourse constructs a 'necessary fiction' about DI that keeps it within the medical sphere. Donovan has elsewhere argued that infertility is a contested concept (Donovan, 2003) whose use, rather than being a neutral descriptive medical category instead constructs a heterosexual norm that can exclude others from access to ACTs (see also Novaes, 1998). Infertility is defined as a condition requiring treatment and DI is defined as a treatment for infertility. However, DI does not treat anybody's infertility. Male partners remain spermatically or genetically compromised and women have to be fertile to have any chance of conceiving. DI 'treats' the desire for a child yet many clinics refuse DI to lesbians or heterosexual single women because they are not infertile. The normative use of the label 'infertility' constructs the necessity of there being a heterosexual couple that are unable to conceive (regardless of who has the fertility problem). Heterosexuality – normality – is inferred, assumed, expected. The potential of DI to be disruptive to facilitate autonomous motherhood is muted, denied and neutralised by its medicalisation.

The fourth way that medicalisation achieves regulation of DI is that donated sperm is successfully reduced to the status of a medicine or drug (in fact in Canada it is controlled under the Food and Drugs Act 1996 [Health Canada, 1996]). Donovan (1993) has argued that donated sperm can be understood, using Douglas's argument, as representing purity or danger which provides a parallel discourse to the medical one, and which is based in social values and the organisation/regulation of risky sperm. Unregulated donated sperm is represented as a risk to the mother and the unborn child and the unregulated donor is constructed as a reckless, selfish harbinger of disease and other unarticulated dangers (Donovan, 1993). The medicalisation of DI and therefore of sperm donation allows the collection of sperm and selection of donors to be constructed as a medico-scientific enterprise with purified, healthy sperm that poses no risk to potential recipients or the potential baby.

The fifth way that the medicalisation of DI provides a rationale for its regulation is the presentation of imminent risk to lay people that use of DI presents can only be addressed by proper medical management. The medicalisation of DI constructs its use as a medical treatment thus lessening the social impact of its use but evidence must be continually produced to maintain its position within the medical sphere. These risks are explicitly for individuals but implicitly for families, children and society. In the provision of DI the medico-legal framework for the protocols surrounding its use implicitly 'promise' prioritising the reproduction of normative heterosexual families.

In this chapter we look at the educational information provided by the HFE Authority to those who may be considering using DI and those who may be considering donating sperm. The leaflets we discuss were downloaded from the HFE Authority website but are also available in hard copy and are themselves both products of and contributions to the construction of a risk discourse around DI. There are four main documents. The *Patients' Guide to Donor Insemination* (HFEA, 2002a), *Issues to Consider* (HFEA, undated a), *Welfare of the Child: Information for Patients* (HFEA, undated b) and *Sperm and Egg Donors and the Law* (HFEA, 2002b). Parts of the *Patient's Guide to Donor Insemination* (HFEA, 2002a) are reproduced in separate leaflets covering specific issues or aimed at either potential recipients or donors. These documents can be argued to present best practice in terms of their content and scope including the legal framework of the HFE Act, 1991. They present basic information about what can be expected if DI is used or if one is to donate sperm. To this extent the literature is educational and can be taken to constitute one method by which lay people as potential recipients and donors gain an understanding about what DI is and what they can expect if they opt either to use it or to become a donor.

What is immediately obvious from the literature is that there is little discussion about the social and ethical implications or consequences of using DI. The medic-legal discourse predominates and the social consequences must be inferred by references made to the medical/technical/genetic aspects of using DI. The language of risk and health is used not only to educate potential recipients about the medical/technical nature of what they might embark on but also as a way of neutralising the broader social implications of the technique. There seems to be several levels at which the information is intended to work. First is to explain to potential recipients of DI or donors of sperm what they can expect if they opt to use the technique or become donors. Second the information given outlines the worst possible health/medical outcomes that may result from using DI as if to delineate both the limits of and rationale for medical and legal regulation. Third, the language of DI as a medical treatment serves to in some way contain the procedure and its social and ethical implications so that it can be understood as a quite benign medical technique that may result in pregnancy and childbirth. The medical/technical language keeps muted the social context of using DI and the resulting implications for kin relationships. The legal language implicitly refers to these relationships but emphasises the legality of the resulting parenting relationships and the integrity of the DI family – as long as all the correct procedures are adhered to. The medical/technical language is infused with notions of risk that coalesce around several aspects of using DI: the medical risks for women; the risks to children; and the risks for the DI family, particularly in relation to the genetic and legal fathers. However because these risks are built around the construction of sperm as a medicine and DI as a treatment, a distance is created from the social relationships that are at the basis of the process.

Medical Risks to Women

One of the first presentations of risk in the use of DI tempers potential recipients' expectations about what DI can achieve:

> All pregnancies carry some risks, and donor insemination does not protect patients from these (HFEA, 2002a, p. 1).

This statement is made very early on in the information and can be seen as a way of establishing that the limits of DI: recipients' expectations should not be raised but neither should they fear anything as a result of using this treatment.

There is a large literature describing the ways in which pregnancy has been reconstructed as a risky medical phenomenon that is in need of careful medical management (e.g. Oakley, 1981). Here the purpose of using the language of risk is not only to present pregnancy as a potential medical problem but also to establish that the use of DI will not take away these risks, thus confirming both the legitimacy of and the limits of medicine.

Another medical risk related to the use of DI is its success rate. Again the language is that of caution and at the outer limits the encouragement of an expectation that DI will not succeed. The limits for the success of DI are bounded primarily by the age of women attempting to conceive using DI. Statistics are given – a characteristic of the medicalisation process wherein empirical evidence is given to scientifically 'prove' the biomedical 'facts' – indicating that with increasing age the chances of pregnancy fall dramatically:

> Women over 40 have only a 3–4 per cent chance of successful pregnancy for each DI cycle (HFEA, 2002a, p. 2).

A caveat acknowledges that the statistics given are only averages and that 'individual circumstances' will affect each outcome. However, the statistical information outweighs this and the information is unequivocal: 'your chances of success decrease with age'. (ibid). Risks here are re-presented as 'chances' in an attempt to present the positive side of risk taking in the use of DI. There are ways and means of using DI that will maximise the chances (risks) of success and medicine has the expertise and knowledge to explain and capitalise on them.

The benefits of using medicalised DI is underlined in the section of the leaflet that explains how DI will be provided. Whilst acknowledging that women will probably be already able to identify when they are ovulating through an examination of changes in the vaginal mucous:

> During this fertile period, blood or urine hormone tests or ultrasound scans are usually used to establish accurately the most suitable time for insemination (HFEA, 2002a, p. 1).

In the presentation of this information, the leaflet simultaneously devalues women's knowledge of their own bodies and creates or confirms the need for the medical management of DI. To maximise the chances of success high tech (and high cost) diagnostic procedures will be used to pinpoint ovulation and the optimum time to inseminate. Franklin (1997) has argued that conception has been socially constructed as the moment sperm and egg meet and merge at ovulation yet the reality is that for many people these conditions even medically contrived, do not result in pregnancy. Nevertheless the patient information states that medical techniques will more accurately identify ovulation and the exact time to inseminate which will improve the chances of DI succeeding. The implications of this for women is that they can expect to visit the clinic every day from about day 10 of their cycle to have their blood or urine taken and analysed until ovulation occurs. They and their partners will experience huge disruption to their lives as they accommodate these medical intrusions into their lives but the hope is held out to them that by so doing they increase their chances of success. Again the medicalised version of insemination is rehearsed as the best chance of achieving conception patients have.

The last set of risks for women related to the use of DI is in the risks attached to the over stimulation of their ovaries. The first risk outlined in *Issues to Consider* is of multiple pregnancy and birth (HFEA, undated a, p. 2). The leaflets spell out quite clearly both the medical health risks to women and children of multiple births and the risks they may face socially bringing up multiple births (e.g. social isolation, financial difficulties). No solution is suggested to reduce these risks – the option to refuse the drugs for example. Taking drugs is presented as an accepted part of the treatment for those patients who might need them to make the use of DI successful. Patients as active subjects are being informed of the risks so that they may understand what to expect if they consent to the treatment.

The second order of risk related to the use of ovulation stimulating drugs is that to women's health (HFEA, undated a, p. 3). At one end of the spectrum patients are informed that they may experience 'mild, unpleasant symptoms' which will be 'shortlived' and may include 'hot flushes, feelings of depression and irritability, headaches and restlessness at night'. These symptoms are 'no cause for concern'. Under other circumstances these same symptoms might be recognised as menopausal causing real enough concern to warrant treatment with hormone replacement therapy. Here, however, they are presented as minor intrusions into women's lives noteworthy only so that women and their partners can recognise them for what they are if they occur. It is interesting to note that the risk associated with the same 'symptoms' is varied by the social context of its articulation.

At the other end of the spectrum ovarian hyper-stimulation syndrome (OHSS) may occur in small numbers of women which may cause the development of cysts, pain, 'mild abdominal swelling' and result in the abandonment of a treatment cycle. In 1 per cent of cases severe OHSS may result in more serious symptoms that may require hospital admission (HFEA, undated a, p. 3). Patients are advised to ask clinics how they try to avoid OHSS and what symptoms to look for so they can be vigilant. Given that the statistical risks are apparently so low it is worthy of comment how much space they give to this risk. In *Issues to Consider*, out of three pages, multiple births and hyper-stimulation takes up just under half of the space and hyper-stimulation takes up nearly a quarter of this section. The impact of hyper-stimulation is relatively small yet the warnings about its possible incidence are relatively great. This is another example of the ways in which the medical discourse of risk serves to define the use of DI as a medical treatment (with the use of drugs to control ovulation) that should be monitored carefully not just by the medical profession but by the patients as well. This exhortation for patients to be vigilant for signs of symptoms, of risks to their health, again constructs them as responsible active subjects who may self-monitor the impact of these drugs. It can serve to create an anxiety in patients that facilitates their compliance with medical regimens of evaluation and monitoring making medical management more necessary rather than the cause of potential iatrogenic effects (Illich, 1976). This is also a reflection of the ways in which the professional interests of medicine influence the construction of risk.

The headlining of the possible health and medical risks and chances of success related to women's use of DI reinforce its status as a medical treatment that is properly within the medical sphere managed by medical specialists. The early presentation of what DI is does not even specifically state that donors' sperm is inseminated into a woman's reproductive tract at ovulation to achieve conception. Instead the leaflet states:

> Donor Insemination treatment (DI) involves the use of sperm from an anonymous donor. It can be used if the male partner has no sperm or very poor sperm or risks passing on an inherited disease. DI may also be used to treat single women or lesbian couples (HFEA, 2002a, p. 6).

This lack of detailed explanation of what constitutes DI can be seen as a further way in which the medical discourse creates a 'treatment' focused version of DI that obscures the nature and function of the technique and allows patients to read a medical rather than a social version of conception.

Risks to Children

One of the first risks outlined for children resulting from the use of DI is in the use of donated sperm. In outlining (and emphasising) the extent to which sperm donors are screened for health and fertility and the fact that they are chosen from within an optimum age range to enhance their potential as healthy fertile donors, reveals the anxieties that exist around accepting sperm from unknown sources. The implications are that not anybody should or would be accepted as a donor, that only the most fertile are chosen that enhance the chances of pregnancy and that only the healthiest are chosen to allay fears about the health of any resulting children. Nevertheless there is an absence/gap in the information for patients that requires some discussion. There is no mention of the genetic screening that donors will be submitted to. This is an interesting absence given the information written for potential sperm donors and the guidance to patients about 'questions to ask clinics'. In the leaflet aimed at potential donors, the message is quite clear:

> A child may be able to sue a donor and a clinic for damages if the child was born with a disability as a result of the donor's failure to disclose inherited disease (HFEA, undated d, p. 3).

A caveat that follows explains that legal action is highly unlikely so long as the donor is 'open and honest about his [or her in the case of egg donors] medical and family history at the time of donation' (Ibid). This warning to donors for honesty is given to explain the only exception to the legal requirement for donor anonymity. Yet its detailed explanation and emphasis underscores the importance of genetic screening in DI and the duty that care donors and clinics are expected to exercise in screening sperm for the safe use by potential recipients and for the best genetic and health outcome for DI children.

It is extremely difficult to speculate on the circumstances that could obtain in which an unwanted genetic disease in a DI child might be traced back to a donor who, it could be established, had deliberately withheld the information. The risks of passing on genetic diseases to DI children are clearly understood as unacceptable and there are strong implications that every measure will be or should be taken by clinics and donors to avoid such risks for DI children. Yet it is only in the 'Questions to Ask Clinics' section of the *Patient's Guide to Donor Insemination* (HFEA, 2002a) that potential recipients are advised to ask clinics what genetic screening they do and whether they include screening for particular diseases (cystic fibrosis is given as an example). This could be because the HFEA takes the view that they will not give general information on genetic screening. It also suggests that protocols for genetic screening are too varied among DI clinics for the HFEA to provide a broad enough description of what to expect. It is also possible that genetic screening is understood as too individualised in its impact to warrant generalising about what might be screened. Rather, individuals are advised to explore genetic screening themselves as part of their evaluation of the appropriateness of the clinic for them.

The second area of risk to children relates to protecting them from inappropriate recipients as parents. The information for potential recipients *Welfare of the Child* (undated b) outlines in great detail the welfare of the child clause in the HFE Act, 1991, and the ways this may be applied by clinics. The welfare of the child requirement includes the welfare of any existing child as well as the welfare of any child born as a result of using ACTs (HFEA, undated b, p. 1). Although the HFE Act, 1991 does not define the welfare of the child, it does explicitly state that it includes the 'need of a child for a father' (Ibid). The HFEA's information about the welfare of the child and how this might be assessed places emphasis on 'who would be legally responsible for any child born as a result of the treatment and who will be bringing up the child'; and situations where the child will have no legal father wherein the clinic 'will pay particular attention to the prospective mother's ability to meet the child's needs throughout childhood' (HFEA, undated b, p. 2).

The leaflet clearly states that the HFE Act, 1991 does not exclude 'any woman' from consideration for treatment and states that anyone is 'entitled to a fair and unprejudiced assessment of their situation and needs' (HFEA, undated b, p. 1). However, in the *Patient's Guide to Donor Insemination* (HFEA, 2002a) section on the welfare of the child, after outlining in summary the kinds of factors that may be taken into account in a clinic's assessment of suitability, we are told:

> Some clinics, as a matter of policy, do not offer treatment to single women or to unmarried couples (HFEA, 2002a, p. 7).

There is a contradiction here between the statement in the HFEA leaflet *Welfare of the Child* which apparently eschews prejudiced selection procedures and the statement in the *Patients Guide to Donor Insemination* that apparently accepts clinics adoptions of policies that are discriminatory on social grounds. If sperm was simply a medicine then this judgement would not be made. Bodies would not be assessed for their social suitability, but would instead be treated. The only legitimate medical interest would be with the risks of the medicine as medicine and not as a social indicator. Sperm clearly has an ambiguous status as medicine.

The location of this statement about clinics' exclusionary policies appears in the section headed Welfare of the Child and suggests the policies have been developed in line with the best interests of the child. It underlines the assumed centrality of normative heterosexual couples (i.e. married) as preferred and assumed recipients. The lack of discussion about or explanation of these policies is also suggestive. Such silence around what could be understood as social engineering is indicative of the hegemony of the normative family in these documents.

Information about how the welfare of the child might be assessed is very detailed in the leaflet on *Welfare of the Child*. The HFEA was given the task of producing guidelines for clinics on how *the Welfare of the Child* should be interpreted and assessed. Potential recipients will be asked about their 'commitment' to having children; their 'ability to provide a stable and supportive environment'; their health; their ages and future ability to provide for their children; their ability to meet the needs of any children including the risk of multiple birth and the effect of any resulting babies on existing children. Incorrect answers imply that a child may be put at risk if DI were to be allowed, and creates an awareness in potential recipients that they will be under pressure to 'perform' correctly in discussions with medical practitioners. This information prepares potential recipients for the kinds of risks to children that clinics will wish to eliminate and encourages recipients to be prepared for discussions about these issues.

It is clear that medical practitioners are expected to carry out assessments that could with some reason be understood to be more associated with the skills, competencies and knowledge of the social work profession. However, there is careful knitting together of the medical and the social in such a way that retains the primary medical nature of the assessment of risk. For example, the history that will be taken of patients will be a 'detailed medical and social one' (HFEA, undated b, p. 2). Its medical nature comes first to designate these matters as primarily medical. Another example of the ways in which

medical and social notions of risk have been brought together in HFEA
information to obfuscate the social is in the following criterion clinics will
screen for:

> Any risk of harm to the child or children who may be born, including the risk of
> inherited disorders or transmissible diseases, problems during pregnancy and of
> neglect or abuse (HFEA, undated b, p. 2).

The notion of harm becomes an umbrella term pulling together inherited
disease, problems during pregnancy and neglect and abuse. With no further
information than this we are only left to speculate on the rationale for bringing
these together. Using the notion of harm as an umbrella term allows them a
grouping together of the most unlikely bedfellows. The imagined 'harm' resulting from genetic disease or problems during pregnancy are of a different order
to that resulting from the action of adults who misuse their power in relation
to children in their care. Here medical and social risks are brought together
with medical risks put first to create an extraordinary sense of association
between them. It is as if a child being born with genetic disease could be said
to have been harmed in the same way as a child who is neglected. Yet it could
also be argued that the underlying goal is to medicalise what constitutes a
social assessment of social risks.

The information given about the welfare of the child does not indicate how
these issues will be explored or by whom. It does explain that clinics may get in
touch with patients' General Practitioner (GP) in order to glean information
and provides a model letter that might be sent to their GP eliciting their recommendations. To safeguard patients from prejudicial GPs the model letter
makes clear to GPs that they are not:

> being asked to speculate on lifestyles or on the probability that a patient of yours
> might behave in certain ways. We are not asking you to assess your patient's
> suitability to act as a parent. You are being asked for relevant factual information
> medical or otherwise, within the scope of the information available to you (HFEA,
> undated b, p. 6).

This statement points us towards an unusually visible attempt to retain
some of the objectivity of predictive risk analysis. The statement strongly
implies that the assessment potential recipients undergo will not be based on
an individual's subjective whim or prejudice, but on a neutral, methodical
assessment of the ascertainable facts. However we might ask whether this is
possible. The assessment being made is a predictive one about a hypothetical
circumstance: might these recipients at some point in the future present such a
risk to a child (who may or may result from using DI) that it would be better
that the child not be born. By presenting the assessment process as if it is a
medical process based on an objective assessment of observable characteristics,
it serves to obscure the profoundly social and ethical nature of the screening
process.

In this construction of risk to children, the welfare of the child is presented as a necessary legal requirement that potential recipients of DI must accept and prepare for if they choose to apply for DI. Entitlement to counselling is dealt with differently in different leaflets. In the *Patient's Guide to Donor Insemination* (HFEA, 2002a) the subject of counselling is referred to straight after discussion of the welfare of the child. Here there is an implicit link made between the sorts of issues that will be explored with potential recipients before a decision will be made and the obligations of clinics to provide patients with counselling. In *Welfare of the Child* (HFEA, undated b) counselling is not mentioned at all.

The other set of risks pertaining to children is their right to know their origins. This is a risk insofar as the security of the family, the legal father and the child, their relationships and the child's sense of self depend on the careful management of this information. This aspect of DI is possibly the most risky. In *Welfare of the Child* (HFEA, undated b), issues related to the children's origins are set out and it is explained that they will be discussed during the process prior to starting treatment with DI. These issues are the child's potential need to know their origins and parents needing to be aware of whether they will or not be able to answer questions from children about their origins; how they might respond to other family members' attitudes to their children and their 'status in the family'; the implications for the child's welfare if the donor is known to the family circle; explaining who will be the legal parents (HFEA, undated b, p. 2). These issues are couched in terms that infer the social implications of using a stranger's sperm yet are not explicit about them. The legal framework is explained as a rationale for patients having to consider the issues. The HFEAct, 1991 entitles children to find out at 18 years of age – or 16 if they are about to get married – whether they are the result of a DI conception, whether their potential spouse is genetically related to them and some limited, non-identifying information about the donor (hair, eye, skin colour and some genetic/medical information). Whilst these requirements are believed to allow adult DI children to have some clearer, albeit genetic, sense of their origins the contradiction embedded in the HFE Act, 1991 is that parents are not obliged to tell their children how they were conceived. The HFE Act states:

> You might consider such matters as whether, and how, you will wish to tell your potential child about his or her origin by DI (HFEA, 2002a, p. 8).

To this extent it could be argued that the risks to children of not knowing their genetic origins are not given as much importance as their parents rights to define their families in ways that protect their interests. There is no discussion about why parents might not tell their children, nor is there any information about what it is to bring up children who are not genetically related to both parents. The sense is that it is only because of the HFE Act 1991 that these issues are being considered at all. This is perhaps because the risks to the DI family of telling children about their conception are considerable and the medical profession in Britain have historically never supported openness in the use of DI (Haimes, 1998).

The Risks to the Integrity of the Family

DI is used in order to provide the opportunity for parenthood for those who otherwise would remain childless. Its reason d'etre is to create families. Yet this method of achieving conception fundamentally challenges the normative assumptions of family life. The legislative and medical framework within which DI is offered implicitly refers to the possible catastrophic consequences of using unregulated, unmedicalised DI. The most compelling reason for using medicalised DI – whether as donors or sperm or DI recipients – is confidentiality. Without this the project fails: the created normative family is revealed as 'abnormal' and the kin relationships are exposed, betraying the legal father as bringing up the children of another man and the donor as having abandoned his genetic children to be brought up by strangers. The theoretical and political threat to society and the normative family are considerable. This condition for using DI – given legal authority – guarantees both the survival and integrity of the DI family as an autonomous family unit not threatened by the donor/genetic father, and protects the donor from any unwanted intrusion into his life by a curious adult who was conceived with DI. Confidentiality, anonymity and secrecy have been fundamentally important to the normative understanding of success in the use of DI because it is through these that normative families who are at no risk of being found out or having their understandings of themselves as family disrupted (Daniels, 1998). The evidence suggests (e.g. Lasker, 1998) that very few heterosexual DI families intend to tell their children how they were conceived and the law facilitates this. Importantly, from April 2005 donors of sperm will be identifiable to their children when the latter reach the age of 18. It is unclear as yet whether this will result in a change in the 'hands off' approach of most clinics in the matter of whether and what recipients of DI tell their children.

A secondary consideration that reinforces the importance of reducing risks to family integrity is the attempts clinics will make to match donors with women's partners. No explanation of why this might be undertaken by clinics is given. The implication is that such an aspect of the treatment requires no explanation:

> Clinics do their best to use sperm from a donor who has similar physical character-
> istics as the male partner, e.g. skin colour, eye colour, blood group, hair colour and
> body build (HFEA, 2002a, p. 6).

Again no guarantees can be given. Matching depends on the supply of donors and in any case the result of matching 'cannot be guaranteed'. The importance of matching is underscored however by the leaflet stating that clinics 'should discuss any deviations from a 'good' match with their patients' (HFEA, 2002a, p. 2). There is then an assumption that by matching the donor with the social father a subterfuge can be worked. The resulting DI child will 'look like' the social father and reduce the risk that the 'real' nature of the family will be revealed to anybody.

Conclusion

In this chapter we have focused upon a specific source of health education and advice which carries within it a range of constructions of risk. We have tried to show the ways in which social discourse and biomedical discourse interact. In particular we have indicated the contradictions inherent in applying scientific discourse to social judgements and the ways in which this leads to a socially normative discourse, masquerading as neutral and impartial information and assessment. The construction of sperm, for example, as medicine neutralises any association with human and social origins and outcomes.

Additionally, the educational information provided by the HFEA is closely linked to a legal framework that implies that all users of fertility services will be treated in the same ways. However, the real availability of services at clinic level is interpreted through normative notions of acceptable families and couples. The information trades upon a notion of active subjects free to choose the 'best' clinic for their purposes. In reality, the choice of clinic is limited as much by personal resources as by knowledge. For example the levels and kinds of genetic screening used with donors may vary between a simple disclosure based upon personal honesty to actual DNA testing, the latter being more expensive for recipients. In the final analysis the educational process articulated through frameworks of risk and biomedicine, is one in which human agency and value are subsumed within a spuriously neutral discourse devoid of connections with the affective context of human reproduction.

References

Ashton, J. and Seymour, H. (1988), 'The New Public Health', Open University Press, Milton Keynes.

Barton, M., Walker, K. and Weisner, B.P. (1945), 'Artificial Insemination', *British Medical Journal*, vol. 1, pp. 40, 43.

Daniels, K. (1998), 'The Semen Providers', in K. Daniels and E. Haimes (eds), *Donor Insemination. International Social Science Perspectives*, Cambridge University Press, Cambridge.

Donovan, C. (1993), *Keeping it in the Family: An Analysis of Doctor's Decision-Making About Access in the Provision of Donor Insemination*, Unpublished thesis, Edinburgh University.

Donovan, C. (2003), 'There's nothing wrong but I can't get pregnant: when assisted conception breaks its promise', Paper presented at British Sociological Association, York.

Douglas, M. (1966), *Purity and Danger. An Analysis of the Concepts of Pollution and Taboo*, Routledge, London.

Douglas, M. (1990), Risk as a Forensic Resource, Daedalus, Fall, pp. 1–16.

Duelli Klein, R. (1984), 'Doing it ourselves: self insemination', in R Arditti, R. Duelli Klein and S. Minden (eds), *Test-Tube Women. What Future for Motherhood?*, Pandora Press, London.

Franklin, S. (1997), *Embodied Progress, A Cultural Account of Assisted Conception*, Routledge, London.

Haimes, E. (1998), 'The making of "the DI Child": Changing representations of people conceived through donor insemination', in K. Daniels and E. Haimes (eds), *Donor Insemination. International Social Science Perspectives*, Cambridge University Press, Cambridge.

Health Canada (1996), www.hc-sg.ca/english/media/releases/1996/96_37e.htm.

Hornstein, F. (1984), 'Children by donor insemination: a new choice for lesbians', in R. Arditti, R. Duelli Klein and S. Minden (eds), *Test-Tube Women. What Future for Motherhood?* Pandora Press, London.

Human Fertilisation and Embryology Act (1990), HMSO, London.

Human Health and Embryology Authority (2002a), The *Patients' Guide to Donor Insemination*, http://www.hfea.gov.uk/HFEAPublications/PatientsGuides/Guide%20to20DL.pdf.

Human Fertilisation and Embyrology Authority (2002b), *Sperm and Egg Donors and the Law* http://www.hfea.gov.uk/ForDonors/Donorsandthelaw/Introduction/sperm%20and%20Egg%20Donors%20and%20the%20law.pdf.

Human Fertilisation and Embyrology Authority (undated a), *Issues to Consider*, http://www.hfea.gov.uk/ForPatients/PatientsGuidetoDI/Issuestoconsider.

Human Fertilisation and Embryology Authority (undated b), *Welfare of the Child: Information for Patients*, http://www.hfea.gov.uk/forPatients/welfareofthechild/Introduction/welfare%20of%20the%20child.

Illich, I. (1976), *Limits to Medicine. Medical Nemesis: The Expropriation of Health*, Penguin Books Ltd, Middlesex.

Lasker, J. (1998), 'The users of donor insemination', in K. Daniels and E. Haimes (eds), *Donor Insemination. International Social Science perspectives*, Cambridge University Press, Cambridge.

Nettleton, S. (1997), 'Governing the risky self. How to become healthy, wealthy and wise', in A. Petersen and R. Bunton (eds), *Foucault, Health and Medicine*, Routledge, London.

Novaes, S. (1998), 'The medical management of donor insemination', in K. Daniels and E. Haimes (eds), *Donor Insemination. International Social Science perspectives*, Cambridge University Press, Cambridge.

Oakley, A. (1981), *From Here to Maternity – Becoming a Mother*, Penguin, Harmondsworth.

Saffron, L. (1994), *Challenging Conceptions. Planning a Family by Self-Insemination*, Cassell, London.

Snowden, R. and Mitchell, G. (1981), *The Artificial Family. A Consideration of Artificial Insemination by Donor*, Unwin Paperbacks, London.

Warnock, M. (1984), *Report of the Committee of Inquiry into Human Fertilisation and Embryology*, Cmnd, 9314 HMSO, London.

Index

For Product Safety Concerns and Information please contact our EU
representative GPSR@taylorandfrancis.com
Taylor & Francis Verlag GmbH, Kaufingerstraße 24, 80331 München, Germany

www.ingramcontent.com/pod-product-compliance
Lightning Source LLC
Chambersburg PA
CBHW070357270326
41926CB00014B/2597